B
Louis, J.   c.1

ASTOR.
       "... AND A CREDIT TO HIS
RACE".

1974   7.95   1-75

B
Louis, J.   c.1

ASTOR.
       "... AND A CREDIT TO HIS RACE".

1974   7.95   1-75
1990
  1

". . . And a Credit to His Race"

"… And a Credit to His Race"

The Hard Life and Times of Joseph Louis Barrow, a.k.a.

JOE LOUIS

by

Gerald Astor

New York
Saturday Review Press | E. P. Dutton & Co., Inc.

B
Louis,
J.

Grateful acknowledgment is made to Random House, Inc., for permission to quote from *I Know Why the Caged Bird Sings,* copyright © 1969 by Maya Angelou.

LIBRARY OF CONGRESS CATALOGING IN PUBLICATION DATA

Astor, Gerald, 1926–
"And a credit to his race."

1. Louis, Joe, 1914–2. Boxing. I. Title.
GV1132.L6A84   796.8'3'0924 [B]   74–9609

Published simultaneously in Canada by Clarke, Irwin & Company Limited, Toronto and Vancouver
ISBN: 0-8415-0347-8

For Sonia, true courage

". . . And a Credit
to His Race"

1

The temperature in Las Vegas ranged between 105 and 110 degrees. Inside the stone-façade ranch house the air conditioning labored noisily while kids gamboled back and forth through the living-room's sliding glass door on their visits to the swimming pool that filled almost the entire backyard. On the couch sat 58-year-old Joseph Louis Barrow, the former heavyweight champion of the world. He wore only white undershorts, a white undershirt from which his huge biceps poked, thick black socks and his golf cap with the Caesar's Palace emblem. His attention focused upon a color TV set where Randolph Scott, who regularly destroyed Western villains in the same era Louis shot down heavyweight contenders, shot his way through the traditional struggle between cowmen and sheepherders.

It was more than three decades since Louis cheered the anti-Fascist world by knocking out Nazi Germany's Max Schmeling, more than two decades since he retired from boxing after a comeback attempt ended in a knockout by Rocky Marciano. Louis's eyes followed the adventures of Randolph Scott with the same heavy-hooded impassiveness that marked his ominous deliberateness in the ring and caused some observers to question his level of intelligence. Beneath the golf cap lay the same bald spot that perhaps more clearly marked his age during the Marciano fight than even his flat-footed tired responses to the Brockton, Massachusetts, strong boy whose professional debut began after Louis's first retirement in 1948. A mound of stomach beneath the undershirt showed Louis a good 40 to 50 pounds above his best fighting weight of 200.

The comfortable home, the joyful cries of the kids, the quiet presence of his third wife, Martha, a successful Los Angeles criminal lawyer, napping in the study, the still-powerful body of a retired champion . . . it could have been a scene of a man approaching the twilight of his life with content, if not with wealth.

But in fact, this seemingly tranquil vessel of humanity, the man, considered by many the greatest heavyweight champion in history, was more like some huge ship with a defective rudder. The man who had risen to the most prestigious achievement available to men of his race and background at the time had spent four months in the psychiatric wards of Colorado hospitals, and several more months being treated as an outpatient. Now, living in Las Vegas, beyond the reach of the court order that had committed him for therapy in Colorado, the former heavyweight champion, a man whose public heart had once been noted for how easily it became glad, saw the world as thickly populated with sinister forces bent upon his destruction.

One night he placed a long-distance call to *New York Post* boxing writer Lester Bromberg. "I want to write a book," announced Louis.

"About your career?" inquired the newspaperman.

"Naw, it would be bigger than about boxing. I got enemies." Louis was convinced organized crime had a contract out on him.

Joe Louis had come into the world as the son of sharecrop-

2

pers in Alabama, at a time when white America blew away the last vestiges of the Reconstruction and Jim Crow laws legalized a more sophisticated system of control and oppression of black people. His family joined the great migration of rural southern blacks northward to urban centers where Jim Crow wasn't in legal codes, but racial oppression was just as real.

He matured during the final years of prohibition, when America's rackets went from adolescence to vigorous young manhood. It was a time for wide-open gambling, prostitution, violence and conspicious consumption. Showgirls, diamond stickpins, big black cars and professional fighters were standard ornaments of the crime figures. Although Louis himself was clean, his co-managers, John Roxborough and Julian Black, made their stakes outside the law. His trainer had served time as a murderer.

It was a quiescent time in America's race relations, because blacks were too oppressed for the luxury of challenging the system and whites too unchallenged to require any self-justification.

But if they were as yet unprepared to fight for civil rights, the blacks of the rural South, New York's Harlem, Chicago's South Side and Detroit's Paradise Valley knew Joe Louis as their champion. Down South, on fight nights, they flowed to the general store or farm that had a radio. In the cities, they poured into pool halls and bars on fight nights to cheer for Louis, usually against a white challenger.

In her portrait of life in the southern black belt, Maya Angelou recorded in *I Know Why the Caged Bird Sings* a montage of the Joe Louis experience:

The last inch of space was filled, yet people continued to wedge themselves along the walls of the store. Uncle

3

Willie had turned the radio up to its last notch so young-sters on the porch wouldn't miss a word. Women sat on kitchen chairs, dining room chairs, stools and upturned wooden boxes. Small children and babies perched on every lap available and men leaned on the shelves or on each other.

The apprehensive mood was shot through with shafts of gaiety as a black sky is streaked with lightning.

"I ain't worried 'bout this fight. Joe's gonna whip that cracker like it's open season."

"He gonna whip him till that white boy call him Momma."

. . . "They're in a clench, Louis is trying to fight his way out."

Some bitter comedian on the porch said, "That white man don't mind hugging that niggah now, I betcha."

. . . Even the old Christian ladies who taught their children and tried themselves to practice turning the other cheek, would buy soft drinks, and if the Brown Bomber's victory was a particularly bloody one, they would order peanut patties and Baby Ruths also. . . .

"He's got Louis against the ropes and now it's a left to the body and a right to the ribs . . . it's another to the body and it looks like Louis is going down."

My race groaned. It was our people falling. It was another lynching, yet another Black man hanging on a tree. One more woman ambushed and raped. A Black boy whipped and maimed. It was hounds on the trail of a man running through slimey swamps. It was a white woman slapping her maid for being forgetful. . . . This might be the end of the world. If Joe lost we were back in slavery and beyond help. It would all be true, the accusations that we were lower types of human beings. Only a little higher than the apes. True, that we were

4

stupid and ugly and lazy and dirty and unlucky and worst of all that God himself hates us. . . .

". . . and now it looks like Joe is mad. . . . Louis is penetrating every block. The referee is moving in, but Louis sends a left to the body and it's the uppercut to the chin and the contender is dropping, he's on the canvas, ladies and gentlemen. . . . The fight is all over. . . . The winnah and still heavyweight champion of the world— Joe Louis."

Champion of the world. A Black boy. Some Black mother's son. He was the strongest man in the world. People drank Coca-Colas like ambrosia and ate candy bars like Christmas. Some of the men went behind the Store and poured white lightning in their soft drink bottles. . . .

It would take an hour or more before the people would leave the Store and head for home. Those who lived too far had made arrangements to stay in town. It wouldn't do for a Black man and his family to be caught on a lonely country road on a night when Joe Louis had proven that we were the strongest people in the world.

In the cities, the sense of Joe Louis as Avenger, Champion, the Dark Destroyer gladdened the heart of oppressed blacks. Earl Brown, then writing for the *Amsterdam News,* said of Louis, "He is the current natural pride of his people, a heavyweight champion every Negro hopes and prays for. His huge picture in fighting togs adorns every ham hock, fish fry and liquor joint in the community. The Depression, getting on home relief and singing of the black blues because they didn't hit the number have been forgotten at least until after the great event by the Harlemites."

Fascist Italy and Nazi Germany were forced to note that

5

a descendant of black Africa, a non-Aryan, claimed world supremacy. Even at home, in Louis's native United States, millions cheered when a German beat the native son. But for other white millions in America, this black man became their champion, an ally against the Nazis, especially to Jews whose relatives in Germany were victims of persecution.

The rise of Joe Louis forced one highly visible segment of America to recognize race as a fact of life. Sportswriters, working in an era when almost all sports figures were white, had to deal with the fact of Louis being a black man. And what was written about him is revealing of America's condition during the period.

In the *New York Daily News,* John Chapman observed that sportswriters had labeled Louis everything from the "Brown Bomber to Zooming Zulu. But not even those who considered Carnera a bum, called him [Louis] the Black Hope."

Jimmy Cannon's statement—"He's a credit to his race, the human race"—was enlightened for the time, even though, a quarter of a century later, it carries a faint whiff of condescension. Some oldtimers of boxing praised Louis only on the basis of his comparison with his single predecessor as a black heavyweight champion, prideful Jack Johnson. Mushky Jackson, a boxing functionary during the golden days of Louis, remarked, "You know why he'll be remembered long after a guy like Jack Johnson is forgotten? Because he knew his place—nobody could point a finger at him with white women." The distinction was really one of manners, though. Johnson had flaunted his white female companions. Louis did not restrict himself to black women but he was discreet.

With Joe Louis, the fight game procured some undeserved respectability. Promoters continued to cheat the public and the Internal Revenue Service, managers still stole from the fighters and fixed fights, and contracts were manipulated. But the sport didn't fall into total disgrace largely because the man at the top of the heap, the heavyweight champion, appeared to be without sin. He had his personal weaknesses, though. Louis became a juicy prey for the hustlers who hang around money-winning fighters. Although he had earned roughly $4.6 million as a fighter, he lost most of it to bad investments—and bad people. Worse, no tax lawyer took him in hand until it was too late. And, as one old friend said about him, "Joe was an absolute chump when it came to women."

None of these failings, however, damaged his reputation; in fact his vulnerability may even have made him, as a black man, less of a real threat than latter-day black athletes. It was acceptable for white children of the 1930s and 1940s to admire him. And he was the only black national figure for black children to idolize. There were no others that the white-controlled media so favored.

Now, more than three decades beyond Joe Louis's prime, Las Vegas was host to a heavyweight fight between Muhammad Ali and Jerry Quarry. Ali, like Louis, was a southern black with an abysmal public school education. Unlike Louis, he had refused to make any concessions to the white establishment once he won the heavyweight championship. He chose a religion that degraded whites and rejected his country's uniform, unlike Louis who enlisted before he could be drafted. Unlike Louis, he was as adept with his mouth as with his fists. And Ali would undoubtedly regard any attempt to make him a credit to the whole human race as an insolent effort by whites to co-opt his virtue.

It was the opportunity to see Muhammad Ali in action that brought to the Nevada desert these 1972 June blooms of the black ghetto, exotics of show biz, heroes of sports and

7

overachievers in hustles, legitimate and otherwise, as well as the more prosaic business men. The high rollers surged through the Las Vegas Strip in a cacophony of colors. Pigeon breasts and pot bellies tucked behind high-priced couturier and tailor names as well as the off-the-rack garb of younger whites touring the West for a vacation, all this became a gray backdrop for bush hats, spangles, beads, shirts, vests and pants of leather, britches, jump suits, creamy white suits. The new blood wagered at the tables with a fierce joy. Among them, at Caesar's Palace, moved a tower of flesh, Joe Louis.

Beside the roulette table he called to a white man, "Put five on twenny-seven for me, put five on twenny-seven." A chip covered the number, the wheel spun, the ball stopped on 19. Louis, clutching several $25 chips in his huge hand, shuffled toward the crap tables where he took a privileged position beside the stickmen. Occasionally, he'd lean forward and whisper and laugh with a matchstick-sized white man who would continue to spread his chips on the green felt.

As he ambled about the place, offering a genial nod or a hand to the regulars, he would be stopped, not by the young black people intent upon the action but by the middle-aged whites. A woman halted him and asked for an autograph, which he granted. It all appeared so placid, so much a portrait of a man in harmony with himself.

But earlier in the day, fresh from a good afternoon on the golf course, Joe Louis stood amid the black-jack tables frowning. Suddenly he wheeled, grabbed a slender black man by his shirt front and lowered his massive round head, fury spreading across his face. Security men packing side arms held their ground uncertainly, mute but apprehensive. Louis bulled his man away from the tables, and a sergeant of security hurried over. Words were exchanged, Louis relaxed his grasp. The freed man departed and Louis turned his attention back to black jack.

Later in the Noshorarium, the Caesar's Palace coffee shop, Louis sat in a corner with friends talking about the fight. Harry Belafonte came by and sat for a couple of words, Joe DiMaggio paused for an exchange, and Louis tried to secure some tickets for a wizened tiny white man. "Gimme a phone dahlin'," said Louis to a waitress and he kept ringing the convention hall ticket office fruitlessly, finally discovering an acquaintance with two undistinguished $50 seats.

I came to his table during a lull, introduced myself and explained my desire to do a book about his career. For weeks I had tried to reach him with letters and by telephone, never quite succeeding until on a hunch I asked for his friend Ashe Resnick, who manages Caesar's Palace Casino. Louis was sitting with Resnick when I called. He told me to come on out. Before I did, though, his wife, Martha, telephoned to make certain that I saw her when I arrived.

After introducing myself, Louis put one very large hand on my arm, an invitation to sit. We talked a little bit about my project and tentatively arranged a meeting a day after the fight. Toward the end of our conversation, I asked, "What happened with that guy you grabbed this afternoon?"

The former champion's mouth turned down, his eyes seemed smaller, remote. He mumbled, "Mafia, but I don't want to talk about it."

Later I joined Mrs. Martha Louis while she ate a steak and salad in the Noshorarium. Throughout the meal she kept her eyes on the corner where her husband held court, now in earnest conversation with a newspaperman taking notes. As he rose to leave, Mrs. Louis asked me to intercept the newspaperman and ask him to speak with her. "I want to find out what Joe said and then explain to this fellow. He's not one of the regular reporters." To the chagrin of Mrs. Louis, the interviewer escaped me as he entered the crowds around the gambling tables.

Still distracted, Martha Louis confessed, "I'm at the end of my rope. My law practice is shot to hell. I've done my part." She has been married to Louis since 1957, his marriage to Marva Trotter in 1936 lasted six years, his union with Rose Morgan of 1955 only two years. "I have nothing to gain," continued Martha Louis. "I love him but what can I do. I told his daughter if I ever get involved with a man again, she could shoot me. She laughed, she understands."

She continued in what soon became a nonstop soliloquy. "He suddenly gets the idea to rush down to my mother's house and stay there, that nobody will know where he's hiding. I don't drop in unannounced even at my Momma's. But he thinks that if he calls then there'll be somebody up on the roof waiting for him.

"He has a gun. A man in Detroit gave it to him. He sleeps with it under his pillow. One night he got up. I said, 'Where are you going?'

" ' I'm going to kill that boy I seen there,' he says.

" 'Joe, there's nobody out there,' I tell him. But he keeps prowling around in the dark with that gun. I just hope he doesn't kill somebody. I hope it isn't me that he shoots.

"Caesar's Palace gave him one of their cars to use. I always try to drive him. But they give him a car and what'll happen if he thinks that someone is chasing him in another car? The other day at Caesar's Palace, he kicked a man in the leg, twice.

" 'Why did you do that, Joe?' I asked him.

" 'He coughed, he's trying to give a signal about me.'

" 'If you think that way,' I tell him, 'you'll have to kill

10

everybody with a cold.' I tell him the Mafia must have an awful lot of manpower to be able to watch him like that. All of his friends will do anything to protect him, but he's sick. Maybe some good would come out of an incident. Maybe people would realize that he's sick and he needs to be hospitalized. I know that I won't do it again."

Martha Louis had made one painful effort to get her husband the kind of medical treatment that she believes he so desperately needs. A version of the events that culminated in Joe Louis being taken by Colorado sheriff's deputies to the psychiatric hospital appears in *Brown Bomber,* a book by Barney Nagler. Shortly after *Brown Bomber* was published, the subject, who was paid for his cooperation, talked angrily of suing the author for failure to clear the manuscript with him and for allegedly falsifying facts. Martha Louis complained mildly that Nagler had failed to submit the work before publication as had been agreed. She did not contest the truth of his book.

According to Nagler, Louis began to show signs of emotional instability late in the 1960s. Throughout his marriage to Martha, as he had in his previous attempts at matrimony, he associated with other women. But at his age and with the decline of his fortunes, he more often fell in with a group of women scrambling between survival and crime, in many instances achieving the former only by dipping into the latter. Narcotics were a fixture on the scene.

One of these demi-monde friends, a casual bedmate for a period of years, introduced Louis to cocaine. Perhaps he took it as a stimulant to sex. Louis never touched alcoholic drinks or smoked until after he suffered his breakdown, but faced with a lessening of his almost legendary abilities as a lover, he may have felt insecure, as many men of his age do. Cocaine has been known to produce psychoses.

11

Joe Louis's tumble from mental stability appears to date from the period in which he dallied with this girl who introduced him to coke. Over a period of months Martha Louis noticed a marked change in her husband's behavior. He started to smoke cigarettes, gave up his beloved game of golf and embarked on a more than usual series of hide-and-seek adventures in which she would have to telephone his old friends across the country to track him down. Disappearing acts, usually in connection with flings with one or more women, had been a characteristic of Louis even when he was heavyweight champion. But these latest adventures occurred in sordid surroundings, lasted longer and when they were over Louis himself seemed unable to recall where he had been. During one of these sprees, the ex-fighter fathered a child. Martha Louis gathered the boy up and took him home with her to raise.

Louis's condition worsened. He was often vague and torpid and at other times he was frenetic. The symptoms were all too obvious to Martha Louis. In her practice of criminal law, she had often dealt with drug addicts. Indeed, the client who had attracted her to Denver, onetime heavyweight champion Charles Sonny Liston, had succumbed to an overdose of heroin in Las Vegas. Once after discussing business on the telephone with Martha Louis, Liston turned to his manager, Willie Reddish, and remarked admiringly, "That Joe, all he wants to do is stay in bed with a woman all day."

Monogamy had never been among the baggage of Joe Louis's life; it rarely is among professional athletes, military men or other individuals who spend enforced periods of time isolated from women and away from home. Of far more concern to Martha Louis than her husband's infidelity was Joe's conviction that a giant conspiracy had been created to destroy him. One night, according to Nagler's account, while

12

the Louises were staying at Caesar's Palace, Martha heard sounds coming from the terrace outside their room. She found her husband laboriously pasting masking tape over the decorative scroll work on the façade of the building. "They're shooting air in through here," he explained. "I'm stopping up those cracks where those assholes are putting poison stuff in on me." This fear of being secretly gassed by agents of the Mafia caused Louis on occasion to paper over air-conditioning ducts and other openings into his room and led to his wearing a cap to prevent a sneak attack upon his bare head. Once he smeared mayonnaise over some ceiling cracks to protect himself against omnipresent would-be assassins.

His paranoid behavior eventually reached such a level that Martha Louis and her husband's children by his first marriage—Jacqueline Burton and Joe Louis Barrow, known to his father as Punchy—felt forced to act. The three, though plagued by the doubts anyone has who commits a relative for psychiatric treatment, agreed they had no choice. The actual papers to commit Louis bore Punchy's signature. When the sheriff's deputies served the writ, they found their subject surprisingly docile. Had he physically resisted, the scene could easily have degenerated into a violent tragedy.

Even in the Colorado Psychiatric Hospital, Louis continued to protest that he was not ill. He agreed, however, to waive a right to appeal against the commitment writ, in return for a transfer to the Veterans Administration Hospital. There he proved almost a model patient, demonstrating understanding and sympathy for other patients.

Louis was given a heavy dosage of thorazine, a strong tranquilizer that falls under the heading of psychotropic drugs. Often employed for alcoholics, it has a depressant quality that alleviates emotional stress. While Louis never

13

conceded that he was ill, he seemed comfortable with his therapist and his conversations indicated his obsession about hostile forces had lessened. It never disappeared completely though. During a pleasant visit with Nagler on a summer day, Nagler asked Louis if he was worried, and Louis answered matter of factly, "I'm just thinking about them assholes blowing gas in on me."

The psychiatrist in charge of the case decided that Louis could continue to improve as an outpatient. Some of the ex-heavyweight-champion's friends had not forgotten him. Ashe Resnick, a good basketball player at Long Island University just before World War II, had known the former champion from the time he worked as a shill for the Thunderbird Casino in Las Vegas. Resnick, who was in charge of casino operations for Caesar's Palace, gave Louis a post with this new Las Vegas hotel.

For several months thereafter Louis shuttled back and forth between Caesar's Palace and his psychiatrist in Denver. But then the physician was forced to call a two-week recess because of a personal problem. The thin connection between Louis and professional help was severed, and his progress toward mental stability ended. He again tortured himself, and his wife, with the delusions of a Mafia plot against his life.

Worst of all, Louis now lived in Nevada, beyond the reach of the Colorado court order that had originally incarcerated him in a hospital. Unless he voluntarily returned to Colorado, there was no means to force him to continue treatment, unless Martha Louis and his children applied for a new court order in Nevada. None of them felt inclined toward another court action, particularly since he might fight it, and in Nevada he enjoyed, through Caesar's Palace, enough friends to make any action against him difficult. Meanwhile,

Louis stopped taking tranquilizing drugs, convinced that these medicines contained poisons prepared by his enemies.

When I saw him at his Las Vegas home, Louis said that he had not seen Barney Nagler's book, although it had been available for weeks. Then a dark look appeared in his face, an expression that early in his career caused Paul Gallico to describe him as "mean spirited." He asked what Nagler had written about the Mafia and cocaine; he wanted to know if Nagler had suggested that there was no plot against him, that he was instead deluded by the use of coke.

Martha Louis had told me earlier: "He should have been treated like anybody else, not something special because he's Joe Louis. His friends will do anything to protect him, to cover up for him. But they're really not helping him to get well."

2

In 1914, the president of the United States was Woodrow
Wilson, a southern-born white aristocrat, and the heavyweight champion of the world was Jack Johnson, a Negro.
Wilson, a Democrat, brought to his political party, and to the
nation, a liberalism that gently curbed the power of big business, loosened the grip of high tariff protectionists upon the
national economy and finished the wrecking job that had
been started 30 years earlier upon the Post-Civil War Reconstruction programs designed to assimilate the newly freed
slaves into the American mainstream.

Woodrow Wilson issued decrees that firmly segregated
such government agencies as the Treasury and the Post
Office Department. The mood of blacks was expressed by
Booker T. Washington: "I have never seen the colored people so discouraged and bitter as they are at the present time."

A delegation of Negroes, protesting the spread of segregation into the federal bureaucracy, met with Woodrow Wilson
in 1914. Said the president: "The white people of this country, as well as I, wish to see the colored people progress, and
admire the progress they have already made, and want to see
them continue along independent lines. There is, however, a
great prejudice against colored people. . . . It will take one
hundred years to eradicate this prejudice and we must deal

with it as practical men. Segregation is not humiliating but a benefit, and ought to be so regarded by you gentlemen. . . ."

Segregation was now the order of the day. It was maintained even at the price of considerable inefficiency in the military forces mobilized under Wilson upon the entry of the country into World War I. A War Department directive provided for separate toilet facilities for women, but not men. Perhaps more serious was a new regulation that required a photograph to accompany applications for Civil Service jobs, a tactic that the youthful National Association for the Advancement of Colored Peoples suspected of being used to screen out nonwhites.

White southerners made big gains in the 1912 and 1914 elections and swept Negro postmasters and other minor federal officials in the South from their jobs. The Georgia Collector of Internal Revenue appointed by Woodrow Wilson announced, "A Negro's place is in the cornfield."

State governments, particularly in the South, passed statute after statute to limit the opportunities and the freedom of black citizens. Congress not only failed to redress these assaults upon civil liberties and civil rights but in fact became an accessory to the oppression of nonwhites. Congressional fury reached a peak with the marriage of Negro heavyweight champion Jack Johnson to a white woman. The Mann Act, the federal statute that makes it a crime to transport a woman across state lines for "immoral purposes," was supposed to be a weapon against prostitution but it owed its passage to the furor over Johnson. Georgia Representative Seaborn A. Roddenbery introduced a 1912 constitutional amendment to ban racial intermarriage. Roddenbery called the Johnson marriage, "more revolting than white slavery." In the heat of passion to protect womanhood, Roddenbery

17

declaimed, "No brutality, no infamy, no degradation in all the years of southern slavery possessed such villainous character and such atrocious qualities as the state laws which allow the marriage of the Negro Jack Johnson to a woman of the Caucasian strain." The Senate allowed Roddenbery's proposed amendment to perish in committee, although 92 northern and southern representatives favored it; only 10 opposed. From 1907 to 1921 more than twice as many bills to bar interracial marriage as statutes to halt lynchings were tossed into the Congressional hopper.

In fact, the only force that saved the United States from a total codification of segregation was the inertia of Congress which refused to put its sanction upon executive orders that separated whites and blacks.

In New York the appalled New York State legislature passed a law that forbade bouts that pitted a black against a white. Nearly thirty years after Johnson demolished ex-champion Jim Jeffries, the greatest white hope, sportswriter Bill Corum of the *New York Journal* recalled his childhood fury, "Man alive, how I hated Jack Johnson in the Summer of 1910! Nor did I ever quite get over it. In recent years it became an aversion rather than a stronger feeling. But when he knocked out Jeffries at Reno, I hated him."

Jack Johnson was, to his own delight, a perverse person in the eyes of the whites, though a far more understandable one today. Far from knowing his place as a black competing with whites, he thumbed his nose at white superiority and did not stop short of the white woman's bed. Possibly because it had always been considered an animal-like endeavor, and often outlawed, the ring had been one of the few ventures open to nonwhites. But Johnson very nearly caused that avenue to be shut down. It was more than 20 years after Johnson lost his title in a controversial match that another black was permitted to compete for the heavyweight title.

On May 13, 1914, while Americans were fuming over the antics of Jack Johnson and Europeans were rapidly maneuvering themselves into a war, a midwife named Susan Radford came to attend Lillie Reese Barrow in a sharecropper shack about half a dozen miles from the tiny Alabama village of Lafayette. The area lay in the Buckalew Mountains, a series of hills undistinguished in either history or geography.

A burly 28-year-old black woman, Lillie Barrow, like the wife of any sharecropper, had spent her life in the fields, picking cotton, staggering along behind the plowhorse and bearing children between chores. As the wife of Monroe, or Mun, Barrow, Lillie had already given birth to four daughters and two sons.

Mun Barrow's mother and father had both been slaves on a plantation owned by a man named James Barrow, whose holdings supposedly included roughly 100 black chattels. Victoria Harp Barrow, the paternal grandmother of Joe Louis was thought to be part Cherokee. Certainly, a photograph of her indicates face-bone structure that seems Indian.

The child brought into the world on that May 13 was named for Mun Barrow's brother-in-law, Joe Louis Nichols. According to an interview that his mother gave some years later to writer Earl Brown, "He weighed about 11 pounds when he was born and 'cept for an earache when he was a kid, he has never been sick a day in his life. He's always been healthy and strong 'cause I fed him plenty collard greens, fat back and corn pone. He didn't talk 'till he was six. He always like to sleep too much. It was worth my life to get him outa dat bed."

Louis's own recollections, at least in his autobiographical reports, match his mother's memory of a slow-developing child. "My mother says I was a worse crybaby than any of

19

her others. I would holler longer and louder when she had to whip me, or when I'd stub my toe. She remembers I was 11 months old before I got around on my own legs. That was slow for a Barrow.

"My mother says I liked to stumble a lot when I was a baby. She says she couldn't leave me indoors alone when she went out to work in the cotton because I'd knock things over. I had the strength when I was a baby to knock over the churn when she set it by the fire. She says that I did that two, three times. Once I spilled the cream she was fixing to churn."

When his seventh child had turned three and a baby sister, Vunies, had been added to the family, Mun Barrow abruptly deserted. He eventually was committed to a state mental institution. A neighboring widower, Patrick Brooks, with five children of his own to raise, decided to join forces with Lillie. "He was a good stepfather. He was the only father I ever knew," said Louis many years later.

The family had lived in an unpainted. windowless shack that backed up on a cotton patch. It did not even belong to Mun Barrow but, apparently, to a maternal uncle. Struggling to survive, Lillie and Pat Brooks moved their family some miles deeper into the Buckalew Mountains to Mt. Sinai, a settlement so insignificant that maps do not list it. "I remember most was how cold I used to get," said Louis. "We didn't wear shoes much and we kept our good clothes for Sundays. We had only kerosene lamps in the shack." The six-year-old boy now shared a bed with his two older brothers.

They all worked in the fields, although at his age Joe was mostly a messenger who carried lunch out to the other members of the family. For recreation, there was an occasional horse or mule to ride, fish to be caught, snakes to be stoned.

Scrabbling in the stingy soil of the Buckalews for existence, the Barrows and Brookses had formed a harmonious

20

union. The Brooks brood included Pat, Jr., a boy Joe's age. "We got along good. We liked to lay in the cotton when it went to the cotton gin. The mules would go slow down the dirt road and we would bounce on the cotton in the car. On hot days we would fill a bucket at the well and me and Pat would catch hold of the handle and carry cold water into the crops."

Even though there was not enough money for warm clothing against the mountain chill, the family farm did produce enough to eat—corn, potatoes, bacon, chicken—and there were fish in nearby ponds and streams. The big adventure was a trip to nearby Camp Hill, an oasis with stores along the main street. Pat Brooks would drive in on a Saturday evening, leave the two boys in the wagon, then appear with cheese and crackers as a treat. Christmas meant a stocking filled with fruit and peppermints.

For the most part, Joe showed no particular aptitude for what was to become his trade. In the Buckalew Mountains, after Louis ascended to the heavyweight championship, folks remembered brawls among kids that were called "knockin." A great-uncle of Joe Louis Barrow, hunted down by a reporter after the nephew had risen to fame, claimed that "Joe used to knock four boys at a time." But the champion himself disclaimed any such distinction as a youngster; he considered himself the most pacific member of the family. Once, though, he got into a scrap with another boy at school, and a teacher who witnessed the fight, seized Louis and whipped him. Louis attributed his punishment to his size; he was bigger than most of his contemporaries.

Louis's school, which he attended intermittently, had only one room for the 15 or 16 youngsters. An outhouse was in the backyard. Some 20 years later, when Louis went back to Alabama, the place was still standing.

21

As a boy in Alabama, segregation had little impact on Joe. "I don't remember any racial things from Alabama," he admitted while living in Las Vegas almost 50 years later. "The farm next to us belonged to white people, named Landers I think. His two sons and my brothers were close friends. The kids were nice to us and we played together. Maybe I was too young to hear about anything."

A hard-shell Baptist, Lillie Barrow Brooks made certain her children got to church every Sunday. Vunies, the youngest child, recollected that Pat Brooks owned an old Model T Ford. "Every Sunday, all of us would pile into that old car and go to church, some six or seven miles away," she said. "There were no paved streets, lots of large holes and ditches in the road. We were lucky not to break an axle every time we went." For his part, Louis mostly remembers when he would have to walk several miles to the place of worship.

The grinding contest to stay alive in the Buckalew Mountains goaded the family to look elsewhere for survival, to the northern cities. The first great migration of blacks from the southern farms had occurred while Joe Louis Barrow was struggling to take his first steps. The Arsenal of Democracy created after the incident at Sarajevo needed manpower to work the factories. In 1917 to 1918, field hands, followed by their families, had renewed routes of the old underground railway that brought freedom to southern slaves. Detroit had actually published advertisements inviting Negroes to come to the motor city for work. In 1910, a census put the non-white count in Detroit at 12,000. By 1920, the number had risen to 40,000.

Along with the blacks pouring into the city of Detroit, arrived a great many southern whites, bringing with them the ways of the rigidly segregated South. There was racial trouble all over the country. Black United States soldiers

22

who had served in segregated units during World War I had come home rebellious at having risked their lives for an idea of freedom and equality which was not available to them as civilians. A counterreaction came from whites, worried about Negro demands for civil rights in the competition for jobs. Lynchings and racial confrontations increased sharply immediately after World War I.

In the mid-1920s, while the Barrow–Brooks combine pondered its future, Henry Ford was gearing up to face the challenge of auto-manufacturing upstarts General Motors and Chrysler. His answer to them was his Model A Ford, the kin to the Model T whose success had been built upon the assembly-line system which he started in 1914, the year of Joe Louis's birth. For all his narrow-minded ignorance and quirks, Henry Ford showed a surprising willingness to grant nonwhites a semblance of employment opportunity.

Like so many others, Pat Brooks left the subsistence Alabama fields for the insecurity of industry in Detroit in the mid-1920s, probably early in 1926. He left his family back in Mt. Sinai. Brooks did not immediately find work in Detroit but he was favorably impressed enough to return to Alabama and bring everyone north, where they shared rooms with kin while Brooks looked for work.

"The place we lived in on Macomb Street," Louis told Barney Nagler, "was crowded, but it had something we didn't have in Alabama, an inside toilet. And there were electric lights. It was nice." When Brooks succeeded in getting hired by Ford, the family moved into a tenement on Catherine Street.

Almost 13 now and already a big kid, Joe was put in the fifth grade. The separate and unequal system of public education had destroyed any real possibility that he could cope with the Detroit public schools. Vunies, his younger sister,

23

explained, "We lived quite a distance from the school in Alabama, and it wasn't easy to get there every day. And we didn't start until we were six or seven years old.

"When we came to Detroit, for example, my sister Eulala [who was older than Joe] was put back into the sixth grade." Joe himself was not prepared to participate with boys and girls who were so much younger than he, so much smaller. He looked really out of place there and as the years passed he fell further and further behind.

In the Detroit classrooms, the ordeal of performing before youngsters half his size but considerably more able to recite from books was an emotional burden on Joe—one shared by many black youngsters who came north and found themselves among white kids with a better background in basic academic skills. Young Joe Louis Barrow's reaction was to develop the stammer, and a reticence with strangers that later caused newspapermen to think of him as either phlegmatic or stupid.

Vunies remembers her brother in Detroit as anything but introverted or silent during his boyhood. "Joe was a jovial fellow and very verbal. He talked plenty around the house and even then he was quite witty."

The Barrow–Brooks family, that was eventually to swell with nine more children borne of the union of Lillie and Pat, lived in what was an integrated neighborhood on the east side of town. In fact, at the time the family took up residence on Catherine Street, the ghetto did not exist. "There was segregation in Detroit," says Vunies. "Only one theater downtown with a live show admitted blacks. And we knew that the hotels and restaurants were closed to us. But we had Italians and a few Germans living in our neighborhood. My first girl friend was an Italian girl. That lasted until she went off to a Catholic high school. I went to an integrated school.

24

Then the junior high school in the area was converted into a senior high. That was done to prevent the black students from going to Easton which at the time was where Grosse Pointe kids went."

"We had an *Eye*talian family cross the street from us," is Joe Louis's memory of the integrated neighborhood.

Joe struggled through the fifth grade at Detroit's Duffield School but never made it through the sixth. "He's going to have to make a living with his hands," a teacher decided. So Joe entered the Bronson Trade School to learn the art of the cabinetmaker.

"In those days, education for blacks," says Vunies, "meant training their hands, not their minds."

Whatever his failings as a student in the Detroit educational system, the country boy eagerly joined in the city excitement for his age group. Although Vunies claims that Joe never joined one of the street gangs that populated the east side of town, he did participate in the fun and mischief of his contemporaries. In one of his autobiographies, he reported, "Nights I hung out on the corner with the Catherine Street gang. We had fights, but nothing much; just gang fights the way kids do. You got into a fight and you just punched the best you could. I had no haymaker then, no more than any other East Side kid."

Earl Brown, managing editor of the *Amsterdam News,* suggested that the future champion's behavior brought him to the narrow edge of trouble. ". . . Louis played with a tough gang. Sometimes they would steal fruit from a wagon or throw mud at policemen and then enjoy the long chases through the dirty twisting streets. The supreme achievement for the gang was to sneak into the movies when the cashier's back was turned. Joe never thought up these amusements, never started the fights or baited the cops. But although not

25

a leader, he presently became recognized as pound per pound, the best fighter in his social circle."

Meanwhile, the fortunes of the Barrow–Brooks family sagged. Hard times had hit the automotive industry and Pat Brooks could count on perhaps three days of work a week. Then he was injured and the family, along with millions of other Americans, began to depend on that new United States institution, home relief. "We were always hungry," said Lillie Barrow Brooks, "Joe didn't even have shoes to put on when he went to school."

Along with a friend, Fred Guinyard, Joe worked on a coal truck occasionally in winter, an ice wagon in summers and delivered groceries. The receipts for his efforts went toward household expenses. "Up north," recalled the fighter in 1940, "we didn't eat as good as we did in Alabama, stuff cost too much."

In spite of their poverty, the matriarch insisted on a certain code of behavior. Everyone was expected to attend church on Sunday and the girls, like Vunies, were forbidden to attend school dances because their mother considered such activity as the first step toward sin. Aware that one avenue of higher income open to nonwhites was music, Lillie Barrow Brooks propelled her youngest children toward musical instruments.

"I wanted to play the violin," says Vunies, "but Mama said Joe would do that and I would study the piano." From some hidden resources, Mrs. Brooks dug up enough to pay for a cheap fiddle and her son embarked upon a musical career at one dollar a lesson.

Actually, the boy violinist took no more than one or two lessons before he found a more attractive use for the weekly dollar. At the Bronson School where he studied cabinet making, the recreation program included boxing in the gym.

26

Thurston McKinney, a youth a few years older than Louis and also a student at Bronson, watched Joe spar in the gym. Already involved in an amateur boxing program, McKinney advised the younger boy to abandon music for fighting. He pointed out how much a black fighter, Kid Chocolate, earned, how much more Jack Dempsey received. "Jack Dempsey was the one hero that I had when I was a kid," Louis has said. "We listened to his fights on the radio. It was always Dempsey does this, Dempsey does that."

The teenaged Louis was not a wholehearted enthusiast of boxing at the time. As an untutored novice he was on the receiving end of fists often, and "some of those kids could really sock." On the other hand, the violin as a career tempted him very little. Vunies still remembers her brother pretending to practice and barely getting any sound out of the instrument. He never even learned to play a scale.

Thurston McKinney dangled before Louis a more immediate reward than the far-off riches of Kid Chocolate or Jack Dempsey. He explained that as an amateur, he would receive up to $25 worth of merchandise every fight. Convinced, Louis abandoned the violin and instead used the lesson money to pay his amateur dues and the quarter a week it required to participate in the boxing program at the Brewster Recreational Center. A two-story red-brick building, Brewster was a Detroit Department of Parks operation. It contained a swimming pool, gym for basketball, rooms with Ping-Pong and a boxing ring.

Alter "Kid" Ellis directed the training at the Brewster Recreation Center, and in one account of his career, Louis said that for the first nine months of his enrollment, Ellis kept him out of matches that brought the merchandise checks and used him solely as a sparring partner.

Although he was not participating on local-amateur cards,

Louis did request an application to enter the Golden Gloves competition, as a novice. "I beat my mother to the mailbox to get the application and letter which said where I was to fight," remembers Louis. "It was to be in the naval armory. I had to hide the letter and application where she couldn't find it. I put them in a light fixture in my room. But one day, I came home and there was my violin teacher, telling my mother that I hadn't shown up.

" 'What you been doin'?' my mother asked me.

"I broke down and told her about going to be a fighter. She took it fine, said okay, 'I'll help you.'

"I went upstairs and got the letter off the light and I told her I'm fighting in a few days."

His career shift apparently was made easier by the fact his music instructor had informed Lillie Barrow Brooks that her son showed no aptitude for the violin.

About the same period, it was decided that there was little point in Louis attending the Bronson School any longer. With his older brother Alonzo, he went to the Briggs plant early one morning to apply for a job. "When it came to noontime we were like dead," Louis told writer Margery Miller. "Alonzo took the dollar we got from my mother and went out to buy some hot dogs while I held his place in line. We didn't know any other kind of meat but hot dogs in those days. Finally in the late afternoon, we got to the employment window. Alonzo didn't get a job but I was lucky. They hired me for $25 a week. Our feet were aching so we thought they'd fall off by the time we got home."

At Briggs, which next to Ford offered the most jobs to Negroes, Louis shoved truck bodies mounted on dollies to a paint spray station on the assembly line. It was a long arduous day that left him with no energy to drop in at the Brewster gym after dinner. Only on Saturdays could he muster enough interest to spar. For about half a year he continued in this fashion, his progress as a fighter stunted by the need for employment, now that Pat Brooks was unemployed.

As the Depression deepened, Franklin D. Roosevelt whipped Herbert Hoover and the heavyweight championship bounced amid a flock of contenders like a greasy football. In 1932, weighing just under 170, Joe Louis entered the ring for his first formal bout, a stag event at the Edison Athletic Club. His opponent, a white youth, John Miler, was much more experienced. Miler had represented the United States in the 1932 Olympic Games in Los Angeles and he gave Louis a fearful thumping, knocking him down seven times in two rounds. The loser's reward amounted to a seven-dollar merchandise check which he presented to his mother. The debut discouraged Louis enough for him to abandon boxing temporarily. He changed jobs, going to work for Ford in the River Rouge plant. He was encouraged by Pat Brooks who saw little future in boxing for his stepson and great need for some immediate income for the family.

After a few months, though, Joe returned to boxing, this time under the guidance of a professional black fighter, Holman Williams, a middleweight. At the Brewster gym Louis honed his skills, practicing what Williams told him in front of a mirror and sparring with other aspiring boxers. He took a leave from the Ford plant.

His second amateur fight was at the Forest Athletic Club in Detroit and after two punches, his opponent stayed down for the count. Jubilant, with a $25 merchandise check to tote home to his mother, Louis now began to look forward to a ring career. In his first full year of amateur competition, he fought his way to the championship of the light-heavyweight division of the Golden Gloves. Then he replaced another contestant in the light-heavyweight class for the Amateur

29

Athletic Union championships. In the title fight in this tournament he met a skillful former Notre Dame football player named Max Marek who outboxed the less experienced Louis.

A new trainer had taken over instruction for the Detroit prospect. George Moody, who directed boxing at the Detroit Amateur Club, instilled further fight science in the willing pupil. An amateur named Stanley Evans beat Louis easily by a decision, but, after a few more months under Moody's direction, Louis defeated Evans in a return match to take the United States Golden Gloves a second time. Louis looked forward to revenging his defeat by Max Marek, but he never got the chance because Marek moved to the heavyweight class.

Young Joe Louis suffered one other grievous disappointment when he went to Chicago to participate in the International Golden Gloves championships. Louis was in the dressing room, his hands already bandaged for the fight when Arch Ward, sports editor of the *Chicago Tribune* which sponsored the fights, came to see him. "He asked me if I had ever been to South Bend, Indiana," Louis recalled.

"I said I'd never been out of Detroit, except to Chicago. He told me that a man killed his wife in 1926 and I had been identified as that man. Seems like some preacher in South Bend saw my picture in the paper and identified me as that man. I had only been 12 years old then, but I had to go to the police station in Gary. I was never in the jail, just sat in the captain's office and talked to him. Some boy substituted for me in the Golden Gloves and he won. The police just talked to me, then let me go, said it was humanly impossible for me to be the one who killed that woman."

For all of the instruction and the merchandise checks that he was receiving—he had a total of 54 amateur matches—Louis remained a basically unskilled and hungry fighter.

Even though he had learned how to get cash in place of the merchandise, he could not afford fresh wrappings for his hands and used the same bandages to guard his knuckles fight after fight. Instead of real boxing shoes he wore high-topped sneakers. Worst of all, he existed on a diet of less than championship potential. "Mostly I lived on frankfurters. I liked them. I loved ice cream too. When I lost to Evans, I had eaten only some hot dogs and apple pie." But Louis could punch hard; his 18-year-old body had hardened and grown through constant workouts and exercise.

George Moody's most impressive contribution to Louis's future had nothing to do with his capacity as a teacher. It was Moody who introduced the young fighter to a well-known black businessman in Detroit, John Roxborough. While he had done well enough as an amateur, Louis could not hope to progress in his boxing career without some sort of sponsorship. John Roxborough proved to be the patron who opened the glory door.

3

John Roxborough had come to Detroit long before the World War I migration of rural southern Negroes. His ethnic heritage included Scots, Jamaicans, Spanish and Creole. His father, a lawyer in New Orleans, moved the family to Detroit in 1899, when John was seven years old. The family settled in an all-white neighborhood, mostly a Polish community.

"I had a little trouble making myself understood," said Roxborough 70 years later. "In New Orleans I spoke nothing but French and Spanish. I couldn't even speak English. But these Polish people were wonderful. I never knew I was Negro until I made my first trip downtown."

Roxborough learned more about the color line as he aged. His older brother, Charles, who became the first black member of Michigan's state legislature, had earned a law degree. But after one year at the University of Detroit, studying to follow the same course, Roxborough sized up the job opportunities for a Negro college graduate and decided it was not worth the effort. "You'd ask for a job, tell them you were a college graduate, and they'd say, 'Oh yes, we have a porter's job for you.' "

Roxborough's reaction was, "To hell with education. What good would it do me? I made up my mind that when

I got a chance to make money, no matter how, I'd take it. I would avoid embarrassing situations, like asking for a job when I was qualified. I also promised myself I'd help myself first and then I'd help my black brothers."

Despite the fact he had only one year of college, in Roxborough's later years reporters constantly referred to him as a graduate of the University of Michigan and a lawyer. There is no evidence that Louis's manager ever tried to disabuse them of their mistake.

In his quest for money, Roxborough discovered the career of bail bondsman. It struck Roxborough that the financial return to a bondsman was quicker than to the lawyer and required no substantial investment in schooling. When an individual found himself in jail he would accept any key to the cell door without inquiry into the racial background of the source. The courts and police too seemed more or less color-blind when it came to the source of bail money.

Of course, it helped to have police and court officials who pointed customers in one's direction. One evening the police turned to Roxborough with a case that altered his life. "We've got a policy hood from Kansas City down here," Roxborough remembers hearing. "Nobody else wants to get out of bed to bail him out. What about you?"

The ambitious young Roxborough scrambled into some clothes and got the racket man out of jail. He, in turn, was grateful enough to invite his benefactor to Kansas City to observe the workings of the policy, and he offered Roxborough a sound investment tip. "We've got a gold mine in Kansas City and you've got no game in Detroit. The way Ford is bringing Negroes into the city, you can't miss."

Policy in one form or another had been a part of the American gambling scene for 50 to 75 years by the time Roxborough first began to investigate it. It was a poor people's game from the start, with penny bets that promised to return better than 200-fold winnings. In the beginning, pool selling, as it was known in New York, flourished among lower-class whites. When Roxborough began to consider the possibilities of the racket in the early 1920s, the syndicate considered the Negro population in most cities too lacking in money to be worth any heavy operations.

Based upon what he learned during his visit to Kansas City, Roxborough created his own policy bank and called it the Big Four. His territory was Paradise Valley, the burgeoning slum that belied its name. Roxborough pioneered in the Detroit policy field. But within three years, other prospectors, hungry for the pennies of blacks, opened shops.

In the primitive period, policy players had bet buttons and beads, and winners were determined by pulling marked beads from a sack. After a little more than 50 years had passed, the game had progressed only to the point that pennies were the medium of exchange and the fortunate few were those whose numbers had been drawn from a barrel or drum. The temptation to finagle with the winning figures produced a lack of confidence in some potential bettors, and the operators constantly had to worry about someone conspiring to pull off a big score. The happy solution was the numbers. The payoffs were bigger, although the odds in favor of the bankers increased substantially. Stock-market transactions or mutuel handles at a race track provided the winning digits. All players could see what numbers had come up simply by reading a newspaper and no longer could anyone rig a winner.

Roxborough's interests spread out through Wayne County. Like others in his trade he worked at auxiliary services. He published guide books to winning numbers, based upon interpretation of dreams, omens and experiences.

Later, he was sued for plagiarism in this field. A former associate claimed, "John controlled gambling for all the Negroes in the County. He was the payoff man." The entrepreneur involved himself in politics, forming alliances with such men as Detroit Mayor Frank Murphy, later to become U.S. Attorney General and a Justice of the Supreme Court. However, Roxborough's ties to the other local politicos brought him unhappy results in his later years.

Like many blacks who managed to achieve some economic power, albeit from illegal means, Roxborough plunged into the role of a race man. He contributed to the Urban League and the Young Negroes Progressive Association. On a more personal level he doled out money for rent, food and coal. These contributions were traditional to men intent on planting some political crop; but Roxborough seemed to have a genuine interest in the fortunes of people of his race. He sponsored promising young men seeking higher education, and supposedly at least 30 people went through the University of Michigan as a result of Roxborough's generosity.

Roxborough's behavior wasn't unique. Successful Negro racketeers enjoyed considerable status among lower-class nonwhites and aid, however tainted, was readily accepted by organizations bent on improving the status of Negroes.

A Negro reporter said of Chicago's black racket man, Daniel M. Jackson, "I don't like to admit it, but an open town is far better for the Negroes than a closed town. . . . Of course these bosses make a lot of money, but while Jackson was in control he donated thousands to charities, the N.A.A.C.P., working girls' homes and the like. While Jackson was in power the colored people always had a friend to go to. . . ."

It was again a system that however beneficent in its peculiar way, emphasized exploitation of the blacks. Because the

35

local people scored some immediate visible gains through vice, there was small incentive among the nonwhites to root out gambling and prostitution in their midst. Apart from charity, the rackets stimulated other business: taxies, restaurants and nightclubs. People were, of course, unaware of how much of their hard-earned capital left the black community; the toll exacted by politicians on every nonwhite racket entrepreneur and the hired hands—numbers runners, bookies and hookers—forced all of the purveyors of vice to intensify their activities.

A white writer, a few years after the association between Louis and Roxborough began, wrote of the latter, "an American archetype machined by those attitudes that operated to exclude him from sharing in the decenter, larger prospects society offered to white men of half his talents, training and ambition. He was cunning, he was callous and he was involved in transactions that were shady . . . still he donated to Race."

In his efforts to improve the quality of life in Detroit, John Roxborough had supported a number of local black athletic teams. According to Roxborough's memory, in the early 1930s Thurston McKinney, the young fighter who had tutored Joe Louis Barrow at the Brewster Recreation Center, approached the numbers man and complained, "How come you're always laying out money for basketball and softball teams and you never help us boxers. We need help too." Roxborough responded by reaching into his wallet.

Some months later, said Roxborough, McKinney accosted him again. "Mr. Roxborough, there's a sweet-looking amateur you might want to look at. He could sure use some help. He doesn't even own a pair of trunks. But can he punch." Again, the patron went to his bankroll. After learning the prospect's name, Joe Louis Barrow, he said, "I'll be down to see him the first chance I get. And here's a couple of dollars. Take the Barrow kid out and buy him a meal."

In some of the authorized accounts of Louis's life appear slightly different versions of this first meeting with Roxborough. One story has it that Roxborough just appeared at the Brewster Street Gym and after watching the young man box a few rounds asked, "Boy, what's your name?"

"Name's Joe Louis Barrow."

"That's too long. We'll just call you Joe Louis."

However they came together, Roxborough was shrewd enough to see that his protégé would need more than instruction in the finer points of boxing. He also needed to change his whole way of life if he were ever to progress beyond a skilled clubfighter. The only satisfactory method for reshaping the young fighter would be to take him totally in hand. Roxborough brought the youth home to live with him. In place of the hand-me-downs from elders that failed to reach the ankles, Roxborough outfitted the fighter with clothes from his own wardrobe; extensive alterations were required since Roxborough was a pudgy man much shorter than the six-foot Louis.

If we are to believe what Roxborough told one interviewer many years later, the manager was confronted with extremely raw material. Tutors of English, math and manners were hired, claimed the numbers man. He instructed his housekeeper that the guest could not have his breakfast until he had showered and brushed his teeth. "It was tough at first," remarked Roxborough, "but what did we have to work with? It certainly wasn't Joe's fault. Where could he have learned how to hold a fork?" Such reminiscences are undoubtedly exaggerated. Louis's manners may have been improved, but, considering his later financial difficulties, he does not seem to have learned much math. In one account,

37

Roxborough generously doled out a five-dollar-a-week allowance, but in actuality he used his political connections to get Joe Louis a job at the Ford plant assembly line for $6.80 a day.

Meanwhile, Louis was continuing to destroy amateur opponents. When he finally turned pro he had waged 58 fights, winning 54 of these. Roxborough saw to it that Louis's appearance in the ring improved as much as it did outside the ring. The fighter now was clothed in a terrycloth robe, selected by Wilhelmina Morris, later to become Roxborough's wife. Fresh bandages protected his knuckles before every fight and leather boxing shoes replaced the high-topped sneakers. And he dined on meat, the way champions were supposed to eat.

By June of 1934, the 20-year-old fighter was becoming less enchanted with the life of an amateur fighter in spite of the comforts afforded through his association with Roxborough. He told his sponsor that he wanted to turn professional and make a stab at bigger money than the $25 and $50 merchandise certificates.

"I tried to talk Joe out of it," remembered Roxborough. "I thought it was too soon. I asked him to wait until he had won the Golden Gloves heavyweight championship. He said, 'Mr. Roxborough, I want the money.' That I could understand. That was why I was in the numbers business—and I've never been ashamed of it—and I said, 'O.K. Joe. I'll find you a good manager and a good trainer.'"

"No, Mr. Roxborough," said Joe to the numbers man. "Just find me a good trainer. I've got a good manager—you. I won't fight unless you agree to manage me."

Roxborough was reluctant, for several reasons. It may well have been that he felt Louis was not ready, either in skill or in deportment, for the pressures of professional competition. Also the venture would move into areas where Roxborough had little background. He had no professional ring experience and knew little about matchmaking. And finally, John Roxborough was financially strapped at this particular time.

But his protégé was adamant on the subject. And Roxborough found the necessary partner to put up the initial $2,000 that it would take to finance Louis for the first months of a professional career. The new partner was a Chicagoan named Julian Black.

A native of Wisconsin, and a Negro, Julian Black spent his early years shuttling between Oshkosh, where his father was a barber, and Milwaukee, where his dead mother's sister helped raise him. "My uncle was a maitre d' at the Pfister Hotel," remembered Black. "But finally, I went to Chicago to stay with another aunt and I attended Wendell Phillips High School."

As a young man, Black studied the embalmer's trade. "I passed the exam, but it wasn't what I wanted." While working at the craft, Black discovered more lively commerce. His employers in the funeral business were Charlie and Daniel Jackson both of whom were hip-deep in Chicago rackets. After an apprenticeship as an employee of the Jacksons, Black graduated to his own enterprises. He managed the Colonial Club, "a rich Jewish" playpen on the South Side where he did everything from running the elevators to managing the bowling alleys and billiard rooms. He operated a speakeasy known as Elite Number 2. Like Roxborough, Black was also a policy man. Truman Gibson, who was a lawyer for Black and involved in some of the post-World-War-II operations of Joe Louis, knew Black as "an extremely wealthy man, who had a white partner." Short and chunky, in the mold of Roxborough, Julian Black never earned the affection his Detroit partner did. "I liked Roxie," said one associate many years later, "but Julian Black was cold and calculating."

"Roxborough and I had been friends for a long time," said Black explaining their alliance. "I used to see him in Mt. Clemens [Michigan] where I went for my arthritis." Black has contended that in 1934 he was no better off financially than Roxborough. "John may even have had more money than I. But there wasn't much of an outlet for a fighter in Detroit and that's why he came to me." Still, subsequent events indicated that Black held more contractual power than the Detroiter.

Roxborough and Black undoubtedly considered themselves skilled enough businessmen to penetrate the jungles of professional boxing without being devoured by conniving promotors or sacrificing their proprietorship to the avarice of the gangsters who controlled much of the fight game. Roxborough's involvement with syndicate chiefs may have been less solid, but Black had operated close enough to the top to expect protection against third parties muscling in.

Still, neither man was foolish enough to believe that their hopeful possessed enough of the sweet science to enter the professional ranks and straightforwardly punch his way to the top. They needed a trainer. Roxborough's experience in this area was limited, but Julian Black's Elite Number 2 had become a gathering place for all of the local sporting world. As a professional evaluator of talent, Black turned to a former fighter named Jack Blackburn.

Born in Versailles, Kentucky, in 1883, Blackburn was a former lightweight who fought more than 100 bouts. His record was not terribly impressive, but he did meet such headliners as Joe Gans and Sam Langford.

Blackburn suffered from one ultimately fatal weakness,

alcoholism. A ferocious barroom brawler, in 1909, at the peak of his pugilistic phase, he stabbed a man to death in a Philadelphia saloon. Convicted of manslaughter, Blackburn spent better than four years in a Pennsylvania penitentiary. Another souvenir of his street fighting was a long scar across his face where an opponent slashed him. The violence in Blackburn would surface one time during Louis's career, threatening a rupture in the alliance.

Following his retirement as a fighter, Blackburn had converted himself into a trainer and had been in the corner of a lightweight and a bantamweight champion.

Some 40 years later, Louis remembered, "Roxborough said to me, 'I'll send you to Chicago to Julian Black. He'll find you a trainer.' It was the first time I ever rode on a train. Black met me, and got me a room with some nice people. I went down to the gym and met Blackburn. He was strict and he called me 'Chappie' [Blackburn's favorite form of address] from the first day.

"For two weeks he put me in the gym, to work on fundamentals. Blackburn believed in balance, balance first. I had to learn to start with my left, always open up for the right hand after the left.

"Blackburn told me that if you never make a mistake, you won't get hit. In the gym in Chicago we would box and he would throw punches at me. I had to block it, I wasn't allowed to duck. When he threw a right hand, I had to catch it and he told me that any time somebody missed, you should hit him. He taught that if you can throw one punch, you can throw two, you can throw three because you're always on balance."

At their first encounter, Louis weighed 175 pounds and Blackburn recognized that he could not survive as a heavyweight unless he put on at least 20 pounds. After advising the

41

young prospect of his deficiency, Blackburn said, "Starting tonight, you'll have to go to the stockyards and drink two quarts of hot beef blood. You got to do that every day. That's the only way you'll put on weight. You hear?" Louis nodded.

But that night he rapped on Blackburn's door. "Mr. Blackburn," said the fighter, "I've been thinking about drinking that blood, I just can't drink it, Mr. Blackburn, and I thought I'd better come 'round and tell you." What Louis had failed to realize was that for all of his severity, Blackburn possessed a sly sense of humor.

Many reports from this period stress Blackburn's concern for Louis to wipe out the alleged stigma left by Jack Johnson. "You're colored, Joe. And a colored fighter's got to be lots better than the other man if he's gonna go places," Blackburn supposedly lectured. "But you gotta have more than just two good hands. You gotta do the right thing. And never leave yourself open so people can talk about you."

Roxborough recalled a session with Louis in which he lectured the young fighter. "To be a champion you've got to be a gentleman first. Your toughest fight might not be in the ring but out in public. We never, never say anything bad about an opponent. Before a fight you say how great you think he is, after a fight you say how great you think he was. And for God's sake, after you beat a white opponent, don't *smile.*"

Julian Black reminded, "That's what Jack Johnson did."

Roxborough added, "Joe, you're going to get a lot of invitations to nightclubs. But you never go into one alone. And above all you must never have your picture taken with white women." Louis honored the first restriction only until he achieved enough prominence to be able to reject the advice and counsel of his managers. But no photographs of him alone with white women ever appeared.

At the end of this solemn meeting, Blackburn offered his own advice on conduct. "There's one more thing," he said. "You never, never lose a fight," and he then burst out laughing at the perplexed managers. Blackburn was a hard-bitten man. He knew how to play the soft-spoken black role but he was not a handkerchief head who would counsel submission.

Satisfied with the progress of his pupil, Blackburn flashed the word to the co-managers that their fighter was ready to move out of the gym and declare himself a professional in the ring. Fittingly enough, the day chosen was Independence Day, July 4th, 1934, and the announcement was in the form of a four-round match with a fighter named Jack Kracken.

Before the Kracken fight, a white manager remarked to Izzy Klein, welterweight champion Barney Ross's trainer, "Those guys must be nuts. Kracken will kill that boy. Louis is in over his head." Louis knocked out Kracken in the first round.

For his labors, Louis received a purse of $59. The managers took nothing at this point. Jack Blackburn was on a straight salary. At the original session of observing Louis, Blackburn had said, "If I take him and I ain't saying I'm gonna, how much you gonna pay me?"

"Thirty-five dollars a week for four weeks," answered the managerial team. "After that we'll see what's happened." Although some accounts claim that after Blackburn's student began to stretch for big money at the top, the trainer received a percentage, the evidence is that he stuck to a salary. When Blackburn died in 1942, his estate amounted to only $6,000 and if he had been cut in for even a tiny share it seems likely his fortune would have been greater.

In 1934, the original salary, four weeks in advance, seemed eminently satisfactory to Blackburn, who at the moment had been marking time with a pair of undistinguished white

43

fighters. Roxborough said that when the deal was completed, Blackburn cackled, "This will be the best job I ever had. Usually got to whip my man to collect my pay. I got to tell you, you'll never make a success of this kid, but I need the job. He ain't going to make no money worth shaking your finger at, remember he's a colored boy."

One week after Kracken fell in Chicago, Willie Davis went down for the count in the third round. Less than three weeks later it was Larry Udell's turn in two rounds. Then Jack Kranz hung on for eight rounds but Louis had the decision. Finally, at the end of August, Buck Everett stretched out on the canvas in the second round.

With five wins, four by KO's, the chiefs of staff agreed that the time was propitious for a return of the native, a match in Detroit. Louis signed up to fight a white boxer, Alex Borchuk.

In the Motor City, his home town, John Roxborough met the first challenge to his right to manage Joe Louis. The Michigan State Boxing Commissioner, Bingo Brown, according to Roxborough's memory, summoned him to a conference that included Brown, Roxborough, five local fight managers, all of them white, and Eddie Edgar, the white sports editor of the *Detroit Free Press,* invited as an observer for some inexplicable reason.

"Roxborough," said Brown, "I'm a little annoyed at the set-up with Louis. You're a Negro, Black's a Negro, Blackburn's a Negro and, of course, Louis is a Negro." Brown's facts couldn't be denied.

"We'd like to have a piece of Louis," chipped in one of the white managers, "but Roxborough, you're blocking us."

Brown judiciously summed up his sentiments, "I think we had better let a white man in with Louis. Yes, I think that's what we had better do. It doesn't look right having nothing but Negroes around him."

Suddenly, Roxborough found an ally, Eddie Edgar, the *Detroit Free Press* editor. "You must be kidding. Sure Roxborough has Louis. He's laid out a lot of money, he's fed him, he's put clothes on his back. Who did these guys ever feed or clothe? Six months ago they wouldn't even say hello to Louis."

"Wait a minute," said Brown hurriedly, "Don't misunderstand." Turning to Roxborough, he offered a quick compromise. "We aren't trying to cut you out completely. Why don't you just pick one of these fellows as a co-manager and that will settle everything. You can still have a piece."

"No," stubbornly resisted Roxborough. "These guys think I'm young and easy [he was 35 actually]. Well, I'm not. And one thing I'm not doing is what they are doing, loud mouthing, running to newspapers and telling them how much they are doing for their fighters, which is nothing. I wouldn't take one of them as a partner for a million dollars."

From authority, then wheedling, Brown turned to ugly threats. "I can't force you," said Brown. "But you either do what I tell you or Louis will fight nothing but colored fighters in this state." Not only would that have seriously restricted Louis's career but it would have meant a string of small purses since promoters diagnosed all black fights as box-office failures.

Roxborough remained unconvinced, however. "Then Joe won't fight in this state. We sure as hell don't need Michigan. But when people start yelling to see the hometown boy, I'm going to tell them exactly what happened."

Roxborough has stuck to this account of white oppression. However, Eddie Edgar could not recall the confrontation.

"We used to sit around at night and talk and drink. Roxborough and Bingo Brown were often present. But I never heard Brown make that kind of a demand."

On September 11, 1934, in Detroit, as scheduled, Joe Louis, knocked out Alex Borchuk, the white heavyweight. Roxborough and Black were still the sole managers.

The swiftness of the Borchuk fight result is deceptive. The white man dealt Louis a punch to the jaw that broke a tooth and the pain nearly caused Louis to quit. Before the year ended, Louis had counted up six more impressive wins, with five KO's and another white victim, Jack O'Dowd again in Detroit. Louis had, in six months, scored a dozen victories. He had not been simply thrown into the ring to survive or perish, however, particularly in the first year of his development. Louis was carefully matched, put in against men that the crafty Blackburn felt his pupil could take.

The Detroit whiz had begun to attract a following, but mini-fame had not yet altered his personality. Louis at 20 was a diffident young man. He still addressed his seniors as Mister, and he even had to struggle to drop the formal address with trainer Blackburn. Unlike some members of the Louis entourage, Blackburn scorned any rituals of respect. He received it in spite of his diction or alcoholic failing because of his personality rather than from his position. In later years sparring partners for the champion would always talk of "Mr. Roxborough" though Blackburn insisted that they call him "Jack."

Apart from some local fans, Louis had also begun to attract attention from the sachems of boxing and the piranhas that circulated in the murky waters of the fight game during the era. But one element gave pause to even the greediest, most foresighted potential investors in Louis—his color and what it meant in terms of boxing and America.

4

Joe Louis's early boxing career was stalked by the specter of Jack Johnson, the flamboyant black who so aroused white racist passions that no black had been allowed to fight for the heavyweight championship since Jess Willard had won the title from Johnson in 1915.

The first black fighter to achieve recognition by boxing historians appropriately enough was an American, Bill Richmond, the "Black Terror" who was born on Staten Island, New York, in 1763. The justly celebrated historian of the British ring, Pierce Egan recalled, "I saw Richmond when he was fifty-five years enter the lists with a tall strong and young navigator, and won the battle in twenty minutes. If there had been prejudice against men of colour appearing in the P.R. [prize ring] the fancy would never have let Richmond beat some of the best men of his time. This is a decided proof that the love of fair play belongs to the P.R. and that country or color is of no consequence so that a man proves himself an honest man to his backers."

When Richmond married a white woman, advanced himself enough to own a pub and an academy to instruct in Egan's "Sweet Science" the historian recognized that outside of the "P.R." he suffered "taunts and insults."

In 1810 the British demonstrated that fierce emotions over

integrated sports competition were hardly a monopoly of America. The Cribb–Molyneaux fight was the first recorded interracial match of modern recorded history and some 20,-000 spectators appeared in response to what boxing historian Trevor Wignall described as "the opinion that Negroes were not fit and proper persons to oppose white men." Tom Molyneaux was a South-Carolina-born former slave, while Tom Cribb was the hometown WASP.

Later in the nineteenth century John L. Sullivan, the acknowledged heavyweight king in the United States drew a strict color line, however, and no black contenders ever met him in the ring. George Godfrey once managed to schedule a bout with Sullivan but John L. canceled.

John Arthur Johnson was born in Galveston, Texas, in 1878. In his autobiography, *Jack Johnson Is a Dandy,* he wrote that as a 12-year-old boy he suddenly developed an overwhelming desire to see Steve Brodie, the man who supposedly jumped off the Brooklyn Bridge and survived. So he stowed away on a ship that he thought was bound for New York where he might glimpse his idol, but instead the vessel put to port at Key West, Florida. Stowaway Johnson was discovered and beached, "penniless, friendless and hungry." To earn money he became a sponge fisherman; once he survived a terrifying encounter with a 23-foot shark that capsized his boat.

Eventually, Johnson shipped himself to New York, met Steve Brodie and drifted around the Northeast for a year before returning to Galveston. He worked on the docks where fighting was almost a part of the job. Johnson's autobiography reports of one of his earliest battles: "I had been attacked in the streets by a young man much older and larger than myself. I did not have the courage to fight him, and was casting about for an excuse to evade him. My sister came along at this juncture, and noting that the older boy was taking advantage of me, she became angry enough to demand that I fight him. In fact, she pushed me into the fray. There was nothing to do but fight and I put all I had in it. The little I had learned in boxing stood me in good stead, and after a mauling and pounding that lasted several minutes with the results considerably in doubt, I finally whipped my antagonist." The somewhat ponderous language employed by Johnson in the autobiography owes nothing to any ghost writer. Although uneducated, Johnson picked up an ability to express himself that went well beyond what his boxing descendant, Joe Louis, ever managed.

Street fights in Galveston slowly built Johnson's reputation. As a 16-year-old, Jack Johnson took on a bullying grown man in a bare-knuckles encounter. "I gave him a tremendous beating," reported Johnson. As a result, folks in Galveston began to call him "Lil Arthur." Johnson's autobiography typically spells the Christian name properly, though most histories of boxing refer to him as "Lil Artha."

Wanderlust again seized Johnson and he hopped freights to the Midwest. At a stop in Springfield, Illinois, he engaged in a "battle royal," a sports exhibition that exploited blacks. Battle royals—four to six men, usually black, fighting in a ring with the survivor to take all—entertained clubs and stag gatherings as late as the 1940s. Johnson triumphed and with the jackpot moved on to Chicago for what he reports as his first professional fight, a bout with a man known only as Klondike. *The Ring Boxing Encyclopedia and Record Book,* however, lists half a dozen professional fights before the Chicago one. Klondike defeated him, but Johnson had tasted the glory of the ring and wanted more of it.

Finding few opportunities to fight in the North, Johnson returned to Galveston where he fought Joe Choynski. According to Johnson the fight ended with a raid by the Galveston police. Other accounts say that the cops interfered only after Choynski had knocked out the 17-year-old hometown boy. In any event, both men served three-week jail terms. It turned out to be a fortunate experience for Johnson. Choynski, an experienced ring expert, tutored his former opponent in fancy footwork and boxing defenses, skills that became Johnson's trademark in later years.

From this point Johnson's career was one of almost uninterrupted success in the ring. He fought close to 80 times before he finally got his chance at the heavyweight championship, and he lost only twice, once on a decision to Marvin Hart and once on a foul to Joe Jeanette; he avenged his defeat to Klondike twice. Johnson and Jeanette, another black fighter, met 10 times over this period. Good black fighters found it difficult to get white contenders into the ring with them and were forced to compete against one another often.

While Johnson continued to batter all available opponents, Tommy Burns, a Canadian who was born Noah Brusso, held the championship. Burns went on a world tour, punching out challengers in London, Dublin, Paris, Sydney and finally Melbourne. Johnson followed him about, calling for a shot at the title. After evading the American Negro for some time, Burns finally agreed to meet him in Sydney in 1908. Such a title fight might not have been possible in the United States at the time, since resistance against interracial activities was growing stronger. Johnson's autobiography reports that Burns had, while fending off the challenger's demand for a match, spoken harshly of him and contributed a generous amount of racial slurs. After the agreement had been made, both men built up interest in the fight with comments on their opponent's character.

Johnson, who was slightly over six feet, weighed 192 for the fight, some 25 pounds more than Burns. The 30,000 spectators quickly saw that Burns was overmatched. He took a fearful thumping and Johnson admittedly heaped humiliation upon injury with a drum-fire of verbal abuse. In the 14th round, a police inspector decided the carnage was enough and Johnson assumed the heavyweight throne. One of the spectators was Jack London, novelist and white jingoist. He was outraged with Johnson and his "villainous golden smiles" (produced by a mouth that sparkled with gold teeth).

With the heavyweight championship his, and his second wife a white woman, Johnson easily captured the furious imagination of the white supremacists. Immediately after the triumph abroad, he returned to fight four no-decision fights with white boxers, including Victor McLaglen who shortly afterward abandoned that form of entertainment to become an actor. The search for a "Great White Hope" to put the black man in his place became frantic and the first to be sacrificed was a fierce middleweight named Stanley Ketchel. Ketchel was a great knockout puncher but he was giving away almost 50 pounds. The shrewd Johnson, serving as his own manager and matchmaker for the encounter, foresaw no real threat to himself but a great box office draw. In fact he awarded the middleweight a larger percentage of the gate than he might ordinarily have granted because Ketchell would attract customers.

Johnson contended that he permitted Ketchel to make a good showing in order to give the customers their money's worth, although the heavyweight champion felt he had complete control. Toward the end of the fight, Ketchel fired a punch that landed on the black man's jaw. "My brain had been working rapidly—so rapidly that I recognized this to be a clean cut blow with apparently much force back of it,"

Johnson later wrote. "I said to myself, 'Now's your time! Here's your chance,' and so I hit the canvas. . . . As I got to my feet, I pretended to be groggy, but in reality I was ready to deliver the knockout. Ketchel rushed me. . . . I met him with a murderous blow that put him out instead. It was a right uppercut. . . . Stanley lost several teeth and when I returned to the dressing room I found one of his teeth embedded in my glove."

Johnson might have been exaggerating the extent of his control over the fight, but whatever his strategy or the potency of Ketchel's punch, they became close friends and Ketchel joined Jackson's group when he trained for his 1910 title defense against Jim Jeffries. It was this fight that solidified the Negro fighter's position as the blackest villain in white America. Jeffries, a 220-pounder, had been heavyweight champion until he retired in 1904 to become a farmer. Jack London, leading the pack seeking the white hope, importuned, "Jeffries must emerge from his alfalfa farm and remove the golden smile from Johnson's face. Jeff, it's up to you."

At last the former title holder acceded to the demand and George L. "Tex" Rickard, former soldier of fortune in South America, Klondike gold prospector and now boxing promotor, arranged for the match, to be held in San Francisco. It was an entrepreneur's dream. The contest symbolized something beyond the fighters themselves, just as did the second Louis-Schmeling battle 28 years later. Said Johnson in 1928, "I realized that my victory in this event meant more than on any previous occasion. It wasn't just the championship that was at stake—it was my own honor, and in a degree the honor of my race."

With an arena hammered together and $300,000 in ticket

sales already counted at the box office, all parties were suddenly stunned by the decision of California's governor to ban the fight. At a cost to him of an additional $50,000, Rickard transferred the show to Reno, Nevada.

Meanwhile, the campaign of vilification intensified, with the racism pouring out of the Jeffries camp. Rumors of an agreement to fix the fight in Jeffries's favor circulated. Threats on the life of the black champion were heard. In short, the pre-fight build up was the delight of any promotor. Some 50 Pullman cars in the Reno station served as hotel annexes. People slept in bathroom tubs.

The day of the fight dawned hot and clear; 25,000 spectators choked the wooden stands. Johnson entered the ring first and seized the shady corner. When white hope Jeffries appeared, he suggested that the two men flip a coin for the place out of the sun. Shrewd showman and superb gamesman, Johnson refused; instead he simply relinquished the shade to his opponent. As a fight, it turned out to be a near massacre with the "good guy" in the eyes of most Americans, on the wrong end of the meat ax. For two rounds, Johnson carefully felt out the 35-year-old Jeffries, then concluded that "the fight was mine." Shucking off Jeffries punches, Johnson kept up what Alexander Johnson, a sportswriter, termed, "his accustomed barrage of offensive chatter, 'Come now, Mistah Jeff, let me see what yo' got.' Since Jeffries remained silent, Johnson addressed a series of remarks to Jim Corbett, another former champion who worked Jeffries's corner. Said Johnson, "In the gathering of spectators who saw the encounter was another huge group of newspaper writers and photographers. . . . I recall that occasionally I took time during the exchange of these blows to suggest to telegraph operators what to tell their newspapers."

Flashing the golden smile, Johnson bloodied Jeffries until the 15th, then decked him with a left for a full nine count. Another left ended the fight.

In the wake of this blasting of the Great White Hope, riots occurred across the nation. Some 19 deaths, 251 injuries, 5,000 cases of "disorderly conduct" were attributed to emotions over the fight. Nat Fleischer, founder of *Ring Magazine,* remembered Johnson's appearance in New York afterward. "Thousands of Negroes crowded the streets, parading, shouting, shooting off fireworks, and carrying on in hilarious fashion. They were celebrating a Roman holiday. There were some fist fights, but the anticipated disorder on a large scale was missing in contrast to the street riots which Johnson's triumph over Jeffries caused in other cities. . . ."

Johnson paid a heavy price for his victory. He became a hounded man; the numerous love affairs which he conducted openly continued to vex white American manhood sorely. Congress passed a law that forbade interstate commerce in the showing of his fight films. Johnson found it difficult to survive economically in this country because of harassment and he toured Europe. Eventually he traveled to Havana to fight a new white hope, the moody giant Jess Willard. In the 26th round, under the blazing sun, Johnson went down and was counted out. He later insisted that he agreed to take a dive. While he was on the canvas, he kept his right glove raised above his face to shade his eyes from the sun, and Johnson and others cited that as proof he had complete control of his senses. Others claimed that the heat and the age of the 37-year-old champion had finally done what no fighter could do, and that although conscious, Johnson lacked the will to continue.

Johnson fought a few more times, then served a prison

sentence on the charge of violating the Mann Act, which prohibited transporting a woman across a state line for immoral purposes. The action was brought by the mother of one of his conquests. The eight months he spent in a penitentiary didn't completely end his boxing career, though. He didn't fight his last exhibition until he was 67.

To the end of his life Johnson insisted that he had never been an antiwhite racist. To Nat Fleischer he confided, "Nat, why would they bring in the black race against the white race in athletics? I licked Tommy Burns fairly. I did the same in my fight with Jeffries. My battle with Jeffries was not a contest between a black man and a white man, but between the two boxers. . . ."

One British observer, Trevor Wignall, reflected how the liberals of the era viewed the black fighter: "Johnson had many defects. He was a swaggerer by nature, but this is not altogether surprising when it is recalled that for many years he was an absolute idol. . . . If he had not been so insanely pestered by women, and if he had not been so ridiculously flattered by men, he would probably have been a better fellow!" In support of his statement Wignall reported that on one visit to see Johnson "I was compelled to force my way into the building past crowds of women. . . ."

Wignall found Johnson quite conscious of his blackness. "He was firmly convinced that he had a mission in life. He told me this in so many words—he believed that it was his duty to 'lift the black race,' that it would be superior to the white. . . . He did considerable harm to boxing but the men to whom he rendered the greatest disservice were pugilists of his own hue."

Even if Johnson had behaved in the manner that white America believed correct, the history of other sports suggests that the paths would still have closed off to nonwhites. Before the turn of the century, blacks had already been barred from major-league baseball.

College football teams had a few black players in the early 1900s. Fritz Pollard of Brown made All-America in 1918, and Paul Robeson, before his singing career and before his politics forced him to seek exile, starred at Rutgers after World War I. But the costs of college education and the complete exclusion of blacks from admission to southern universities and a good many northern private ones, kept blacks from complete participation. In the pro ranks, black players were rare until after World War II when Paul Brown of the Cleveland Browns abandoned any limitations based upon race.

Golf and tennis were never friendly to blacks. Both games developed in private clubs that usually restricted membership to whites by costs and by choice, even in the 1970s.

Horse racing in America started out almost exclusively with black jockeys. In the first Kentucky Derby of 1875, 14 of the 15 riders were black. Color bars began to appear in the next 25 years. By 1911, blacks had been excluded from the Kentucky Derby.

In basketball, few colleges used blacks; too many games were played in the South. Pro basketball kept its color line until 1949.

In track and field, the pattern of entry, disappearance and then a resumption of participation again marked the black athlete's role. In 1904, a 400-meter man, George Poage, became the first Negro to represent the United States in the Olympics. Several Negroes competed four years later, but they seemed nearly to vanish from meets during the 1920s, only to reappear for good in 1932 with Eddie Tolan and Ralph Metcalfe, the dashmen, preceding the triumphs of

56

Jesse Owens at the 1936 Berlin Olympics.

In boxing, long before Jack Johnson antagonized white America, black fighters had found it difficult to become champions. Nat Fleischer believed that Sam Langford, Sam McVea and Joe Jeanette, contemporaries of Johnson, were probably the equals of Marvin Hart and Tommy Burns, successors to Jim Jeffries as heavyweight champions. But none of the blacks ever got into the ring with the champions.

In view of all this, it seems unfair to blame Lil Artha for the closing off of the heavyweight ring to blacks after his defeat. But, as an immediate consequence of his battering of Jeffries, Tex Rickard, the top boxing promoter of the day, absolutely refused to countenance any mixed matches for the rest of his life. Since Rickard controlled fights at major arenas, including Madison Square Garden, that effectively curbed the climb of aspiring Negro boxers. It took the death of Rickard and the punch of Joe Louis to provide for the ascendancy of a black fighter to the top.

The most immediate loser, because of Rickard's decision, was a strong Negro heavyweight, Harry Wills. Although he defeated dozens of white and black fighters, including some considered fit opponents for the reigning heavyweight champions of the 1920s, Jack Dempsey and Gene Tunney, Wills never received a title fight.

When Louis became champion, Johnson denigrated his spiritual successor whenever interviewed. But on their first meeting, although he had been cautioned not to emulate Jack Johnson, Louis recognized that he was in the presence of a champion. "Every man's got a right to his own mistakes," Louis said. "Ain't no man that ain't made none." Years later, Louis again defended Jack Johnson. "He was pretty smart in the ring. When people said to me, 'Joe, don't make the mistakes Johnson made,' I'd think that was right, but lots of white fighters made mistakes outside the ring also. When I got to be champ, half the letters I got mentioned Jack Johnson, lot of them from old colored people. They thought he disgraced the Negro, but I figure he did what he wanted to do, and that didn't affect me."

The life of Jack Johnson may not have been in the mind of Joe Louis, but it weighed heavily with those who invested in and controlled the fortunes of the sport.

5

While the boxing establishment anxiously observed the progress of the black fighter from Detroit and worried about his effect on ticket sales, some entrepreneurs reached a decision that Joe Louis was a potential money-making project. One day early in 1935, as Roxborough, in his chauffeur-driven limousine, rolled to a stop before his office, the door to the Lincoln was opened. Before Roxborough could emerge, a local gambler named Lefty Clark slid onto a seat.

"One of the syndicate people told me Louis was for sale," said Clark.

"Somebody's pulling your leg, Lefty," Roxborough answered. "He's not for sale, at any price."

The chauffeur did not wait to see the outcome of the curbside exchange; he fled the car and ran to find Louis at Roxborough's offices. "There's a gangster out there trying to buy you from Roxborough," the chauffeur shouted.

The fighter hurried outside and ran to the car where Clark continued to talk with Roxborough. "Mr. Roxborough," Louis yelled, "you tell that man I ain't for sale." Louis slammed shut the car door and went back to the office.

"Roxy, I'm sorry," said Clark, "but this syndicate guy, well, I thought he knew what was going on."

"Forget it," said the manager. "They tried to move in on

Joe before and I blocked them. They're just sore. They told you that, trying to stir up trouble."

Detroit's hoodlums belonged to the Purple Gang, which didn't have quite the clout of the bigger combines operating out of Chicago and New York. Roxborough alone may not have been able to fend off Detroit hoods but in Julian Black he had an ally who could reach to the top of syndicate activities; this offered the best protection against Purple Gang hoods muscling in on Louis.

The incident with Lefty Clark may not have posed much of a threat to Roxborough and company, but it was a reminder that an aura of gold had begun to suffuse the operation. Major fight promoters began to take notice of the new prospect from Detroit. One telephoned John Roxborough to offer fights at an arena that he controlled. "I can help your boy," he advised Roxborough, "but you understand he's a nigger and can't win every time he goes into the ring."

"So am I," answered the manager and hung up. The brain trust could only wait for the right opportunity to knock. Meanwhile, the fighter continued to punch his way through the lists. With his limited skills he had been carefully matched early in his career against relative pushovers. But progress meant standing up against better opponents. Fortunately, Blackburn's lessons had begun to take effect. "Joe was easy to teach," the trainer remarked in his later years. "You only had to tell him something once. But at first he sure didn't like fighting. At least he often showed a lack of enthusiasm for it. Sometimes he hated the ring and it was all I could do to put enough steam into him to make him fight." Success and the money that it brought eventually made Louis more enthusiastic.

When asked about Blackburn as a teacher almost 40 years later, Louis said, "He talked to you in a way that you could understand that what he said was right. Even if you thought he was wrong, you'd still take a chance that he was right because of the way he would explain his ideas."

Besides teaching him balance, Blackburn helped Louis develop his left jab—a weapon that can keep an opponent from being able to move forward and, if delivered with enough snap and frequency, wear down an opponent enough to set him up for a knockout punch. The most powerful punch in Louis's arsenal was the left hook, but he hit hard with his right hand also. Louis employed a shuffling gait in the ring, and he experienced the most difficulty with opponents who kept skipping around the ring, staying out of range. But while his footwork could never be labeled fast, Louis, under Jack Blackburn's tutelage, learned to throw his punches with extreme rapidity. "His feet moved slow," said a sparring partner, "but his hands were very fast." Against an opponent who came to slug, instead of box, the swiftness of Louis's hands exploited minute openings.

The training routine insisted upon by Blackburn was hardly attractive to a young man who had just begun to find ready cash in his pockets and a growing public. Roadwork began before sunrise; every morning Louis would run six miles around Chicago's Washington Park. When he finished, he could climb back into bed until 11 o'clock. After a breakfast, Blackburn took Louis to Trafton's gym where he drilled his pupil incessantly in footwork, balance and blocking punches.

"Sometimes at night," remembered Louis, "he would let me go to a movie, but mostly we would sit around and talk boxing. He would show how to throw punches without losing balance. I told him I won all my amateur fights with my left hook, and he saw how my right hand pulled me in and left me off balance. He kept after me until I could shift my

61

left foot to put me in position to throw that right without letting myself open for a counterpunch. He saw I couldn't follow a left hook with a right without picking up one foot. He said it was no good, that a fighter had to keep both feet planted to get power or take a punch." Louis suffered a bad scare in his eighth pro fight when he met Art Sykes at Chicago's Arcadia Gardens. "I hit him a hundred times but couldn't keep him down. I didn't want to hit him any more. When he went to the floor in the eighth and got the count, I was glad it was over, but when I left the club the doctors were still with him in the dressing room. I called the hospital all night to find how he was doing." Later, Louis met Damon Runyon, who had rooted for Sykes as a fellow New Yorker, and Runyon remarked, "You almost killed my boy."

Art Sykes retired from fighting and, reviewing the event, Louis once said, "They come in there to give it to me. I can't say it's a sorry feeling, but I don't like to do it."

In his 12th fight against Lee Ramage, Louis received a boxing lesson for eight rounds before catching up to him. "I think that Ramage was the best boxer I ever had against me [most likely an overstatement that says less about Ramage's skill than Louis's lack of it at the time they met]. I could hardly lay one right on that boy." In the corner, Blackburn told his student to keep boxing, to tire his man out and then capitalize on an opening. "In the eighth I saw his arms drop a little. Chappie had taught me to watch another fighter's arms. He said, 'When a fighter is fresh he keeps his arms at regular height. When he's tired and wants to make believe he's fresh, he lifts too high, and that's the giveaway.' I knocked Ramage down three times in the eighth. His corner threw in the towel."

The country was deep into the Great Depression, but Louis had begun to prosper. By Christmas of 1934, just after the Ramage fight, Joe Louis was no longer a poor boy who collected little better than pocket money from his fights. One fight brought him a $1,400 purse. He took $270 of his share and repaid the Detroit home relief agency for the money advanced to the family while Pat Brooks was unable to get work.

"Mr. Roxborough and Mr. Black let me come home for Christmas with the family and it was a big Christmas. I had money to buy clothes and watches and such for all my kin." Until this time, Louis had been living in a room rented in the home of a Chicago chef named Bill Bottoms. His host later became the official cook at Louis's training camps. And while the prospering young fighter bestowed gifts upon his family, he did not neglect his own creature comforts and tastes. Louis bloomed in a variety of striped suits with wide lapels, and he sported the light-colored, broad-brimmed hats of the day, made more famous by Chicago's fashion plate, Al Capone.

In the first months of 1935, the investment returns soared for all concerned in the Louis operation. In early January, Patsy Perroni, a six-year veteran with no future in sight, helped lure a full house to Olympic Stadium in Detroit. Although Louis could only manage a decision against Perroni, he received better than $4,000. In a Los Angeles rematch with Lee Ramage in March, Louis earned $3,000 for a second-round knockout.

It was at this time that Louis began to be known as the Brown Bomber. Several accounts of Louis's life credit a Detroit promoter, Scotty Monteith, with the nickname. Eddie Edgar insists that Monteith had nothing to do with it, that the staff of the *Free Press* had a habit of sitting around bouncing possible labels for athletes off one another and Brown Bomber came out of one of these sessions.

Louis's reputation by the close of 1934 was sufficient enough to give pause to a number of managers intent upon building up their own fighters. For example, Mushky Jackson was managing fighters at the time. "I handled nothin' but heavyweights," said Jackson. "I had heard of a prelim boy, a colored boy from Detroit who was doing four rounders and knocking everybody out. Scotty Monteith, a Detroit matchmaker, called me and said he could set up a fight for me with my fighter Red Barry. 'I'll give you six rounds with this Joe Louis.' I said I don't want to fight him, I don't want no part of him."

While dodging the challenge of Louis to his own hopeful, Jackson kept in mind that the Louis management was in search of fodder. Shortly after, Jackson entered into a discussion with a Chicago promoter, Benny Ray, who wanted an opponent for Louis. "I had a fighter, Stanley Poreda. He had a reputation but he was going backwards. I asked Ray how much we could get. They offered a $1,000 guarantee, a week's expenses, the hotel bill, plus two round-trip tickets.

"We came out for the fight and Poreda looks a little wobbly. I didn't want the boxing commission to see him in a gym and I said he'd done all his working out in New York.

"But the boxing commission insisted that Poreda would have to work out, show that he was in shape. I agreed only to have him limber up. We're in the same gym where Louis is and he's knocking his sparring partners all over the place. Julian Black, the manager, is there too. I says to Poreda, 'Don't look over there.' I put up a punching bag with a swivel and I tells Poreda to hit it. The bag flies off and I say, 'Wotta puncher. That's enough, you'll break the bag.' Black's new in the business and I figure they won't catch on.

"The fight itself was something nobody ever heard of. My fighter took a count of 39 in one round. The first punch from

Louis put him down for nine, the second punch for another nine. The third punch knocked Poreda out of the ring and the referee kept counting until he got back, he got up to 21.

"When I got back to New York, I tell everybody what a fighter that Louis is. But nobody paid any attention. He was colored, and colored fighters were a dime a dozen."

Jackson's path crossed that of the Louis entourage again, however. The New York manager had traveled to San Francisco with hapless Stanley Poreda for a benefit fight with the heavyweight champion of the time, Max Baer. Louis had just knocked out Lee Ramage in Los Angeles. This time Jackson was willing to consider "my palooka, Donald Reds Barry" as a foe worthy of Louis—for a $3,000 guarantee. The encounter took place in San Francisco two weeks later and Barry failed to survive the second round.

Jackson claims that Black and Roxborough, taken with his acumen, offered 10 percent of their fighter if Jackson could arrange an outing in New York. "I said it was too tough to get matches for a colored fighter." In spite of his lack of faith in the economic future of Joe Louis, Jackson brought the word of the black fighter's skill to the ears of one promoter who was astute enough to sense the possibilities—Michael Strauss Jacobs, the Uncle Mike who dominated boxing for 12 lush years.

6

During the 12 years that he promoted fights, Jacobs staged 61 championship bouts and arranged a total of 1,500 shows; on Joe Louis alone, he grossed $10 million. While he reigned, the boxing world turned on a Yes or No clacked from his ill-fitting false teeth. Some fighters swore by him, others at him. Typically, Sugar Ray Robinson did both. While desperately seeking a crack at the welterweight championship in 1946, an alienated Robinson growled, "Mike will manipulate anybody for a buck. He's always sore if I fight without his okay. If you don't do what he wants, he'll try to prevent you from getting fights anywhere. You don't earn the championship on merit anymore, you buy it." Several years later, however, having bedded down as both welterweight and middleweight champion, a snugger Robinson said, "You check the records and you'll find the total income of main-event fighters doubled or maybe tripled while Mike was in the driver's seat. Mike's business was good for two, three, four, sometimes five million a year. You've got to figure that the fighters were cutting in for 50 percent of that."

Someone hung on Jacobs the nickname of Uncle Mike. But to so many observers the avuncular image hardly squared with his restless pursuit of a dollar. When presented with a proposition Jacobs would lisp through his false teeth,

"What's in it for Uncle Mike?" Columnist Dan Parker, on Hearst's *New York Mirror,* thought that Jacobs deserved to be called Uncle Wolf because the manner in which he downed food mirrored his business practices. Parker regularly scolded Jacobs for his easy tolerance of Frankie Carbo, a known underworld power who controlled a string of fighters. Parker pointed out the frequency of these performers on fight cards arranged by Jacobs and suspicious results in bouts involving betting coups. He accused the New York State Boxing Commission of nonfeasance for its failure to investigate such Jacobean maneuvers. Parker also reported that Carbo on one occasion placed his pistol on a desk during a meeting with Jacobs and only a call for assistance to Mafia don Frank Costello averted a potentially bloody confrontation for Uncle Mike.

But Joe Louis's evaluation of Mike Jacobs, made 20 years after the promoter's death, was all on the plus side of the ledger: "He was one of the finest men I ever knew."

At the peak of his career, Jacobs operated both from Madison Square Garden on Eighth Avenue and 49th Street and his ticket brokerage office in the Forrest Hotel on 49th Street between Broadway and Eighth Avenue, a block from the Garden. The site became a hangout for fight managers, fighters and hangers on. Supplicants often waited their turn on the sidewalk, catching pale sun rays on what became known as Jacobs Beach while hoping for a golden flash from Uncle Mike. Occasionally, police officers attempted to chase the throngs, which often included men familiar with the wrong parts of station houses. But Uncle Mike could be counted upon to confer with the officers and the lawmen would depart, probably several bills richer.

Jacobs's beginning, like that of his future superstar, Joe Louis, was rooted in poverty. His parents, Eastern European

Jews, fled from the oppression in their homeland and settled for a time in Dublin before coming to New York. The sojourn in Ireland put one peculiar mark upon the Jacobs family. When it come to New York, it chose to locate on the lower West Side of the city—"Hell's Kitchen," which was the Irish district—rather than in the heavily Jewish environs of the East Side.

Young Mike, born in 1880, grew up in a more pugnacious atmosphere than if he had been raised among East Side Jews. As a 10-year-old newsboy he had to fight off competitors who would steal one's stock or, failing that, burn it. To supplement his income, he also took up the trade of a "digger," someone hired by ticket scalpers to purchase seats in advance at a box office. The brokers then levied whatever the traffic could bear for hard-to-get tickets. By age 12, Jacobs was shrewd enough to see that as the middleman, he received the least profit in the operation. He began scalping on his own. When an indignant former employer threatened to assault him, Jacobs smoothly played the role of ingenuous kid. He tearfully hollered for a policeman and accused his assailant of the crime of scalping. The cop found a pile of tickets in the offender's pocket. The older man considered himself lucky to escape from the boy rival with neither a jail sentence nor the loss of his investment.

Jacobs's father, Isaac, was a tailor who added to the family income by working as a professional greeter and message runner for new immigrants. Mike worked with the father on the piers as a candy butcher and purveyor of refreshments on the excursion boats.

When the excursion boats shut down for the winter, and the ticket-hawking business fell slack, Mike Jacobs worked as a waiter. Even there he got himself an edge, for he worked at Tammany Hall, the center of New York politics. His customers included the ranking politicians of the day, men like Boss Richard Croker and Police Chief William Devery; men under whom corruption flourished like orchids in a hothouse.

Even as a boy, Jacobs was not content merely to offer his wares. He knew how to create demand where there had been none. On the excursion decks, he was generous with his portions of peanuts because they created a thirst that pushed the lemonade. He would make a swing around the deck where couples enjoyed the sea air and drop a bag of candy on the woman's lap. It had the air of a sample, a free offering. But Jacobs would return later to collect from an escort too embarrassed to refuse in the presence of his date. He sold seasick remedy, a concoction that amounted to tea with lemon.

When the Hudson–Fulton Celebration stirred New Yorkers in 1907, Jacobs earned the name of Steamboat Mike for his skirmishes with the Iron Steamship Co. "I had a couple of tubs and an old scow," said Jacobs. "But I had people in uniforms selling tickets all over town." The rival company flexed its political muscles and an ordinance forbade salesmen from hawking tickets in the streets, and restricted the business to sheds or booths. Steamboat Mike arranged for carpenters to construct flimsy, lightweight booths that a man could tote with him, setting up shop wherever the traffic seemed lively. The ordinance had not specified that the booths be stationary and Jacobs triumphed again over an institution with much greater financial resources.

At sixteen, Jacobs claimed a stake of $1,000 and he began to concentrate on the ticket-brokerage business. He pounded the pavement so hard, pushing tickets to the boats and to the biggest attraction of the day, the Metropolitan Opera, that his feet actually bled. He secured an edge at the Met through his friendship with the Met impresario, David Belasco; with stars such as Caruso, Melba and Galli-Curci around, Jacobs profited fiercely.

The connection with the theater enabled him to become something of a showman himself. He signed Enrico Caruso for a series of one-night stands, guaranteeing the singer $1,000 a night. The concerts made $80,000 for Jacobs. He also sent Barrymores, Ethel and Lionel, off on a successful tour.

When British Suffragette Emmeline Pankhurst arrived in New York before World War I, the astute Jacobs counted the house of devoted listeners. To the astonishment of Emmeline Pankhurst, he proposed a lecture tour with paid admissions. The women's-rights leader at first protested that her message could not be commercialized, but Jacobs persuaded her that everyone would profit, including the cause. The pilgrimage of Emmeline Pankhurst fulfilled the vision.

While World War I was making the world safe for Democracy, Jacobs made money by supplying services to men away from home. He established concessions at army camps up and down the East Coast, and the enterprises controlled by him—bus lines, barbershops, snack stores—brought in $5,000 a month. He sold out the operation for $1,000,000 shortly before the market vanished with the Armistice.

Jacobs became involved in sports through his ticket business. He scored a notable killing in 1905 with the first of the modern World Series. The contests between the New York Nationals and the Philadelphia Nationals were close enough to Jacobs's home base for him to do a brisk commerce in tickets. But it was not until 1916, that Jacobs became fully involved in sports promotions. Everything grew out of an unlikely partnership between the Hell's Kitchen Jew and an honest-to-God, former cowboy named Tex Rickard.

Rickard and Jacobs turned out to be a well-matched pair,

but on the surface, except for their cunning in extracting wealth from the labors of others, they were an unlikely match. Born on the edge of the Kansas–Missouri border in either 1870 or 1871, George Lewis Rickard caught the tail end of the Western frontier as a trail rider. While his future partner grubbed for a living in the streets of New York, Rickard spent his long hours in the saddle tending to the welfare of beef cattle. The cowboy became town marshal of the hamlet of Henrietta, Texas, about the time that Jacobs was starting his career as a candy butcher. Death of an infant and then of his wife sent Rickard off to frozen spaces of Alaska after gold. But Rickard spent most of his life in Alaska operating gambling halls and saloons, harvesting his gold from the pockets of prospectors, rather than panning for it himself.

Rickard made and blew several small fortunes in Alaska and then drifted down to Goldfield, Nevada, where he ran a gambling saloon The Northern. Goldfield residents decided to boost their gold-mining interests by focusing public attention upon their town. The promotional scheme hit upon was hosting a lightweight title fight between Joe Gans and Battling Nelson on Labor Day, 1906. It was Rickard who dreamed up the idea of piling up the $30,000 purse in $20 gold pieces in a bank window, a publicity stunt that produced photographs in newspapers around the country. Rickard was not a novice in fight promotions at the time; he had already staged bouts in his gambling saloons and in theaters in Alaska.

The fight went to Gans on a particularly flagrant foul by Nelson in what has been described as one of the foulest bouts on record, but Rickard not only had made Goldfield famous (although the expected mining-stock profits failed to accrue), he pocketed a good sum of money to boot. He would remem-

71

ber the effectiveness of the golden purse when he beat out other contenders anxious to stage the Jack Johnson–Jim Jeffries contest.

Jacobs also had the ability to think in the grand style, but unlike Rickard he was much less of a gambler; he did not invest unless he saw for himself a sure thing. Jacob's first tie to Rickard came when he advanced the promoter cash for a 1916 fight between Jess Willard and Frank Moran. His advance to Rickard for the Willard–Moran fight brought him blocks of good seats which he could unload at high profits.

The Jacobs relationship with Tex Rickard solidified with the 1921 match between heavyweight champion Jack Dempsey and the French contender George Carpentier at Boyle's 30 Acres, an open field near the car barns of Jersey City. Rickard had now permitted his lively imagination to consider the first million-dollar gate in the history of the sport. His initial flush of enthusiasm for the project pushed the promoter and his backers to the edge of a fiscal abyss. Dempsey, through his manager Jack Kearns, refused to accept a percentage of the gate (as high as 40 percent); he wanted a flat guarantee of $300,000. The challenger, a French war hero, insisted upon $200,000 for his appearance. The old Madison Square Garden with a capacity of only 12,000 could not possibly provide enough revenue to cover these sums. Rickard leased Boyle's 30 Acres, so named for a printing plant that owned the land, and set about construction of a bowl that would accommodate 60,000 spectators.

The size of Rickard's commitments froze the minds and wallets of his original backers, however. Rickard's project appeared on the verge of collapse. He needed $100,000 cash just to satisfy the demands of his contractor. But Mike Jacobs, impressed by the heavy early demand for tickets from his regular customers, threw the drowning promoter a lifeline of nearly a quarter of a million dollars. He put up $25,000 and convinced eight other ticket brokers to advance the same to Rickard. In return, Rickard dished out to his benefactors big blocks of choice seats. In fact, advance sales went so well that Rickard installed nearly 30,000 more seats. As a favor to his angel and to himself as well, Rickard planted a newspaper story to the effect that all of the expensive ringside seats were gone. Free-lance speculators beseeched Jacobs for any ringsides he might have, and of course, as the friend of the house, he held a sizable number.

The fight, an artistic promotion, fell something short as a sports event. Dempsey demolished the challenger in the fourth round. And the suspicion is that Dempsey had to carry Carpentier that far in obedience to Tex Rickard who feared that a quick KO might sour future promotions. As a financial operation, the 30 Acres extravaganza exceeded the wildest hopes with 80,000 people paying better than 1.7 million dollars. The returns on the fight actually were much greater since Jacobs and the other brokers taxed the public ruthlessly. In fact, Jacobs supposedly disposed of more than 5,000 tickets at an average profit of $50 a seat, for a profit of $250,000. Some of the unsold admissions actually were in the hands of speculators who had paid a stiff fare to get them from Jacobs. The only participants to walk away with deep regrets must have been Dempsey and Kearns; a percentage would have brought them several hundred thousand dollars more than the flat guarantee.

Mike Jacobs had now become firmly entrenched in the boxing world. Through his connection with Tex Rickard, who not only controlled the heavyweight champion Dempsey and also enjoyed the post of matchmaker for the new Madison Square Garden that opened in 1924, Jacobs was guaranteed access to the best tickets for any major fight promotion. During this period, Jacobs actually operated out of a secret office in the Garden, a windowless storage room area, while his visible business address was the Forrest Hotel a block away.

Rickard, who had been instrumental in building the new Madison Square Garden, had depended upon Jacobs in deciding on the right place to build the Garden. "The trend for amusements is to the midtown section. It will soon be the heart of the theatrical district. Everything is moving up toward Fiftieth Street," Jacobs advised Rickard, as reported in Nat Fleischer's memoirs.

Boxing and Jacobs might never really have flourished in New York, however, were it not for the intercession of sports-minded politicians, those same individuals whom Jacobs had so carefully cultivated while he waited on tables at Tammany Hall. The old Frawley law that had banned decisions had been repealed, along with restrictions on racially mixed fights. A state athletic commission was named to supervise fight promotions, and standards for lengths of fights and officiating were made statutory. The sponsor of these reforms was state legislator James J. Walker, soon to become mayor of New York and a devoted fan of the kind of entertainments produced by Rickard, Jacobs and their friends.

When Tex Rickard died in 1929 of pneumonia, Jacobs, as one of the thinkers behind the new Garden and a silent partner in Rickard's enterprises, expected to be named his successor as the promoter of fights at the Garden. Instead, the executives of the arena reached out for a talkative, diminutive, dapper former fight manager, Jimmy Johnston, also known in the trade as "Little Larceny" or "The Boy Bandit." At a Garden party to celebrate the appointment of Johnston, Jacobs supposedly took over the position of beer

74

dispenser. Johnston, a man apparently never at a loss for words, remarked to Mayor James J. Walker, "Leave it to Mike to ace his way into the job that makes everybody come to him."

Unfortunately for Jimmy Johnston, and quite possibly through faults of his own, boxing began to sag almost immediately upon his capture of the job of promoting the sport. Johnston's primary handicap was the absence of a popular heavyweight champion. Gene Tunney had beaten Jack Dempsey for the championship in Philadelphia in 1926. In a return bout in Chicago one year later, Dempsey's left hook in the seventh round smashed Tunney to the floor, but referee Dave Barry held up his count because Tunney took advantage of the extra seconds and didn't rise until the count of nine. He then went on to decision Dempsey in the "battle of the long count." Tunney defended his title only one more time, against Tom Heeney, the Australian Hard Rock, in 1928. Employing his usual skill, Tunney, who never showed the devastating knockout punch of a Dempsey, sliced up Heeney for 11 bloody rounds until the referee called a halt. But this was Rickard's first failure in a heavyweight fight; he claimed to have lost better than $150,000. Tunney then retired, leaving the heavyweight title vacant.

Jimmy Johnston struggled to make attractions out of an elimination tournament to determine the new champion. English heavyweight champion Phil Scott, with an awesome lack of credentials for serious contention, had once been a Jimmy Johnston fighter. So he participated in the elimination series, meeting Jack Sharkey. While under the guidance of Jimmy Johnston, Scott had earned the title of Phaintin' Phil for his habit of clutching himself in the groin and falling to the canvas while gasping the word "foul." During the match with Sharkey, Scott bellowed his traditional complaint. The referee disallowed the protests and Scott, after several more body blows from Sharkey, eventually relaxed on the canvas to the disgust of spectators.

The logical contestant to meet Sharkey was a heavy-browed German named Max Schmeling. He possessed a strong right hand but otherwise seemed less than impressive. And when he entered the ring in New York in June of 1930 for one of the few successful promotions by Johnston, the expert opinion seemed confirmed. Sharkey piled up points in the first three rounds. But in the fourth round a wild swing by Sharkey clearly landed well below the German's belt line and left him unable to continue. Officials were forced to declare Schmeling the world champion. In a rematch Sharkey outpointed the champion over 15 rounds. Then Sharkey was defeated, under suspicious circumstances, by Primo Carnera, the graceless Italian giant.

Along with this less-than-exciting series of heavyweight championship fights, Jimmy Johnston had to buck the Depression. The big money from Wall Street was no longer around to snap up tickets for the big fights, to say nothing of the regular fight cards that were supposed to be a staple of the Garden's diet.

Meanwhile, Mike Jacobs continued to prosper, selling tickets when he could, not burdened with any overhead. Brokers in that period often took tickets on a consignment basis. If the $30 seats wouldn't sell at $30, they could mark them down, take their profit and pay off the promoter at a rate of say $20 a ticket. Opportunity for Jacobs to get fully immersed in the fight game arose out of a short-sighted decision by the Garden management. In a step to maintain revenues, the chiefs decreed that henceforth the Garden would no longer sponsor charity events in which the arena split the proceeds with some worthy cause and the participants. Among the dispossessed was the Milk Fund, a pet project of Mrs. William Randolph Hearst.

In an attempt to propitiate their employer's wife, three Hearst writers, Damon Runyon, Bill Farnsworth and Ed Frayne, agreed to stage their own fight for the Milk Fund. They signed Barney Ross who had surrendered his light-weight title to become a welterweight and in 1934 held a bastard crown known as the junior welterweight champion-ship, and Billy Petrolle, sometimes known as the Fargo Express, although his home town was Berwick, Pennsylvania. To handle ticket sales, the three newspapermen engaged Mike Jacobs. The fight, which was won by Ross, produced $10,000 for the Milk Fund, a modest enough sum. But Jacobs perceived a marvelous opportunity to strike out on his own against the fumbling Garden boxing operation. As was customary, he secured himself an immediate edge by forming a partnership with the three newsmen and creating the 20th Century Sporting Club, with plans to run regular cards at the Hippodrome, an arena at 6th Avenue and 44th Street. Garden officials struck back at the competition with a bitter complaint to the Hearst papers that their writers ought not to be permitted to be parties to sports promotions they would be writing about. Officials of the Garden made no reference to their many sub-rosa arrangements with writers.

In a decision based upon pragmatism, Hearst officials forced Frayne and Farnsworth, the lesser members of the paper, to choose between journalism and promotions. They opted to go with Jacobs. But Runyon, the headliner for Hearst, faced no such ultimatum; he was allowed to continue in both roles as a reporter and a Jacobs partner. Later, Run-yon split with the 20th Century Sporting Club and became an acidulous critic of Jacobs.

Coincidentally with the formation of the 20th Century

Sporting Club, Jacobs began to think seriously about the highly touted Negro fighter from Detroit. The promoter was apparently astute enough to see that when it came to hand-and-hand combat, the public would accept a black man, provided he was destructive enough. If Jacobs held any racial sentiments, the potential for making big money off a black fighter stifled them. In point of fact, throughout Louis's career, Jacobs exhibited no antiblack attitudes. He often invited Louis to his home in Rumson, New Jersey, fed not only the champion but the black sparring partners as well and, when he visited Louis in camp, he even shot crap with the working stiffs, regardless of their color. On the other hand, Jacobs could hardly be considered a militant believer in equal rights. Shortly after World War II, Jacobs sat glumly talking about the lack of box-office challengers for the welterweight title then held by Red Cochrane. Fight buff Budd Schulberg listened and then mentioned, he claims, his own candidate, Ray Robinson. "Aah, we got too many colored boys on top now; the public's gettin' tired of 'em," growled Jacobs. Schulberg hastened to excuse the promoter of bias. His perception of the market rather than racism spoke on this occasion, theorized Schulberg.

Mushky Jackson was not the only one to pour tales of the Detroit prospect into the calculating mind of Jacobs. Nat Fleischer, who now had his own publication, *Ring Magazine*, also did publicity work for Jacobs and handled radio materials for the promoter. In his memoirs, Fleischer claimed to have spotted Louis's talent while he participated in the National AAU Championships in Boston "and recognized a future world titleholder. Then I saw him three times in professional fights in the Midwest and came back to New York raving about the young Negro whose clouting ability was a reminder of the early days of Dempsey."

Jacobs contacted Roxborough and Black, but he was not the first promoter to see the potential of Joe Louis. As the representative of Madison Square Garden, Jimmy Johnston also made a pitch. But according to the Louis executive board, he betrayed a certain coolness. He indicated that the Garden could survive without the Brown Bomber. And there was a suggestion that more money perhaps could be made if Louis did not reach the top, which badly wounded Roxborough's sense of pride.

Roxborough claimed that he was so anxious to tie in with the new 20th Century Sporting Club—Jacobs and his newspaper partners—that he offered 10 percent of Louis to Sam Pian and Art Winch, co-managers of Barney Ross and good chums of Jacobs. In what must have been a singularly disinterested gesture for boxing, Pian supposedly rejected the offer, but agreed to approach Jacobs. Whatever Jacobs had heard about Louis, he now had confirmed by Pian, whose judgment of talent could not be faulted. Jacobs, unlike the too crafty Jimmy Johnston, played easy to get and brought Black and Roxborough to New York.

The initial agreement was simply a handshake. Roxborough, in fact, never signed his name to any paper with Jacobs. On the other hand, Julian Black did make a binding commitment with the 20th Century Sporting Club and, however much Roxborough's arrangement with Jacobs rested on simple trust, Louis was in fact legally bound to the New York promoter.

Barney Nagler's account insists that there was a written document to which all parties, including Louis, affixed their signatures, and it seems unlikely that Jacobs, as fully versed in the slippery quality of verbal agreements and the knavery endemic to boxing, would have settled for less than legal control.

But an aura of good feeling did envelop the new boxing trust. When Jacobs made his pitch a cautious Roxborough had inquired what the fighter might be obligated to do in fulfilling the contract. To the manager's delight, Jacobs answered, "He can win every fight he has, knock 'em out in the first round if possible. I promise if Joe ever gets to the top, he'll get the shot at the title." Throughout his career, for all of his scheming to hike the box-office take and for all his easy tolerance, even compliance with hoodlums and their fighters, Jacobs achieved basically a reputation for promoting honest fights. Jacobs was intelligent enough to know that while customers would accept heavier and heavier prices for admissions, dumped fights, particularly in feature attractions, would destroy the business. Ironically enough, the fight that brought both Louis and Jacobs enough power to dominate boxing was against the man whose career was most shadowed by corruption and fixed fights—Primo Carnera.

7

Once Louis had become his property, Jacobs undertook to develop him with consummate skill. On the eve of Louis's ten-round fight on March 28, 1935, against a clever boxer named Natie Brown, Jacobs reserved an entire railroad car and carried as many as 30 of New York City's sports writers to Detroit, lavishing upon them food and liquor en route. It was on this occasion that Louis met Jacobs for the first time. From that first meeting on, nothing ever shook the fighter's confidence in the promoter. And there was never any suggestion that Jacobs ever cheated the fighter of his share of the proceeds. Whenever Louis came to New York, he visited Jacobs's offices, often taking the promoter's chair, putting his feet on the desk to hold court with reporters, while Jacobs would dart off to a corner of the Garden, or, as sometimes in his zeal for secrecy, drag the immediate object of his deal off to a small toilet that ensured privacy.

Natie Brown proved too evasive for the new Jacobs protégé. While Louis repeatedly drove home punches and cut up Natie Brown badly, he failed to score a knockout and had to settle for a decision. If that disappointed the Louis–Jacobs combine, it did not seriously damage the reputation of the fighter. The New Yorkers whom Jacobs had carted to Detroit filed glowing accounts of the winner. Harry Markson, at the time a reporter for one of the papers, later a Jacobs employee, and ultimately director of boxing for Madison Square Garden, said, "Even though he didn't KO Brown, Louis was exciting and impressive. You could see this kid had it, the way you could the first time you'd seen Ray Robinson or Willie Pep." Later, Louis, knocked out Natie Brown in a rematch.

While Jacobs sought a suitable foe for Louis's New York debut, Blackburn, Black and Roxborough kept the fighter busy. Following the decision over Natie Brown, Louis scored a third-round KO of Roy Lazar in Chicago, a two-round knockout of Biff Benton in Dayton, a six-round KO over Roscoe Toles in Flint, Michigan, took two rounds to put away Willie Davis in Peoria and three for Gene Stanton in Kalamazoo. None of these adversaries seriously threatened Louis, or anyone else, and they served chiefly to help publicize Detroit's dark tiger. For meeting a journeyman like Roy Lazar, Louis's end was worth $12,000, double what he got for Natie Brown. In other fights, however, the money ran as little as $750.

And while Louis marked time on the chins of these opponents, Jacobs found the opponent he sought in Primo Carnera, the 6-foot 5¾-inch Italian circus strong man who had briefly held the heavyweight championship, winning it from Jack Sharkey, then losing it to Max Baer. The date set was June 25, in New York, and although the 20th Century Sporting Club was but a year old, Jacobs recognized that he had an attraction that demanded more than the sleazy Hippodrome and he rented Yankee Stadium for the big fight. In a fatal failure to protect its flanks Madison Square Garden had not signed up the local ballparks to prevent Jacobs from a coup.

Louis arrived in New York City by train four weeks before the fight, and the publicity buildup, begun by Jacobs, snowballed. Newsreel cameramen shoved around the crowd of curious spectators and newspaper reporters. The commotion outdid anything that Louis had experienced before. He had begun to enjoy the shock of recognition that would greet him in the streets of Detroit, but he was unprepared for the mass press interview. To some reporters he appeared sullen. He retreated into silence when confronted by a situation that overwhelmed him, as he had in the classrooms of Detroit.

A brief tour of celebrities and places dazzled the newcomer. He met his former idol, Jack Dempsey, dropped in at City Hall for a brief visit with the town's first citizen, Mayor Fiorello H. LaGuardia, and he even savored his initial seductive taste of Harlem high life, making an appearance on stage at the Harlem Opera House. Customers watched him do a simple turn, "I punched the bag! Made like I was training and went on stage with the girls."

But occasionally he was reminded that he wasn't, after all, a white fighter. As part of the promotion, Mike Jacobs had arranged for the fighter and his trainer to drop in on a number of newspaper editors. Louis remembered one stop at the *New York Daily News,* where a journalist delivered a lecture ". . . on our color. He finished up saying that we had two strikes on us. Jack Blackburn turned to me and said, 'Let's go Chappie, we're going to have a lot of fun with that third strike.' " The memory of the incident brought one of Louis's wider grins.

With the obligatory promotional activities over, Joe Louis, Jack Blackburn, Bill Bottoms, John Roxborough and an assorted group of sparring partners moved into Doc Bier's training camp at Pompton Lakes, New Jersey. Some of the other residents of the area complained about the influx of black skins. But Joseph Bier, a physician, shrugged off the anti-Negro sentiments.

For Louis, rural New Jersey proved a delight. Russell Cowan, a young man assigned to serve as a sort of aide-de-camp to Roxborough and coach Louis in grammar and manners, wrote several letters to his sponsor, John Dancy, then secretary of the Detroit Urban League. "The boy is living the life of Reilly," Cowan informed Dancy. "After the rest period in the morning, I drive him over to a riding academy where he warms his buttocks on the back of a nag. . . . Mr. Roxborough has been accompanying him on the gallop. Both have become rather tender behind from the bumping. And they have been chasing the elusive globule around the golf links, much to the amazement of the citizenry in the hills and hollows." (Contrary to what most accounts claim, Louis had taken up golf well before his disastrous first meeting with Max Schmeling.)

Russell Cowan reported that local legend claimed George Washington slept at the Pompton Lakes house while attending the wedding of General Phillip Schuyler's daughter and that Louis had his room—which sounds like a thrust by the Jacobs publicity machine.

In another letter Cowan reported, "We were in New York Thursday to see the Max Baer–Jimmy Braddock championship fight at the Madison Square Bowl on Long Island [*sic*]." After observing the match, Louis supposedly commented, "Ain't nobody gonna tell me these are the two best fighters in the world!"

Cowan offered John Dancy a modicum of sociological research. "This is wonderful country up here. Met some bright, fine people in towns like Passaic, Montclair. . . . all high-class, colored people who are doing very well as far as it appears on the surface. And they have been entertaining us on a high scale. As well as the Congressman, Mr. Hartley of this district. He had a special spread for Joe the other evening." Ten years later, Congressman Fred Hartley achieved national recognition as co-author of the Taft–Hartley law which restricted practices of labor unions.

"All the public places have been thrown open and many of the private spots, much to the efforts of the State Police who have given us the right to rush pell-mell through the countryside with an escort. It's good to be with a winner," concluded Cowan.

An almost carnival atmosphere surrounded the Pompton Lakes camp. Although the Detroit fighter had been a professional less than a year, the promotional build-up attracted as many as 6,000 people to the weekend sparring sessions. Vendors hawked souvenirs, hot dogs and soda pop. There seemed to be no limit to the pre-fight demands of the press and the newsreel cameramen. On one occasion, a photographer requested Louis to pose with a huge slice of watermelon. Louis flatly refused, to the amazement of the photographer, and in answer to the question of why not, Louis snapped, "Because I don't like watermelon."

"Joe likes watermelon very much, as a matter of fact," said Harry Markson years later. "But he was aware enough of what the guy wanted and he knew how to say no without making a fuss."

Jack Blackburn kept atop his pupil to be certain that he would have all of his skills for the fight. A photograph of the period shows a seemingly diminutive 6-foot 1-inch Louis standing with three sparring partners. They averaged 6 feet 4 inches. Since Carnera stood nearly 6 feet 6 inches, Blackburn wanted his fighter to become accustomed to facing an opponent who towered over him.

Meanwhile, the Hearst press in which Jacobs had allies, puffed the character of Louis vigorously. He was presented as a bible-reading, former violin student of exceeding kindness to his mother.

There were still some unhappy moments around the camp. Local racketeers vied for the gambling concessions that usually surrounded such fight camps, but Roxborough resisted open gambling, although certainly not from moral scruples. The mob again made overtures to Roxborough for a hidden partnership, but the Detroit numbers man managed to stave off the outsiders. In Primo Carnera's camp, the mob didn't have to try to muscle in. They were already on the inside.

On January 1, 1930, the *New York Times* carried an item that read, "The Cunard Liner Berengaria docked at its West 14th Street Pier late yesterday and deposited the bulkiest piece of fighting machinery ever known in the ring." The particular devastator, to become known as the Ambling Alp, the Vast Venetian, the Merchant of Muscle—as well as the Tall Tower of Gorgonzola to those less impressed with his skills—was Primo Carnera, considered to be the classic case of the gangster-managed fighter. He was less a fighting machine than a large slab of raw meat, and in fact Jess Willard was actually bigger.

At his birth in northern Italy in 1906, this first son of a stone-cutter, Sante Carnera, supposedly weighed a staggering 22 pounds (the world's record stands at 24 pounds).

"My childhood was miserable, very miserable," Carnera told writer Jack Sher. "We were always hungry. I worked hard, extremely hard. At school I was not happy. I was too large to be accepted. I did not take part in sports then. I was too large and clumsy."

By age 12, the adult-sized boy had left home and drifted through the Alps into France. A circus hired him as a strong man, capitalizing on the freakish nature of his build; his weight ballooned well over 260 pounds. When interest flagged, the carnival billed Carnera as a wrestler, matching him against all comers in the villages and towns. Sometimes experienced grapplers drubbed him fearfully. He survived mainly through his size and strength; he had little skill even in this trade. French fight manager, Leon See, was importuned to examine the potential of the big Italian. At first See resisted the proposition. A seasoned fight manager, with credits from Oxford University as well as connections with the European underworld, See knew that wrestlers could rarely be converted into boxers. A second meeting with Carnera sometime later produced different results, perhaps due to hard times for See, possibly because he had now found a way to translate Carnera's size into a profitable operation without the troublesome job of developing his skills. Certainly, it was not because Carnera had acquired any ring proficiency, for he remained ignorant of the science of the game. See made a minimally effective effort to teach him to defend and attack before the first fight. In 1928, after a couple of weeks of apprenticing himself into the new craft, Carnera knocked out a French gossamer named Leon Sebilo.

An ingenuous writer named Clifford Lewis produced a short monograph on Carnera's life and career in 1932. Leon See glibly explained there that it was good for a young fighter's spirit to win, very destructive for him to be knocked out early in his career. "You must make him feel confident in the ring," said Manager See. "That is why Carnera's early fights were so valuable. They made him feel at home. . . . victories gave him plenty of confidence." Perhaps his faith in himself might have been shaky if the big man had known that the losers were paid or coerced into falling down.

Carnera contributed his own share of bunkum to Clifford

Lewis's with the confession that he possessed "telepathic ability" which enabled him to predict impending punches. He revealed the quality of boxing lore in his entourage with the assertion that two miles of daily road work were quite sufficient because of his great size—from four to six miles had been accepted by leading trainers in the sport. Furthermore, Carnera admitted that he sparred only the last week before a fight, tuning up with a maximum of 40 rounds. Endurance was rarely demanded of Carnera, however. His enemies generally surrendered within one or two rounds.

Within his first year the large Italian had conquered the worst of Europeans in Paris, Milan, Berlin, Leipzig, Marseilles and St. Sebastian, almost as if keeping the show on the road prevented anyone from taking a hard look at the events. Since See's criminal liaisons extended well beyond the borders of France, United States racketeers, abroad during Prohibition to take the spirits instead of the waters, inspected the potential investment and See began selling pieces of Carnera.

At the end of 1929 Primo Carnera boarded the Cunard liner *Berengaria* for a cruise to the golden streets of New York.

The *New York Times* covered his arrival, but without a hint of Carnera's fistic deficiencies; it solemnly noted that he was accompanied by Leon See and Walter Friedman, as the representative of Bill Duffy who, the *Times* declared, had an interest in Carnera. Law-enforcement authorities had an interest in Duffy, a convicted felon, and Walter Friedman's reputation was also less than spotless. As a convicted felon, Duffy, by New York State law, was ineligible to be officially connected with a fighter. In its account, the *Times*, swallowing the publicity bait, inflated Carnera's size to 6 feet 8½ inches and 284 pounds, announced that his walking stick weighed 32 pounds and that he wore a shoe size between 17 and 18. Later newspaper stories stretched Carnera's shoe to a size 22. Actually, Carnera got by with a mere size 13.

On the morning before Carnera made his first appearance in a United States ring, Don Skene of the *Herald Tribune* pointed out that with all his credentials Carnera had boxed only 35 rounds as a pro. Said Skene, "Close students of fistic matters advance the theory that the gondola booted Venetian Giant's astute board of managers . . . would not be likely to toss what they logically call a one million dollar property into the Garden Ring unless they felt practically certain that their ponderous protege would emerge victorious in spectacular fashion." That was very nearly as open a statement about Carnera as would appear during his seasons in the American boxing stage. Quentin Reynolds went only so far as to intimate that there were shady people hovering in the background of the Italian, and just before the Louis–Carnera match the *World-Telegram* noted in an editorial, "There appears to be no secret about the fact that young Louis, for instance, is handled by gents who control the numbers racket in the middlewest. . . . Carnera is financed by New York public enemy Number One. . . ."

There were 20,000 enthusiasts in Madison Square Garden to watch Carnera in his American debut score a one-round KO of Clayton "Big Boy" Peterson. Skene described the action: "Carnera slowly shoved out his left bunch of bananas, or hand, and the glove finally made contact with Peterson's head. . . . He fell down." Then Skene added an unsubtle suggestion of a tank job, that Peterson's seconds jumped into the ring with "water wings."

Goodnatured, somewhat given to fracturing the English language, Carnera furnished the press with fresh material. "What do you think of Hollywood," asked the reporter. "I'll knock him out in the second round," Carnera supposedly replied. Whether he did or did not contribute bright sayings, he was a strong, safe attraction.

In fact, while earning better than $100,000 in his first ten United States confrontations, Carnera boxed only 22 rounds, as foe after foe collapsed to the canvas. But there was considerable doubt about Carnera, even among the hack politicians who dominated the state athletic commissions of the day. His second fight against Eliziar Rioux in Chicago brought the customary one-round KO, but Rioux's failure to throw a punch in the 47 seconds of the fight caused authorities to hold up the purses of both men. Similar official glowers darkened the downfall of George Trafton, a former center for Notre Dame and the Chicago Bears in Kansas City and Leon Bombo Chevalier in Oakland.

Years after Carnera faded from the fight scene, it was revealed that the most effective blows for Carnera occurred outside the ring. Ace Clark, a Philadelphia Negro, was properly primed to take a graceful fall when he was warned by the local authorities, acting on a tip, that they would treat him harshly if he gave an unconvincing performance. Perplexed, Clark boxed the big Italian's ears off for the first five rounds. But then Walter Friedman and a tough-looking yegg eased over to Clark's corner and in the pause between rounds, offered the fighter a glimpse of a pistol. Clark dropped for a 10-count only 30 seconds into the sixth round. Leon Bombo Chevalier, underestimated perhaps by the Carnera management, or else unreached through failure in the chain of command, also threatened to destroy the Ambling Alp's string of victories. He told an investigating body that just before the Oakland, California, fight one of his seconds ordered him to take a fall in the second round. Chevalier, however, rocked Carnera badly in the first round and either through an unwise streak of honesty or seduced by the vision that an upset would catapult him to the top, continued to pound the big target in the second round. Another associate said that if Chevalier didn't lose the fight, he would be shot. Stubborn, Chevalier continued to lash away at Carnera. But Chevalier's seconds rubbed a substance described as capsicum vaseline in his eyes and up his nose, blinding him and sending a searing pain through the nostrils. Even that failed to halt the upset until one of the seconds threw a towel in the ring to indicate that Chevalier had quit. The farce was so transparent that all participants lost their licenses, both in California and in states such as New York, which honored the West Coast ban.

But the Carnera calliope rolled on. The show shifted to Portland, Oregon; Detroit; Cleveland; Newark; Chicago and Philadelphia before leaving the States.

The force behind the whole Carnera swindle was one of the last of the great Irish-American gangsters, Owen "Owney" Madden. Born actually in Leeds, England in 1891, he came to the United States as an 11-year-old and quickly found himself at home in Hell's Kitchen, the West Side of lower Manhattan where New York's impoverished Irish immigrants thickly clustered, not too far from where Mike Jacobs got his start.

At age 21, Madden figured as a prime murder suspect after William Henshaw, who escorted a Madden girlfriend to the Amsterdam Opera House, stopped a bullet in the back as he boarded a trolley car. An absence of witnesses brought freedom for Madden. Several years later, however, a dispute over another woman ended with Madden in a Sing Sing cell. William Moore, better known as Little Patsy Doyle, a burly hoodlum who flashed a pair of gold teeth, sought revenge upon Madden for the loss of a female friend, Frieda Horner.

91

Three of Doyle's acquaintances hit Madden with 11 bullets at the Arbor Dance Hall just north of Times Square. Madden recovered but little Patsy failed to survive a barroom execution squad. Frieda Horner, the woman who had scorned Doyle for Madden, told a court that she heard the accused say, "I want Little Patsy rubbed out because he is a squealer and a rat." After Madden began to serve a 10- to 20-year sentence at Sing Sing, Frieda Horner and two collaborative witnesses recanted. But nobody believed them.

Small in stature, Madden was a dapper clothes horse, argumentative enough to be described by a police sergeant as "that little banty rooster out of hell." But he actually cultivated pigeons, investing in Budapest Tiplitzes, Hollanders, Nun's Capes and other exotic breeds. He was, like some movie fake, incredibly devoted to his aged mother, visited her regularly, even when he went into a sort of self-imposed exile in Hot Springs, Arkansas. His business interests included Brooklyn wet-wash laundries, where competitors regularly suffered unpleasant accidents, and warehouses stocked with illegal Prohibition whiskey. Madden himself was arrested once while riding on a truck with $25,000 worth of liquor but beat the charge. A court battle revealed his ownership of one of the institutions where blacks and whites met, Harlem's Cotton Club. His partner in the Cotton Club was murdered. He also maintained interests in the prize-fight game. Duffy and Friedman both figured as junior partners in the Madden enterprises.

With such backing, it was hardly surprising that "da Preem" should progress as rapidly as he did without pugilistic merit. And when the 1930 visit to the United States ended, Carnera had grossed some $700,000 for his owners. For himself he had little to show except the clothes and a flock of suspensions by state athletic commissions. A short

92

stay in Europe, however, healed all wounds and Carnera sailed to the United States in 1931 free to fight almost anywhere. He had returned to the United States but no longer under the at least partially benevolent guidance of Leon See. The diminutive French manager, either having decided that he no longer wished to be involved with the wolves of America or else forced out of the picture, had retired from the scene. In his place was a man described as an Italian banker, Luigi Soresi, who seemed to lack any regard for his fighter. At Ebbets Field in Brooklyn, a full house watched Primo Carnera learn how inept a fighter he truly was. For 15 rounds, Jack Sharkey, a skilled boxer, slashed the Italian brutally and easily evaded the feeble thrusts put forward by Carnera. The win made Sharkey eligible to meet Schmeling for the heavyweight title the following year, but it failed to retire Carnera. He scored two wins in the United States, including one against Vittorio Campolo in New York that again raised the specter of the fix in the commission's eyes. Then he left for Europe to be rebuilt into a seemingly legitimate contender. Ring experience, plus the skimpy coaching he received, had improved Carnera's skills but not to the level where he was a legitimate heavyweight contender.

Much of the 1932 period, Carnera was managed from Sing Sing where Madden had returned on a charge of parole violation. Following the clever campaign that had kept Carnera moving through cities such as Grand Rapids, Omaha, Tulsa, Antonio, Tampa, Tiverton, Rhode Island, with an occasional stop in the bigger cities, Carnera was scheduled for a 15-round fight against Ernie Schaaf, a tough heavyweight, on February 10, 1933. Schaaf, however, had a few months earlier taken a fearful beating from Max Baer. Although he fought several times after the Baer battle, he had apparently suffered brain damage. Against Carnera he appeared sluggish and collapsed in the 13th round, to die subsequently in a hospital.

Carnera agonized over his role as a manslaughterer. Later he told Jack Sher, "Everyone knows now it was not my fault. I would not do such a thing. When it happened I felt sick. I told everyone it was not my fault."

But to the puppet masters, Schaaf's death provided an opportunity to sweep away insinuations that the Vast Venetian lacked power, that he had been the beneficiary of a well-tailored string of closet dramas. The propaganda was convincing enough to William Muldoon, chairman of the New York State Athletic Commission. Muldoon announced that because of his deadliness, Carnera would not be permitted to meet such ordinary humans as heavyweight champion Jack Sharkey but instead would be eligible only for a new class known as "superdreadnaughts."

The announcement by Muldoon only ensured that Carnera would get another chance against Sharkey. But fight fans were not enticed enough by the power of killer Carnera. Only about 10,000 showed up to witness the fight. There had been some peculiar fluctuations in the betting money with a late surge of Carnera dollars driving down the odds that still favored Sharkey.

For five rounds the champion poked away at his opponent, who outweighed him by 62 pounds. But in the sixth round Sharkey, while grappling with Carnera's hugger-mugger style, slipped to the mat. After Sharkey recovered, and hit his challenger several times, Carnera hurled a wide-slung right. Sharkey, in the words of *Times* writer James Dawson, "slid gracefully to the floor." He stayed down for 10. It was a stunning reversal, so astonishing that some onlookers still claim that the knockout blow was a phantom. Oddly, Nat Fleischer in his *Ring Record Book,* describes "a terrific right uppercut to the chin." But while talking to Jack Sher, Fleischer remarked, "Sharkey should have knocked him out. Carnera won that fight with an invisible punch." Fleischer, even in his memoirs could never bring himself to admit openly that his beloved sport was seamed with corruption. The worst he could bring himself to say in print was: "In most of the contests, the set-up was of the kind that made it almost impossible for Carnera not to win."

Harry Markson who was at the fight insisted that Carnera indeed swung a long right. "But if you're asking me whether or not it would knock a man out, I can't say," admitted Markson.

Primo Carnera returned to his homeland in a strange mixture of triumph and failure. He was the heavyweight champion, although there were whispers of something sinister or something empty about his title. And, although his 79 fights had grossed some $2 million, Carnera declared himself bankrupt one month later and faced a breach of promise suit from a waitress he had wooed. According to Carnera, Leon See had invested some of the fighter's rewards unwisely, but most of it simply went to Duffy, Soresi, Madden and company.

Back home, Dictator Benito Mussolini clasped this famous native son to his bosom and ordered a specially tailored uniform of the black shirt fascisti for the world's heavyweight champion. Photographs of Carnera smartly delivering the fascist salute went to newspapers around the world, and left the big Italian with some hard explaining to do when World War II ended.

For the delight of the Italian people, Carnera bumbled to a 15-round decision over an equally inept Spaniard, Paoline Uzcudun, who was to have one more moment of glory by violently succumbing to Joe Louis. Carnera defended a second time against a 34-year-old light heavyweight, Tommy

Loughran in the United States. With an 80-pound weight advantage, "da Preem" managed another 15-round decision.

But a reckoning was coming. The title could not be kept secure from bona-fide challengers, for all of the art of the mob manipulation. Max Baer ranked as the leading challenger and a match was set. It was one of the few instances in the history of the sport where the champion rated as a definite underdog; the gambling fraternity had not been fooled.

The judgment of the oddsmakers was correct. Max Baer beat up Carnera fearfully. The champion was knocked down three times in the first round, and once every round after that for a total of 13 times before a less than merciful referee halted the action.

Owney Madden was out of Sing Sing now and available to see the slaughter of his innocent, but Bill Duffy had been forced to wait for the results from a federal penitentiary, where he'd been sent on income-tax-evasion charges. When Duffy emerged a free man, he set about to restore the depreciated property. Carnera was packed off to South America for the start of a new slate of wins and then returned to New York to register one victory over a nonentity. Having thus made his fighter "respectable" as an opponent, Duffy could match him with Joe Louis. There was still enough romance to Carnera to draw fans, particularly on ethnic appeal. For the Louis entourage, the match seemed perfect. There was little to fear from Carnera and an impressive win would make an excellent start in the last drive for the summit of boxing.

But nearly 5,000 miles away, a cloud darkened prospects for the fight. In his quest to revive the glory that had been Rome, Benito Mussolini had intimated designs upon more territory in Africa, specifically on Ethiopia. In the spring of

1935, Mussolini sent legions of troops and engineers to the Italian colony in northeast Africa in an obvious attempt to intimidate Ethiopia. The fascist leader bellowed that the little-better-than-spear-armed Ethiopians had threatened him and his possessions.

For the first but not the last time, Joe Louis became the center of a fight that made him a representative of something beyond himself. The Carnera–Louis encounter became to some degree a contest between a representative of fascist Italy and an American of African descent. This stirred nervous apprehensions in the sponsors of the fight, the Hearst Milk Fund, and there was some discussion about canceling the fight. American Negroes had formed the Council of Friends of Ethiopians to make representation at the League of Nations on behalf of the besieged Africans. Professor Rayford W. Logan of Atlanta University, a Negro college, said that the defeat of Carnera by Louis might cause Mussolini to take the final steps to punish Ethiopia. "I am afraid that the defeat of Carnera by Louis will be interpreted as an additional insult to the Italian flag [the professor failed to point out initial insults to the Italian insignia unless he meant resistance to Mussolini's stretch for territory], which will promote Mussolini to start again the recent attempt by Italy to annihilate Abyssinia."

Jacobs calmed the fears of the Hearst management while tickets sold briskly. Trains arrived from Chicago, Pittsburgh, Philadelphia and Detroit. Caravans of automobiles packed with Louis admirers came from Detroit.

The writers covering the fight saw little hope for the Italian and they had finally begun to question openly his qualifications as well as his management.

Bill Corum, a Hearst sportswriter, said, "It is my conviction that Carnera, who won the heavyweight championship of the world from Jack Sharkey with a semi-invisible upper-cut, can't fight a lick and never could. . . . How much he [Primo] knows of the fixing and finagling that has gone on about him since the January day he arrived in the U.S.A. on a trip financed by Owney Madden, I don't know."

Walter Stewart of the *New York World-Telegram* declared, "Louis is reportedly equipped with the most accurate broadside which has come over the horizon since William Tell lanced the apple and shoving him through the ropes with Primo is like giving a chap a battery of machine guns and telling him to hit the Sahara Desert."

The Carnera management professed to be unawed. Luigi Soresi told an interviewer, "I am assuming of course that Joe Louis behaves himself and does not get fresh in the first two or three rounds. . . . If he is a good boy, Primo will make the finish as painless as possible." Carnera boosters theorized that short-punching Louis would not be able to reach Carnera, and the big man would use his weight to wear down Louis in clinching.

The betting authorities agreed with the writers and Louis ranked as a solid favorite with little action except in Harlem. Carnera's odds slipped when Louis's victim, Natie Brown, sparred with the Italian and mauled him. The notables of the day scrounged for tickets. Booker T. Washington, son of the founder of Tuskeegee, complained that "friends from Baltimore and Washington have sent me money to buy them tickets for the fight." Jacob Ruppert, owner of the New York Yankees and a beer baron; New York Giants owner Horace Stoneham; Mayor Fiorello LaGuardia; National Recovery Administration chief General Hugh Johnson; horse-racing figure C. V. Whitney; Judge Thomas S. McAndrews; Alderman Jack Mahoney; Tammany leaders John F. Curry, James J. Dooling and Michael J. Kennedy—New York still belonged to the Irish even if the mayor was an Episcopalian Republican of Italian background—writers Ed Sullivan and Herbert B. Swope; black dignitaries former All-American Fritz Pollard; dancer Bill Robinson; Civil Service Commissioner Ferdinand Delany; Tax Commissioner Herbert Delany; NAACP leader Walter White; musician Duke Ellington; Professor Ralph Bunche, and hoi polloi, including an estimated 10,000 blacks, all filed into Yankee Stadium for the main event.

Earl Brown had remarked in his *Amsterdam News* report that there were fears that the pro-Carnera contingent might turn violent if their favorite lost, but most of the fear in New York centered on the possible reaction of the black fans. Dan Parker of the *Daily Mirror* scoffed ". . . talk of racial trouble . . . is preposterous. Colored sports fans are as peaceful a group of citizens as you'll find anywhere. Their interest in Abyssinia is about as remote as that country is from Harlem."

Apprehensions about civil disorder in New York were not without some foundation in 1935. By this year, half of all Negro families in the North were on relief. In March of that year, the residents of Harlem, beset by the Depression and continued depredation by landlords, shopkeepers and municipal services, burst into a small flame; a flicker of what was to come again in the 1940s and then flourish in the 1960s.

Police Commissioner Mulrooney insisted that fears of disorder because of the Louis–Carnera bout were groundless. "There won't be a Harlem disturbance. The American Negro is by nature law-abiding, kindly, well-behaved. He is also happy and fun-loving. If Louis wins, there will likely be singing and shouting and dancing in the streets of Harlem. . . . a few ashcans may be kicked over, as on New Year's Eve

99

. . . no better behaved and fairer crowds in the world."

Actually Commissioner Mulrooney was preparing for the worst. Some 1,300 of New York's finest ringed Yankee Stadium. Another 300 plainclothesmen mingled with the crowds to sound the alert over incipient trouble. There were four extra patrol wagons parked nearby to haul off potential violators of the peace, and members of the Emergency Squads waited nearby with both tear-gas bombs and grenades.

Into the center of the ring at Yankee Stadium on the evening of June 25 stepped the tuxedoed announcer, Harry Balogh, to give to the tens of thousands an appeal to the ideal of sportsmanship: "Tonight, we have gathered here to watch a contest of athletic skill. We are Americans. That means that we have come from homes of many different faiths, and we represent a lot of different nationalities. In America we admire the athlete who can win by virtue of his skill. Let me then ask you to join me in the sincere wish that regardless of race, color or creed the better man may emerge victorious."

The actual fight between Louis and Carnera established two points: the newcomer from Detroit could hit very hard and the most famous boxer from Italy possessed a rare amount of courage; Carnera's opponents collapsed to the floor in safety from far less painful thumps than those smashed to his body by Louis. Reporter Henry McLemore wrote that seconds after round one began, "Louis feinted, then hit Primo with a left hook to the mouth that drew blood from both corners." From there on it was a night in an abattoir for Carnera.

Supposedly, Jack Blackburn had lectured his pupil on the proper tactics against Carnera: "You lis'ning to me, Chappie? Now you hear me good. A tree like this here you got to

100

chop down. Can't do no fancy whittling. No knife work, ax him, you hear me Chappie?" Blackburn had long been an exponent of the maxim, "Kill the body and the head must die."

Round after round, Louis whacked away at the trunk of the Italian. When Carnera attempted to bull Louis around in a clinch, Louis shocked him by lifting the much bigger man off the floor and swinging him about. In the sixth round, Carnera wilted, his hands hung down. Louis turned his attention to his opponent's head. A punch to the jaw put Carnera down once, a left hook and a right cross when he rose ended the fight after two minutes of the round.

The loser offered a gracious prediction, "Louis, he's a good boy. He'll make a fine champion." It was a widely held opinion, but events succeeding the fight demonstrated again how far Louis would have to go, and how much of America was represented in the Alabama farm boy.

8

Immediately after the fight, Louis limited his comments to "I'm glad I win," and to Earl Brown of the *Amsterdam News* he confided his ambitions, "It's de bucks I'm after." Others were less restrained in their reactions, although between the final punch and the emotional spasms a slight delay ensued. With no radio blow-by-blow broadcast (Jacobs believed radio hurt the gate), those in Harlem and other black enclaves across the country were forced to wait for either a radio news bulletin or a telephone call from some obliging spectator who pushed his way out of the stadium crowd to a booth.

When the news reached Paradise Valley in Detroit the celebrants poured into the streets. One Mary Paplett fractured her leg, "jumping for joy," she said. A 20-year-old woman suffered minor injuries when a passing truck brushed her off the running board of a car.

In Chicago and Cleveland the happiness of the black residents similarly flowed into the streets. But it was in Harlem that the sense of triumph crested and flooded the community. A crowd of 20,000 had gathered at the Savoy Ballroom on Lenox Avenue. Those who squeezed in paid a 75-cent admission charge to be present for the expected celebration and a promised appearance by the new black hope. The word of victory came to the Savoy Ballroom by telephone. The throng shouted with glee and began an impatient wait for their hero.

At another Harlem center, the Renaissance Restaurant on Seventh Avenue, a resident scholar named Gill Holton, sometimes known as Old Broken Leg or Busted Holton, and who had written an essay designed to prove that Shakespeare was a Moor, told a reporter, "It is the greatest night Harlem has had since the riot. . . . Put in the paper that Mr. Broken Leg celebrated the large sums he has won by eating one hog maw, six pork sandwiches, one filet mignon steak, a double slice of watermelon and washed it down with untold quantities of jitter juice." Holton also claimed to have gulped some 15 beers accompanied by gin. "I guess I won about 15 smackers," finished the theorist on Shakespeare.

In the streets, the delighted Harlemites hopped aboard trolleycars to nowhere, goodnaturedly refusing to ante up the fares. Lindy-hopping dancers blocked Seventh Avenue. Some ashcans toppled but injuries during the celebration proved no more than normal for a June Harlem night—one woman treated for a broken leg and three gamblers stabbed after a "misunderstanding."

At the Cotton Restaurant on 142nd Street and Lenox Avenue, another newspaperman discovered the forgotten hero of times past. Sam Langford, the Boston Tarbaby, had gone nearly blind and now lived on handouts. On occasion, a generous fight promoter would lead Langford up into the ring before a main event and permit Langford to pass the hat. At the Cotton Restaurant, however, Langford wanted to talk about the fight: "That boy was goin' to town each time he sent one out, and each time he sent one out he was goin' to town. 'Member the way Carnera backed up and shook his head and couldn't speak? It reminded me of the time Joe Walcott [an early fighter no kin to the heavyweight who held the title 1951–52] landed one on my jaw and I couldn't speak nor swallow for three rounds." To other customers in the Cotton Restaurant, Langford called a stream of greetings, "Hi son, hello Chappie." But then told the interviewer, "I'll leave you now, brother, I got to go beg 35 cents so I can eat. You hear that? I don't like to do it, but sometimes I got to beg to eat." Several years later, during World War II, *Herald Tribune* writer Al Laney discovered the destitute, blind and friendless Langford. His account of the Boston Tarbaby's plight brought a brief surge of funds to keep Langford alive. He survived until 1956.

Langford's contemporary, Jack Johnson, also was highly visible around Harlem before and after the fight. The former champion, a representative of spirits manufacturers, had been rehabilitated enough in the eyes of the press to be a source for pre-fight stories, and Johnson did not disappoint them in their search for extravagance. Dressed in a chocolate-hued sports jacket with a wide-brimmed Panama or in a blue beret, Johnson at the time was promoting Old Champ Lil Arthur Gin, "the gin that'll make you smile." But on the night that Louis whipped Carnera, the dandy substituted a scotch and soda for his testimonial gin. Earl Brown remarked on the "look of respect and wonder the assembled Senegambians gave him—the one and only blackamoor champion of the world."

At the Savoy, restlessness gripped the thousands anxious to shower their approval on their favorite. Bill Robinson, Mr. Bojangles who had dutifully Tommed in the movie roles with Shirley Temple, hurried to the Savoy from Yankee Stadium. At the fight Robinson had attempted to get into the ring to congratulate Louis, and there had been a scuffle with police. But now Robinson gloriously rolled up to the Savoy in his Duesenberg. From every window in the five-story buildings that lined the street and from the jammed rooftops, citizens cheered Bill Robinson.

Shouted Robinson, "I'm so happy I could eat a mud sandwich." But the people wanted most to see and hear from the hero of the evening. The management of the Savoy became increasingly nervous at Louis's delay. Romeo Dougherty, a Harlem sportswriter, tried to keep things calm. "Joe Louis is a fighter, not a talker," Dougherty explained over a microphone. "But he wants to thank you for this reception. He wants to tell you he'll try to bring you the world's heavyweight title." That was not enough to satisfy the multitudes. There were renewed efforts to get a personal appearance from Louis. He had continued to resist pleas for him to appear, saying, "I don't want to go to the ballroom, I'm sleepy. I don't care for this handshaking stuff." At last, convinced that his visible presence was necessary to keep the peace, Louis agreed to visit the Savoy. He arrived at 2:30 A.M. He stayed but a few minutes, spoke into a microphone that was apparently dead and his words could not be heard above the din. But it was enough. Harlem relaxed, sated with an impressive win.

For the loser, there was no where to go but down. He kept fighting, for smaller and smaller purses. In 1936, a journeyman heavyweight, Leroy Haynes, knocked him out in three brisk rounds in Philadelphia. The action pleased spectators enough for a rematch two months later in Brooklyn. This time Haynes required nine rounds to put Carnera away, but the big man absorbed so much punishment that one of his legs became paralyzed. He was in a hospital for five months and when able to totter onto a ship back to Europe, he was once again broke.

The race of Louis continued to loom large in the post-fight reportage. A cartoon in the *Newark Evening News* featured

Louis as a toga-clad, thick-lipped Sambo-style black on a throne. Another figure was identified as Jack Blackburn, who was waving a frond over his head with the line, "Sullivan and Dempsey drew the color line, but not me."

References to atavistic savagery sprinkled some accounts. One writer's copy referred to a moment of emotion in the crowd: "[there] rose a cry that smote upon the ear drums and left them shivering . . . primitive, unnatural shriek of the Harlem belle reacting to the emotions of centuries and strictly reverting to type."

Davis Walsh of Hearst's International News Service, who made no attempt to disguise his attitude toward blacks, wrote of "something sly and sinister last night to strike down and utterly demolish a huge hulk that had been Primo Carnera, the giant. "And high above the clamor of the knockout, Joe Louis, the strange, wall-eyed, unblinking Negro." (No other reporter ever saw exotropia as one of Louis's ailments.)

Photographs of celebrants in early editions described some of the younger celebrants as "Pickaninnies" although that label disappeared in later captions of the same photograph. One newspaper referred to the Savoy as "a darky palace."

One interesting theory on the source of Louis's success appeared in the *Detroit Free Press*. "Louis put the violin under his chin and with his left hand plucked it like a banjo. If Joe Louis ever rises to the heavyweight title, it will be because of the natural instinct to get hot rhythm out of a musical instrument. It was this alone that caused Joe to pluck the violin strings . . . forced him to box."

Grantland Rice, then considered the prince regent of sports writers, also went native for his imagery, describing Louis's body movements in terms of "panther," "savage" and "snake."

Bill Corum advised Louis that he could overcome racial

106

problems. "The people who make race feeling are the people who keep harping on it. Those who do most to kill it are those who never think about it one way or another. . . . Be yourself. . . . Behave yourself. Be an example to your race as well as a champion. . . ."

The *Montreal Daily Star* also struck the theme of Louis's black boxing antecedents. The paper suggested that Blackburn hoped to clear the stigma of Jack Johnson, "a wonderful fighter but one whose record is a smudge on the pages of pugilism. . . . It will be interesting to see how Louis reacts when he is hurled into the vortex of the white way where the chislers, yesmen, sycophants of sock, parasites of punch fasten like limpets to every new celebrity until they lose." If it were a misreading of Jack Blackburn, it was at least a shrewd appraisal of white exploitation of fighters.

A writer in the *London Daily Herald,* with the predictible overseas conviction that perdition lay at the heart of the former colony, remarked, "I seriously doubt whether American public opinion will agree to another match between a coloured fighter and a white champion." To which, however, Grantland Rice retorted, ". . . no chance, Louis has gripped the fancy of the sporting public too smartly to be cast aside."

Among the impressed spectators were Max Baer, the former heavyweight champion, and his manager, Ancil Hoffman. The latter remarked, "If he can take a punch he's the greatest fighter in the world," which may not have been very reassuring to his own client. Baer, however, hoping to recapture his title, said (if we can believe the quotes): "Get me that fellow. He's truly great, but I'll make him jump out of the ring."

Nothing could have delighted Mike Jacobs more than the results of the Louis–Carnera show. The attendance was announced as 57,000 paid for a gross of $340,000 with expenses trimming the net to $277,000. How much, if any, of the "expense money" was skimmed is unknown, but the figures on attendance have been given as 60,000, 62,000 and as high as 70,000. It has been suggested that Jacobs, in the days when the government was less vigilant, managed to sell tickets that never figured in the official gate receipts and therefore never felt the taxman's touch. For the night's work, the press reported Louis collected $45,000, Carnera took home $77,000 and the Hearst Milk Fund was enriched by $52,000. These figures have varied with Louis's share sometimes reported as $60,000. One revenue item, newsreel films, had theoretically been barred from the fight, but the mob bootlegged a set of them, and in later years Jacobs admitted he received an additional $10,000 for the rights to these. It was not until 1940 that it was legal to show films of a fight through interstate commerce.

It was obvious that plenty of paying customers would appreciate an opportunity to witness Baer try to chase Louis out of the ring. Jacobs set about to arrange for the pair to meet in New York in September, only three months after the Carnera match. During that low-tax era, managers had no compunction about keeping a fighter busy. First, though, Louis signed to fight King Levinsky, a heavyweight with the dubious achievement of having lost to Sharkey, Carnera and Baer. Levinsky could at best be described as a tune-up and he knew it. The King was clearly apprehensive about meeting the Brown Bomber. One wiseman suggested that Levinsky be replaced by his sister, Lena, because "She's afraid of nobody," a sentiment that Harry Markson agreed with. In Chicago, on the night of the fight, Mike Jacobs checked the dressing rooms and discovered Levinsky to be so frightened that the promoter himself became fearful; the longer Levinsky waited for his appointment with his executioner, the

108

more possibility that the victim might flee. Jacobs went to the boxing commission and demanded that the match begin half an hour early. When asked why, Jacobs snarled that it was likely to rain, although the skies above Comiskey Park twinkled with stars.

The reluctant Levinsky entered the ring 30 minutes before scheduled. He went down twice, the second time for the full count and the night was over, 2 minutes and 21 seconds after it began.

Now it was back to Doc Bier's camp at Pompton Lakes for Joe Louis, but there was a new element in his life. In Chicago, he had met a handsome 19-year-old, Marva Trotter. Arkansas born, she was a stenographer from a middle-class black family. A mutual friend named Gerry Hughes brought her to Trafton's gym to watch Joe Louis work out.

She has been quoted, "I gave the big man a once over. It was love at first sight." He invited her to visit him at his Chicago apartment. The cautious Marva Trotter traveled to Louis's rooms accompanied by her sister Novella. "We arrived about one P.M.," she told an *Ebony* magazine reporter, "and Joe wouldn't come out of his room until about five." From there on it was a smooth courtship, though slowed perhaps by both Louis's shyness and the demands of his profession.

He selected a four-carat diamond for Marva and a big Lincoln car for himself. His fondness for high-speed driving brought him numerous speeding tickets and eventually a chauffeur from his nervous managers. Louis's win over Carnera enabled him finally to make a clean break with the drag of poverty. For his mother and the other members of the family still at home, he bought an $11,000 brick house on MacDougall Street in Detroit. Lillie Barrow Brooks and the family lived there until she died in 1955.

At Pompton Lakes, the subject of Marva Trotter crept into one of Russell Cowan's letters. "And then this marriage controversy. It was rumored in the papers several weeks. Joe entered a denial [that he was engaged]. I knew all the time because he had told me in Detroit before leaving. . . . Tuesday night the big kid broke down and admitted the truth of the story."

Russell Cowan wrote home to John Dancy of one difficulty: "We were unable to secure competent sparring partners on our arrival. We had a bunch of scouts out scouring the woods but all they brought in was a bunch of stumble bums who gandy dance about the ring."

The party continued to enjoy New Jersey hospitality within limitations. Cowan mentioned that the managing editor of the *Patterson Evening News,* Abe Green, secured for Cowan an honorary membership in the State Association of Police Clubs. He also arranged for a cabaret affair at an exclusive nightclub where, said Cowan, "The proprietor might object to a little colored boy entering the place." With Louis emerging as a race figure, the pilgrims to the camp included more than gamblers and fight buffs. Some 200 National Baptist ministers and laymen dropped in after a convention.

There was mail from Frank D. Fitzgerald, governor of Michigan. He dropped a Chesterfieldian note to the new pride of Michigan:

> Dear Joe: Don't be too greatly impressed by this stationery. I happen to be Governor of Michigan but I'm talking to you as a man more than twice your age just to give a little advice to a young fellow who has a real chance to do something for his people. . . .
> Destiny seems to have pointed you for a high rank in

110

pugilism. Your ability to overpower others by skill and physical force is something of which you may be proud. It's going to make you a lot of money too; more money than is made today by those who excel, let us say, as artists or surgeons, or poets. You'll have world prominence and money.

They will mean little, Joe, if you do not use them as God intended that gifts bestowed by Nature should be used.

Your race, at times in the past, has been misrepresented by others who thought they had reached the heights. Its people have been denied equal opportunity. Its obstacles and its handicaps have been such that it has been saved only by its own infinite patience and its ability to endure suffering without becoming poisoned by bitterness.

For all of the people plucking at his shirttails, importuning him, counseling him, Joe Louis remained what he was, a 21-year-old with little education, diffident in the presence of strangers and uncertain of how to handle the attention centered upon him.

Such was hardly the case for his opponent, Maxmillian Adalbert Baer, a gregarious slugger who might easily have developed into a great heavyweight champion with enormous popular appeal except for an apparent inability to concentrate upon his trade. In his brief moments at the top, Max Baer exhibited a kind of flash that has become a stereotype of the colorful fighter, the jokester, the ladies' man, the street tough with a yearning for the better things. At his best moments Baer was an excellent fighter gifted with an ability to hit very hard.

Baer had been genetically blessed. His Scotch-Irish mother, Dora, stood six feet and weighed 230 pounds and his father, Jacob, measured six feet and 250 pounds. The family started out in the rural Midwest, then migrated to California. Jacob worked in a slaughterhouse and eventually developed his own abbatoir. Max became a butcher for his father. Swinging a meat ax, the husky son killed and dressed 10 hogs or a dozen calves per day. Lifting heavy slabs of meat built Max's muscles, but unlike other fighters he did not spend any of his early years training in a gym.

At 18, a high school dropout, Max Baer and some friends went to a dance. In a typical Baer stunt the group stole a jug of wine owned by a locomotive engineer. When the trainman discovered the theft, he faced the young men and attempted to beat up the largest of the group, Max Baer. The butcher boy threw one wild punch and it felled the burly locomotive engineer. The success inspired Baer to desert the grind of the slaughterhouse for that of the fight ring.

Performing on the West Coast, Baer punched his way through the likes of Chief Cariboo, Tillie Taverna and Sailor Leeds in 1929. Only a month after he began to practice the trade his purses reached $4,000 an engagement. By 1930, he had developed into something of a gate attraction through his gregarious behavior. He had also begun to mismanage his finances, one account claiming that he sold 110 percent of himself. In August 1930, Baer knocked out Frankie Campbell in San Francisco and Campbell died as a result of the beating. Until that happened, Baer had been fighting almost twice a month, but following Campbell's death, cushioned by a $10,000 share from the performance, he took a three-month pause and came to New York to campaign. For perhaps the only time in his life, Baer suffered a spasm of depression. He had actually been arrested after Campbell died and his manager, Ancil Hoffman, posted bail. "They branded me as if I were a blood-thirsty animal," complained an uncharacteristically bitter Baer. His first effort in New York brought him a defeat at the hands of Ernie Schaff, whom he would whip 18 months later with disastrous results.

Baer's fortunes declined further as he dropped three of his next five fights. But he did discover the pleasures of New York, and a woman about town, Dorothy Dunbar, attempted to sculpt away some of his rougher edges. He studied how to dress, putting together a wardrobe of 30 suits, which when added to his extensive haberdashery, filled 10 trunks. While the Depression was putting millions out of work, Baer lolled in a $27-a-day suite at the Plaza. Instead of doing his road work in Central Park, he sat on a bench studying the works of Emily Post, which may have had something to do with his failings in the ring.

Ancil Hoffman, shrewd but paternal, patiently coached Baer back to ring eminence. One of the few boxing shepherds who seemed determined to protect his lamb from the wolves around the fight game, Hoffman straightened out Baer's finances and began to deposit the fighter's earnings in an annuity fund. As part of his reclamation project, Baer even married Dorothy Dunbar. He resumed his climb up the heavyweight ladder with a steady series of KO's and decisions starting in the fall of 1931 on the West Coast. By August of 1932 Hoffman thought it time for Baer to recoup against Ernie Schaaf. For 10 rounds the hard-hitting Baer pounded Schaaf, but the target would not stay down for the count. Baer won the decision. Schaaf slipped into a coma three hours after he left the ring. He regained consciousness and six months later, comparatively light blows struck by Carnera were enough to destroy the fragile tissue of Schaaf's battered brain.

In 1933, Baer met the heavy-browed German contender and former heavyweight champion Max Schmeling in New

113

York. He knocked out the foreigner in 10 rounds. Although Baer was half Jewish, there was no suggestion that the fight incorporated any symbolism; Adolf Hitler had assumed the role of dictator of Nazi Germany only a few months before.

Baer took almost a year's layoff before he finally received an opportunity to take the heavyweight title held by Carnera in 1934. Although this outing promised to be the most important of his career, Baer seemed intent upon making the entire show a farce. At his training camp, he would suddenly burst into a staggering act as an imitation of a punch-drunk fighter. He put on wrestling exhibitions with his younger brother Buddy, who later became a fighter. Baer wrote an open letter to his opponent in which he said, "Be prepared to be flattened along about the 10th round." There was talk that a cable from Mussolini or one of his henchmen had advised Carnera, "You must win." When Baer heard about it he paraded about quoting the telegram and throwing fascist salutes. Not amused was a New York State athletic commissioner named Bill Brown who declared Baer unfit. "His attitude is all wrong. He acts like a clown training to join a circus." There was talk that the Commission would bar the fight. But Baer turned serious enough in some training sessions to satisfy the officials; indeed it hardly seemed likely that even the most courageous of political appointees of the day would have had the fortitude to cancel the match.

When the day of the weigh-in arrived, Baer tweaked the hair on Carnera's chest, chanting, "He loves me, he loves me not"; then he tried to tickle Carnera and said, "Boo, you big palooka." The Italian glowered, unable to respond. It was a harbinger of the night action when Baer mercilessly pummeled Carnera.

During the fight Baer noticed that a San Francisco sportswriter, Harry B. Smith, slumped over, an apparent heart

114

attack victim. The fighter paused in his demolition of the champion to shout, "Take care of Harry."

In the 10th round, Baer actually seemed about to make his promise come true. He landed a smashing right hand that left Carnera, in the words of one observer, "against the ropes, hanging like a crumpled bag of old laundry." To the referee, Baer chortled, "I think he's going to go." But the fight dragged on for two more rounds before the champion was unable to answer the count of 10.

Having worked himself to the top, Baer slid from grace swiftly. He had already divorced Dorothy Dunbar, been sued for assault by a young woman, had a $240,000 breach-of-promise case hanging over his head, and had married again. As champion, he walked through a series of exhibitions before taking on James Braddock, a 30-year-old dock walloper with a history of broken hands and whose record in the 1930s amounted to more losses than wins. Baer clowned a bit and was not prepared to go the full 12 rounds. Braddock, a classic example of the hungry fighter, carried the fight to the champion and lifted the title.

Now Max Baer hoped for a comeback against Louis. Ordinarily, a championship fight such as Baer and Braddock put on resulted in a rematch. But Madison Square Garden officials had no fondness for Baer. Jimmy Johnston considered him too unpredictable, a man who could not easily be controlled. The Garden preferred to dicker with Max Schmeling. The only possibility open to Baer was Louis.

As part of his rehabilitation, Baer had Jack Dempsey in his corner, and the news was duly carried to the Louis camp. When asked whether he thought the adviser might make a difference, Louis responded, "The rules say Dempsey can't hit me, don't they?" It was perhaps the first time that Louis's raw wit caught the ears of reporters.

115

Before the fight, another interviewer asked if Louis had been coached on what to do when knocked down. The fighter answered affirmatively, and then added, "But what bothers me is the thought that if a man gets hit hard enough to get knocked down, he ought to be hit so hard he couldn't remember all that stuff." It was not a prescient statement about the coming fight but it offered some insight into Louis's first professional reverse, his fight with Max Schmeling nearly a year later.

Meanwhile, Max Baer trained very hard at Speculator, New York. While reports flowed out of Louis's camp telling of the slaughter of sparring partners, Baer was too much of a professional to be frightened of the coming confrontation. Unlike Carnera, he possessed the potential for a real test of Louis. It all added up to a healthy stimulus to the advance sale. Despite the soup kitchens and apple sellers on the streets of New York, ticket demands proved brisk. In fact so well did the advance sale move, that Jacobs upped the top-priced seats from $20 to $30.

The betting favored Louis, but the action seemed light. A black Detroit gambler, Tom Hammonds, insisted that he had $8,000 to lay on Louis but could find no takers. In Harlem the betting among the Negroes centered upon picking the round in which Baer would fall. As in the past, newspapermen found copy in the police preparations. "We'll have a detail of 1,000 extra cops here, but most of them will be handling traffic," said a lieutenant, who added that "every member of the dusky fancy" would want to strut on Lenox Avenue after the fight ended in a Louis victory.

The *New York World-Telegram* headlined a sports page, "Everything is golden underneath that Harlem Moon as Boys Rally 'Round." "Harlem near delirium as battle nears," said the head over another story with the subhead,

"If Joe Wins, and 'Cose he will, Black Belt will explode." A set of photographs centered on Harlem bettors and their quotes: "Mah money is on Joe and it couldn't be safer in a bank. It's better than ownin' a piece of the policy game. I'm just relaxin' until collectin' time." A pool player was reported as saying, "Where I is is just where that Mr. Baer is gonna be, behind the eight ball. That Louis will knock Mr. Maxie down so often he'll have to bank th' last one." A barber resorted to his office metaphor—or perhaps it was all done in the city room: "This trimmin ain't nothing like the one that Mr. Baer is gonna get. . . . That won't be any close shave, neither."

Entertainers Al Jolson and Bert Lahr leaned toward Baer, but George Raft, whose early affinity to the rackets undoubtedly supplied better connections into the betting world, saw Louis as the winner. Except for Dempsey and Jimmy Johnston, two less than unprejudiced experts, and Jack Sharkey, the fight game saw Louis as a sure thing.

On the day of the fight, Louis arrived at the offices of the New York Boxing Commission first. He was escorted past several thousand of the curious in the street and inquisitorial reporters who jabbed the same questions they'd asked for six weeks. Inside the New York Boxing Commission suite, according to Henry McLemore, Louis showed his lack of concern: "While waiting for Baer to arrive, in a room that sounded like the Tower of Babel on New Year's Eve, Joe curled up in a chair, pulled a newspaper over his face, and in five minutes was snoring in the soft, rhythmical tones of the true sleep lover. And he didn't wake up until Baer slapped him on the shoulder and said, 'Come on, Joe, let's go down and see what we weigh.' "

McLemore ascribed this phenomenon to "almost psychopathic imperturbability." Conceivably the sleepiness exhibited by Louis whenever he was forced to inaction during tension hours before a fight could also be attributed to a psychological defense against stress, a means to escape from tension. Sleep continued to be a large item in the Louis routine long after he finished his ring time.

Whether his opponent's aplomb disturbed Baer is unknown. But Louis managed to get through the rest of the afternoon before the fight by marrying Marva Trotter at an apartment in Harlem, while 1,000 people anxious for a glimpse of the new black hope waited in the street outside. Her brother, the Rev. Walter Trotter, officiated at the brief ceremony at 7:55 P.M. which was barely over before the groom was hustled to waiting automobiles for the trip to Yankee Stadium.

The Louis–Baer attraction ranked among Mike Jacobs's most successful promotions. Estimates place the crowd that showed up at Yankee Stadium in the neighborhood of 110,-000. Some 90,000 crammed themselves inside the ballpark, a figure topped only by the two Dempsey–Tunney battles in larger arenas. From nearby Bronx rooftops beyond right field, hundreds armed with binoculars peered down at the tiny figures spotlighted like ants in the ring illumination. Behind left field, several thousand other free lookers stood on the platform of elevated trains straining to catch a glimpse of the struggle nearly a quarter of a mile off. Some even rode the subways uptown, then downtown, hoping to catch a few seconds of the action.

The promoter himself appeared everywhere, bawling orders to ushers, telling policemen how to handle the flow of traffic, checking the take at the box office. Louis's share of the receipts was to be $240,000, a figure he exceeded only once before World War II. But the most significant aspect of the evening was the ease with which he handled the veteran Baer.

In the first round, Louis forgot the instructions of Jack Blackburn, "stick and move," and he engaged in a toe-to-toe exchange of punches in the middle of the ring. Baer caught Louis solidly but must have been disheartened when the younger man failed to flinch or back off. Instead, Louis drew blood from Baer's nose. It was all downhill for Baer from here. Louis, finally heeding Blackburn's counsel, shifted his attention to Baer's body instead of the head and boxed instead of permitting Baer to swap blows with him. At the end of the second round, Baer's face was described as "bathed in blood," and he had become so befuddled he was still punching after the bell. During the third round he went down twice: the second trip was interrupted by the bell for the end of the round or the fight might have ended there. A series of left hooks in the fourth dumped Baer for the final time, although the crowd showed some displeasure when the Californian squatted on one knee and removed his mouthpiece while the referee counted him out.

Later Baer remarked to McLemore, "I could have struggled up once more, but when I get executed, people are going to have to pay more than $25 for a seat to watch it." Dempsey told a reporter that fear choked Baer in his corner, that he complained he couldn't breathe.

In his dressing room, which was marked by an uncustomary sobriety after such a convincing victory over a highly rated opponent, Louis phlegmatically accepted the congratulations of visitors. Detroit Mayor Frank Couzens stopped by to say, "We're proud of you, Joe." Barney Ross drew the only glint of happiness from Louis when he said, "I watched the greatest fighter in action I ever saw tonight."

119

Not all appraisals made Louis a superhero, however. Jack Trucott in the *Herald Tribune* wrote, "Joe Louis is an ordinary colored boy, slow thinking and emotionless."

One story that circulated after the fight claimed that Baer had broken his hand a few days before he met Louis and a physician injected novacaine just before he entered the ring. It was a false rumor, but the possibility that Baer hurt his hand when he thumped Louis in the first round can't be discounted.

Jimmy Cannon, as a youthful reporter, was among the highly impressed. "It wasn't Baer removing his mouthpiece as he sat on his legs that I remember . . . it was Louis's face after Baer hit him after the bell," said Cannon, who then described a look of contempt on the black fighter's face.

Over the years, when asked to pick a performance that satisfied him, Louis would name the Baer match. "I felt better that night. I felt like I could fight for two or three days. I threw more strikes at that man than anyone else," said Louis, but he added, "Guess it's true about his having concrete in his chin. It was just like pounding a brick wall." Louis also paid gracious homage to Baer's power. "He can punch," said the winner the night of the fight. "He caught me with a right when we had that mixup in the first round and it was one of the hardest punches I was ever hit. But I came right back after he stung me and I took the play away from him."

The win over Baer brought the expected response in the Negro neighborhoods. "Milling thousands of Negro men, women and children turned the district [Harlem] into bedlam as they surged through the streets, howling gleefully, blowing horns, dancing madly, pounding on pots and pans," reported the *New York Sun*. The news had traveled quickly thanks to radio but the only reported casualty was a detective, struck in the face by an errant watermelon.

There was precious little for blacks to cheer about in 1935. Two whites and 18 blacks were lynched during the year. The vigilante executions occurred while 13 of the victims were already in the hands of law-enforcement agencies. The murdered men had been accused of rape, homicide, organizing sharecroppers and "communistic activities."

For that matter whites had little to sing hosannahs for in 1935. FDR's puffed-up plan to revive the economy, the National Recovery Administration, died of a Supreme Court decision.

More Americans joined the destitute as the dust storms that began on November 11 of 1933 and continued in the droughts of 1934–35 blew United States farms across the landscape, leaving only dead soil. What grew in America was a crop of demagogues. From Louisiana, Huey Long, the Kingfish, phrased his populism in terms of the barnyard and ran his state as though it were a 12th-century barony. And from Royal Oak, Michigan, Roman Catholic Priest Charles E. Coughlin preached "Social Justice," which under close scrutiny appeared to be a vaguely beneficent form of fascism.

While the rest of America thus struggled, Joe Louis was one of the few who thrived.

9

On the surface, Louis appeared to be the number-one contender for the heavyweight title held by Braddock. But Braddock was the fief of Madison Square Garden, and that organization did not relish risking its championship to Mike Jacobs's creature. In the view of Madison Square Garden, and Jimmy Johnston, the Jacobs–Louis combine would have to give up some of its independence before a bout could be scheduled. The Braddock management may also have felt that surely there must be some less dangerous and only slightly less profitable opponents around.

There appeared to be no customer resistance to an interracial match. In fact, the devastation wreaked by Louis on his foes had drawn the kinds of audiences that had not been seen since the days of Dempsey; Americans, if not all boxing fans were always attracted to the heavy hitters rather than the Tunney-like boxers.

While bargaining for a title bout, Mike Jacobs did not intend to ignore the public's desire to see the young black sensation. After his win over Baer, Louis and his wife moved into a six-room apartment in Chicago, and Louis resumed training.

His next fight was scheduled for December 13, 1935, against the Basque Paulino Uzcudun. Uzcudun was an attraction manufactured by a French promoter named François Descamps. After a big Rickard-like build-up in Europe, Uzcudun came to America and scored some wins over lesser talents. But he had been a loser to Schmeling and Carnera and he was never a real threat to the best heavyweights.

Against Louis, Uzcudun came out with both gloves in front of his face, his elbows pulled in close to protect his body. It was a precursor of the so-called peek-a-boo style taught by manager Gus D'Amato and used extensively by heavyweight champion Floyd Patterson. José Torres, another D'Amato pupil, also used the peek-a-boo.

Louis found Uzcudun's style baffling, but he patiently tracked the woodchopper. During the fourth round, Uzcudun apparently became fatally curious. He separated his gloves long enough for a quick peek at his opponent. Unfortunately for Uzcudun, the gap opened long enough for Louis to fire a right hand. It struck with such force that it lifted Uzcudun's feet from the canvas. Two of the Basque's teeth were driven into his lower lip, and blood spurted from the wound. The referee halted the fight. Henry McLemore visited the loser in his dressing room. Uzcudun, after sitting for 20 minutes, said he felt well enough to shower. He rose from the bench and fell over, still woozy from Louis's right. For this encounter, Louis earned $39,612.

Only one incident threatened the seemingly unstoppable march toward ever greater riches and fame. Shortly after the Baer fight, Jack Blackburn's fondness for alcohol and his violent temper when drunk nearly put the trainer back in prison. In Chicago, Blackburn had decided to invest in a piece of property on South Parkway. After several hours in a bar, drinking gin, Blackburn invited a friend to accompany him to inspect his purchase. When the pair arrived, however, the house was apparently locked. Blackburn, seeking en-

123

trance, became outraged and banged on the door and yelled obscenities at whoever was inside.

A man who apparently ran an illegal still in the garage and who was aroused by the commotion appeared and exchanged words with Blackburn. According to John Roxborough, Blackburn identified himself as the trainer of Joe Louis but the other man, possibly suspicious that he faced a government agent, replied, "I don't care if you are Joe Louis. You ain't going into that garage."

Blackburn swung and in his condition missed; the other then felled him with a punch. Blackburn rushed back to his automobile and came back to the alley with his own pistol. The pair confronted each other from perhaps 20 yards apart and opened fire. Neither man was hit but bullets cut down an elderly black man who died in a hospital and a nine-year-old girl.

A coroner's jury, asked to consider an indictment for "assault to murder," weighed the testimony of witnesses and concluded, ". . . from the testimony presented [we] are unable to determine who fired the shot causing the death of the deceased." There have been suggestions that the decision was influenced by a $1,500 bribe. When *Time* magazine described the events it said, "caught in the crossfire were a nine-year-old pickaninny, a blackamoor of 69." Colorful writing was more than a matter of style with *Time*.

In spite of this favorable ruling, Blackburn was still in trouble. The *Chicago Tribune* raised the claim of foul play and an assistant district attorney subpoenaed a dozen policemen to discover what had happened. Instead of a murder charge, Blackburn and the friend who had accompanied him were indicted for manslaughter.

Joe Louis stayed away from the trial until his absence became a subject for comment. On the final day, attired in a brown suit, brown shirt, brown tie, he sat down behind his trainer. Defense attorney Ralph Taylor skillfully seized the opportunity to appeal to the jury: "Please send this old man back to that boy who needs him, so that he may continue to set an example of clean living for the youth of America." The jury found Blackburn not guilty.

Shortly before this incident Louis had attempted to set Jack Blackburn on the wagon. "We were driving from Michigan to Chicago before the Levinsky fight," remembered Louis. "I said, 'If I knock out Levinsky in the first round, will you stop drinking for a year?' He agreed and I kept him on for almost three months. Then he said, 'Chappie, you got to let me off.' So I did." And within a matter of days Blackburn was in deep trouble.

Even after Blackburn escaped from the threat of jail, he retained a pistol. At training camp, he would stash it in odd places. On one occasion, chef Bill Bottoms casually lit his oven only to be badly frightened when a series of explosions rocked the stove. The trainer had stored his weapon there and the heat eventually set off some bullets.

For 21-year-old Joe Louis, the year 1936 began pleasantly enough with a one-round victory over Charlie Retzlaff in Chicago for $23,065. Louis seemed to accept married life. Marva had admitted that at the time of marriage she was perhaps less than adequately trained to fill the duties of a homemaker. "I guess I could keep a person from starving to death," she said of her cooking. "But I guess Joe would rather eat in restaurants."

But her husband's wants were simple; he was not interested in lavish parties and he retained many of his old friends, some of whom came from a side of life alien to his middle-class wife. And some of his new friends from the flash of Harlem night spots may not have been too pleasing to Mrs.

125

Louis. Away from the training-camp schedule, the fighter relaxed at baseball games. Although now a Chicagoan, he still rooted for the Detroit Tigers. He attended an occasional movie, a Western. He played some golf, he passed time with his old and new friends, and he waited for a meeting with Braddock.

But Louis was not to be kept idle for long. His management of Black, Roxborough and Mike Jacobs realized that hoarded assets produce no return; they wanted their capital to be paying dividends. And Blackburn believed that boxing skills could be kept sharp only by frequent boxing in actual fights. For Louis's next major encounter in 1936, the management selected the former heavyweight champion, the heavy-browed German who faintly resembled Jack Dempsey, Max Schmeling.

For all his new fame, Joe Louis at this stage in his life was poorly understood by sportswriters. The *Daily News'* Paul Gallico, one of the early unfriendly voices on the subject of Louis, wrote, "Joe Louis, the new colored knockout sensation features a poker face, cold, expressionless. . . . The crowd will never warm to him as they do to fighters who have the knack of letting the spectators fight along with them. . . . He has been carefully trained in the sly servility that the white man accepts as his due." Gallico in one article described Louis as "a mean, mean man." Meyer Berger of the *New York Times* visited the black hope at his training camp a few days before the Schmeling fight and sketched a somber, almost neurotic individual. "Joe Louis avoids meeting people, hates conversation (even fight talk) and says less than any man in sports history, including Dummy Taylor, the Giant pitcher who was a mute."

Berger quoted Dr. William Walker, who examined Louis before the Carnera fight, "Closest thing to a wooden Indian

I ever saw." Berger remarked that the description fitted Louis outside the ring as well as within. Berger added that another physician who observed the fighter's routine likened him to a "one-celled beastie of the mire-and-steaming-ooze period." It was not that Berger harbored bigotry. He unfavorably compared Louis to another black celebrity, singer, actor and former football star Paul Robeson. Said Berger, "An interview with Robeson evokes rich classical allusions and brilliant, original thoughts." The *Times* writer saw nothing on this level in Louis.

The *Times* writer also brought up the notion of Louis as a race man, and smote the idea dead. "Idealists who see in Louis a powerful influence for raising the prestige of a downtrodden race—a Toussaint L'Ouverture in tights, so to speak, may be a little astonished to learn that he never regards himself in that light. His mind doesn't work that way. If you try to sound him on that point, he's apt to mumble, 'Some my own people bets against me.' Pinned down, he even denies he's at all race-conscious, but submerged in his makeup there is something more than a trace of race consciousness. His managers and promoters, the man who directs the ring campaigns from his corner, his sparring partners, his secretaries and all the hangers-on at his training camp are people of his own race."

In fact the race consciousness probably owed less to any innate sentiments of Louis than those of Roxborough and Black, for they of course did all the hiring. And Mike Jacobs, the real promoter, was white, as were sparring partners on many occasions. Louis, however, probably felt more comfortable in the presence of blacks.

Further on in his article, the reporter discussed what he felt to be a dark melancholy streak in Louis's makeup: "Joe has developed something that in a more sensitive personality

127

might be called temperament. He sulks easily, and when he does, his normal silence takes on richer and deeper shades."

Interestingly, some 10 years later when Louis entered into an agreement with *Life* magazine to do his autobiography, the two writers who worked on it were Barney Nagler and the same Meyer Berger.

Berger's view of the fighter in training for the Schmeling fight may simply have been a matter of catching the young heavyweight on a couple of unhappy days. But there were some sharp contrasts in the ambience surrounding the 1936 meeting with the German and activities during previous years.

Instead of returning to Dr. Bier's remote Pompton Lakes site, the Louis management arranged for quarters at the Stanley Hotel in Lakewood, New Jersey, a clear-air resort for New Yorkers unable to break away to Florida. Besides having more accommodations for visitors and thus an opportunity to draw better for sparring exhibitions, the area also offered an excellent golf course to which the fighter began to devote an increasing amount of his time.

Jack Blackburn considered the pursuit ill-advised. He warned the fighter, "Chappie, that ain't good for you." When Louis rebutted that the walking exercised his legs, Blackburn insisted, "The timing's different. And them muscles you use in golf, they ain't the same ones you use hitting a man. Besides, being out in the sun don't do you no good. You'll be dried out." Louis also countered that Jimmy McLarnin, a welterweight champion, spent much of his training camp time on the golf course. He was becoming less tractable with success and did not automatically respond to Jack Blackburn anymore.

Louis's passion for golf cropped up in the pre-fight stories out of the camp. Some boxing writers, who found Louis less difficult to approach than Meyer Berger, perhaps because they were willing to share an afternoon on the golf course with the young fighter, turned in stories on Louis's golf style. Hype Igoe of the Hearst chain filed one such account which is chiefly memorable for the newspaperman's reporting that Louis addressed him as "Mistuh Hype" and Corum as "Mistuh Bill."

There was a good deal of heavy-handed horseplay in Lakewood. A chair was wired to give an electrical shock. Small-stakes card games passed the time for sparring partners and the entourage. An incident after an evening of black jack revealed, at least to those in camp, that Louis was below the peak he reached with Max Baer. At this gambling session, someone cheated. Breaches of discipline by sparring partners called for Louis to administer severe punishment during the next training session. But instead of pummeling the miscreants, Louis put on a very awkward show and absorbed as much as he gave.

Visitors to the training camp began to notice Louis's sluggish work and some adverse items appeared in newspapers. Jack Blackburn, who had become so furious with his pupil's dilatory work that he threatened to quit after the fight, tried to hush critical voices. "We had him build up a rep as a killer," Blackburn was quoted. "Now Chappie's up on top of the heap. He doan need to murder his hired hands no mo! Stead he speraments with new punches, new shifts, new counters." (Blackburn in this instance got the dialect treatment but when Grantland Rice reproduced his remarks they came through with no trace of so-called black English.)

Contrary to Meyer Berger's account, at least one sparring

partner, Frank Wotanski, was white. This was 1936 and the fight industry could still attract whites to even its marginal jobs because of the Depression.

Wotanski had an eighth-grade education. Illiteracy among whites now figured at two percent; conservatively it was 15 percent for Negroes. When Wotanski could find work it was as a laborer shoveling stone, heaving ties for the New York Central Railroad. He claimed to have had 250 amateur fights but his professional score was an unimpressive 11 wins in 20 tries. For helping Louis get ready to meet Schmeling, Wotanski received expenses for living in Lakewood and $25 every day that he got into the ring with Louis, perhaps three or four times a week. To a reporter, Wotanski voiced the ambition to get enough money to pay off a mortgage on an upstate New York farm.

One of Louis's sparring partners at Lakewood was Jersey Joe Walcott; born Arnold Cream, he had taken on the name of a once famous black fighter from Barbados who campaigned around the turn of the century. Walcott at one session made Louis look very bad and Louis came back the following day intent upon retribution. He succeeded in knocking the sparring partner down, but a reporter noted, "Louis seemed about to suffer another boxing lesson." Relations between Walcott and Louis were never very friendly.

Not the least of Blackburn's problems was that Mrs. Louis arrived to spend a few days with her husband. Then as today, conjugal relations for a fighter in training camp were considered damaging. Historically, trainers have preferred to import a woman for a one-night stand during the long periods of celibacy rather than allow a wife on the premises. One fight manager insisted, "I don't let my guy near a woman for three weeks before a fight. It gets him in the legs." Even when

Marva was not on the premises, Louis did not lack female companions.

Some segments of the press continued to treat Louis in racial sterotypes. The *New York Evening Journal* ran a cartoon with the caption: "Use the word 'defeat' Joseph." "Sho," answered the crude replica of Louis. "I pops'em on de chin and dey drags 'em out by de feet."

A newsreel crew showed up to film some footage on Louis sparring and asked if something could be staged. They wanted to show a knockdown on film. But because of national distribution which included the South, the downed man would have to be black.

For all of the failings he showed in camp, the betting made Louis a heavy favorite, although Jack Blackburn cautioned, "This old German ain't no fool."

Up at Speculator, New York, in the same unlucky camp used by Max Baer, the "old German" meticulously prepared for his fight. Max Schmeling was already 31, presumably past his prime, and had never been terribly impressive when matched against any top-rated United States boxers.

Nat Fleischer was the first United States authority on the fight business to discover Schmeling. Fleischer had an agreement with Tex Rickard to scout for colorful foreign fighters, while he was on the staff of the *New York Telegram*. Arthur Buelow, a German and a well-known international referee, had discovered Schmeling as an amateur, schooled him and now was guiding him as a professional. It was through Buelow that Fleischer made Schmeling's acquaintance.

"If you can bring him to America, you will be delivering to Mr. Rickard the next world heavyweight champion," said Buelow. Fleischer agreed to approach Rickard.

Rickard, however, refused to gamble enough of a guarantee to entice the Germans to the United States. Eventually, Buelow and Schmeling scraped together enough for their fare and simply sailed to New York in hopes of making it on their own.

Make it they did. Schmeling's United States campaigns in the late 1920s grossed better than $4 million. In fact he did so well that he became an attractive property to some of the more ravenous characters who prowled the fight industry. It was Joe (Yussel) Jacobs, no kin to Mike but his near equal when it came to the pursuit of the dollar, who finally secured control over the profitable German heavyweight.

A celebrated mangler of the English language, Jacobs achieved Bartlett's-like fame during a chilly afternoon at the 1935 World Series when he mumbled, within earshot of some sportswriters, "I should'uv stood in bed."

Jacobs and some associates bought out Schemling's contract, and with Jacobs in charge Schmeling won his championship. The heavyweight title had been vacated with the retirement of Gene Tunney after he sliced up Tom Heeney in 1928. Originally, the boxing authorities talked in terms of a strung-out series of eliminations among the top contenders. Several of the principals dropped out due to injuries and unexpected defeats. The final pair of survivors were Jack Sharkey and Max Schemling.

Before the fight, Yussel Jacobs harangued everyone who'd listen about Sharkey's propensity to foul. No less than nine opponents had yelled foul during a meeting with Sharkey. When the German and the American met at the Long Island City Bowl on June 12, 1930, Sharkey took an early lead. Shortly before the fourth round began, Schmeling's seconds were working him over with ice and draughts of smelling salts. Nothing decisive appeared to be happening in the

132

fourth round, when suddenly Sharkey drove a left to Schmeling's body. It appeared to be below the belt. The German went down and, from his corner, Joe Jacobs yanked his cigar from his mouth long enough to bawl, "Foul, foul. Stay down, Max, you wuz fouled." Schmeling remained down; the performance was satisfactory enough for the referee to award the championship to the man on the canvas. Such dubious conclusions led to the development of truly protective devices against low blows. Some two years later, fighters began to wear a belt, or more properly a kind of heavy leather jock strap that prevented any lasting damage from a low punch. At least one method for arranging the conclusion to a fight had been eliminated.

Schmeling successfully defended his crown against Young Stribling in Cleveland in 1931. But in a decision many sportswriters considered unjust, Jack Sharkey outpointed him in a rematch at the Long Island Bowl.

After the second Sharkey fight, Schmeling engaged in one of those crowd-grabbing attractions of the good little man versus the good big man. On the short end was Mickey Walker, the Toy Bulldog, an excellent middleweight who gave away nearly six inches and 30 pounds to his opponent. Schmeling, who could hit very well some evenings, battered the Toy Bulldog for nearly eight rounds before Walker's manager tossed a towel into the ring to end the carnage.

But then Max Baer knocked him out in 10 rounds, and the German appeared to be on the decline. In 1934 a journeyman heavyweight, Steve Hamas, decisioned him in 12 rounds. Schmeling drew a 12-rounder with Paulino Uzcudun in Barcelona. He recouped somewhat in a rematch with Steve Hamas in Hamburg. The native son scored a KO and Yussel Jacobs was observed giving the Nazi salute. When questioned about his gesture, Jacobs replied, "You gotta do it there or else. Anyway, I had my fingers crossed. I'm 560 percent Jewish."

Schmeling registered a win over Uzcudun to complete his restoration as a suitable United States attraction and eligible for Joe Louis. He was, however, lightly regarded by the press and by bettors, and odds hovered between 10–1 and 8–1 on fight night.

Some stories quote Schmeling as having said after watching Louis destroy Uzcudun, "I zee zometing." Since the Detroit boxer did little punching that night except for the one mighty right, it is questionable whether Schmeling really saw something that evening. But he did study films of Louis in action. And he had detected a flaw in Louis's style; a tendency to drop his left hand as he threw his right.

Actually, the German was not the only man to have noticed Louis's defects. One severe critic of the young black was Jack Johnson. During the build-up to the Schmeling fight, Johnson in a French beret, with an English swagger stick and boar-skin gloves, offered an opinion that Louis's feet were not properly aligned, that he lacked good balance. He also spoke of Louis's being open to short right-hand punches. But Lil Artha's comments were suspect. Fearful of any association with him, the Louis braintrust had once barred him from the Pompton Lakes training camp, and Johnson harbored less than friendly sentiments toward his successor as the dark threat to the heavyweight class.

But even members of the Louis entourage recognized a vulnerability. Sparring partner Frank Wotanski admitted to a reporter that his employer was open to a right.

Jack Miley of the *New York Daily News* flat out declared,

"He, Louis, is what you call it, a sucker for a right hand punch."

An undercurrent to the fight was the growing hostility toward Nazi Germany in the United States. The Nazi regime's Nuremberg Laws of 1935 had deprived Jews of both property and legal rights, outraging Jews in the United States. For the rest of America, though, the issue was less clear. Hitler had denounced the Treaty of Versailles but many Westerners had considered it an excessively punitive treaty. He had reoccupied the Rhineland in 1936 but that was traditionally German territory. The United States Ambassador to Great Britain, Joseph P. Kennedy, praised the Third Reich, and within the United States a vocal group of citizens of German extraction had formed what was called the German-American Bund to promote the notions of the new Germany and to influence United States policies in favor of the Nazi government.

Some reporters had sought out Max Schmeling to discover his political sentiments. On his arrival aboard the S. S. *Bremen,* reporters had asked, "Did Hitler wish you luck?"

"Why should he?" answered the fighter. "Why should he come down to the boat to see me off. He is a politician." Perhaps German boxing experts also saw little prospect for Nazi glory in the coming encounter of the Aryan representative against a black.

Ideology caused some of the absence of official support for Schmeling's adventure. The government's *Reich Sport Journal* carried an article in which it declared "not much enthusiasm" for the fight. Julius Streicher, the Nazi in charge of racial purity, had recently expelled a Negro wrestler from a Nuremberg tournament on the grounds that mixed-race encounters were contrary to official policy. The Nazi program

135

had no room for professional sports. Athletics were considered a political adjunct, designed to enhance the state's resources, not a means for an individual to gain wealth and glory.

During the build-up to the fight, Louis had become mildly angered, but not at Schmeling so much as his manager. Yussel Jacobs buttonholed reporters to suggest that Louis owed his success to loaded gloves and sneak punches, blows thrown as the fighters were being separated from a clinch by the referee. It was the same ploy as when Yussel Jacobs characterized Jack Sharkey as a foul winner. The Schmeling manager irritated Louis further by calling him "Mike Jacobs's pet Pickaninny."

Mike Jacobs had believed that the ideological aura surrounding the fight would be good for the box office. He was somewhat disturbed, therefore, when there was a talk of a boycott of the fight. In any event, either because the German appeared to be woefully overmatched or because of the boycott, the advance ticket sale fell well short of what the promoter had expected. To add to Jacobs's distress, rain caused a postponement at Yankee Stadium and some customers demanded their money back. One of his assistants received a telephone call from the advertising department of a local newspaper which had 60 seats and now asked for refunds. Jacobs snarled, "Give 'em an evasive answer. Tell 'em to go to hell. I didn't sell tickets for a date. I sold them for a fight." Jacobs barely grossed half of his hoped-for million-dollar gate. The official figures were reported as 45,000 paying customers who poured $547,531 into the till.

In the opening minutes of the fight, Louis stalked Schmeling using his left hand. The German kept his chin well protected with his tucked-in right hand and a low prodding left.

In the fourth round, Louis committed the move expected by and hoped for by the German. Over Louis's dropped left hand swept Schmeling's right fist to land full on Louis's chin. The black fighter dropped to the floor for the first time as a professional. He stayed down for only a count of three. After he pulled himself to his feet, he managed to evade further damage during the rest of the round.

In Louis's corner, Jack Blackburn reminded his pupil about Schmeling's right hand. But in the next round the German again popped the Detroit youth on the jaw, leaving him dazed. As round five ended, the bell sounded and Louis dropped both hands, but the eager Schmeling swung the right hand again, knocking Louis down and earning himself a warning from referee Arthur Donovan against such post-bell hitting.

Louis hung on stubbornly, scoring with a strong body blow in the seventh. His left jabs and a pair of hooks in the ninth had nearly closed Schmeling's eye by the 12th, but the German kept boxing, shooting effective rights. Louis's left hook caught Schmeling below the belt. Referee Donovan halted the battle momentarily to determine any damage. There was none. When the referee beckoned for the action to resume, Louis tried to slug it out. Schmeling poured several more rights to the head. Louis went down and was counted out.

In his dressing room, the cocky young fighter who had worked out on the golf course near Lakewood became a weeping abject boy. "I quit, I quit. I done everybody wrong." When he left Yankee Stadium he was so ashamed that he held a straw hat in front of his face.

John Roxborough suggested that his fighter had sprained both thumbs because instead of the customary 12 inches of gauze and six inches of tape wrappings for his hands, ring authorities had limited Louis to a mere six inches of gauze and two inches of tape.

Julian Black, who shook hands with the victor after the fight, refused to concede that it was a weakness in Louis's style. Even in 1973, he claimed that the blow Louis took after the fifth round had ended was the "one punch that decided the fight."

Schmeling himself appeared to be a gracious winner, when doing his own talking. "Louis, he is very good fighter, and a game one." He repeated his analysis of Louis's weakness. "I realized that he carried his left too low, that a right hand was the punch to beat him with." (The reporter who transcribed this comment discarded the Low German dialect rendition favored by others.)

A number of writers seemed eager to dismiss Joe Louis now. "Blackburn's tearing tiger was just a cinnamon tabby cat," wrote Jack Miley, who ruled out any possibility of a comeback. Davis Walsh for INS included a reference to Louis's "white master" and called Louis "a myth, a legend that never happened, but the white race more than his own made him so . . . brown bomber, black avenger . . . reverted to type and became again the boy who had been born in an Alabama cabin."

From Germany where there had been so little pre-fight enthusiasm came a telegram from Joseph Goebbels, minister of propaganda. "Congratulations, I know you won for Germany. Heil Hitler."

Jack Dempsey, who spent a suspiciously large amount of time during the 1930s backing various white hopes against Louis, declared, "Schmeling's victory is the finest thing to happen to boxing in a long time. Who did Louis fight anyway? Baer, who was scared to death, Uzcudun and Carnera.

The big bubble broke Friday night. Joe Louis will be licked by every bum in the country."

For white America, the defeat of their countryman seemed of little consequence. The nation was not actively hostile to Germany. One newspaper reported that in the U.S. House of Representatives, still in session late in June in order to wind up its business, cheers could be heard in the gallery after word of the black's defeat was spread. And in Detroit, there were celebrations over the loss by the hometown product. National pride could not be wounded by the failure of a black citizen. The quickest and heaviest number of congratultory messages to the winner came from the United States South.

Only for black Americans was the defeat an unacceptable insult. The goodnatured, boisterous behavior that upset garbage cans, halted traffic and set people to dancing in the streets, turned into rock throwing, window smashing and assaults upon whites who were so ill advised as to venture into black neighborhoods on that night.

It was Louis's recollection that he first became fully aware of his fall from grace when he discovered Blackburn standing over him in a hotel room while icepacks were applied to his head and eyes. His sister Vunies, who was there, said "His head was swollen to watermelon-like shape." Marva Louis was also there, having attended the fight with a woman writer. Appalled by the punishment absorbed by her husband, Marva Louis several times thought she would leave Yankee Stadium, only to be persuaded to stay on. For months later, Marva Louis said she suffered nightmares in which she saw her battered husband stretched out on the ring floor.

Home in Detroit, Louis's mother comforted him. "You done the best you could," she insisted when he allegedly cried that "I let my people down." The reference, if it were made, more likely referred to failing those intimately associated with him than his race.

Joe's brother Lonnie offered one backhanded consolation. "That whippin' will do Joe good. Every fighter needs one." When fully recovered the loser sought no excuses. Asked about a suggestion that he was doped, he replied, "I wuz doped all right—by right-hand punches." Although he had clearly been struck after the bell in the fifth, Louis dismissed that moment, "We wuz both fighting after the bell—he didn't hear it I reckon." Louis summed up, "He jes beat me, tha'sall. He hit me and he beat me."

While some experts now considered Louis an exploded bubble, incapable of resurrection, the triumvirate of Blackburn, Roxborough and Black set about restoring Louis to the path toward the championship. Blackburn relented on his threat to quit after Louis's lackadaisical training and returned the student to the gym to correct the faults exploited so well by Schmeling.

For the comeback, Louis began with a fight against Jack Sharkey two months after the Schmeling debacle. Sharkey was now 33 years old, slow moving and with a tire of flab around his midriff. He served as a perfect specimen to fatten Louis's confidence. Following Blackburn's instructions, Louis boxed carefully, testing his ability to cope with a right hand. He left-jabbed and Sharkey swung a right, which Louis blocked. In the third round Louis pounded a knockout right to the jaw and completed his first step toward a comeback.

Louis then continued on an active campaign. Marva Louis stayed away from training camp while her husband belabored Al Ettore into submission after five rounds, then required three rounds to put away the Argentine, Jorge

140

Brescia. Less than a week later he carried the show to South Bend, Indiana, for a pair of exhibitions in a single night, and both Willie Davis and K. O. Brown were knocked out in three rounds. A repeat show entertained folks in New Orleans; the victims were Paul Williams and Tom Jones. Louis closed out 1936 with a one-round knockout of Eddie Simms in Cleveland. Noticeably, the competition was less than threatening, but the Louis scenario called for him to demonstrate to himself and to potential spectators that he was still the Brown Bomber, and it gave Jack Blackburn time to adjust Louis's skills.

10

Franklin D. Roosevelt took the oath of office to begin the second term of his presidency on January 20, 1937. In his inaugural address in 1933, he had proclaimed, "The only thing we have to fear is fear itself." For his next four years, his keynote was not so much a call for faith as a recognition of problems: "I see one third of a nation ill-housed, ill-clad, ill-nourished."

Violence and lawlessness continued to pervade the country. In December 1936, thousands of workers hunkered-down in automobile manufacturing plants in Detroit. The sit-down strike, a tactic that originated in a United States meat-packing plant in 1934 and was then exported to Europe, now came back to paralyze General Motors. The vice president of the company, William S. Knudsen, refused to recognize the newly formed Congress of Industrial Organizations as the representative of GM workers. The company called upon the governor of Michigan, Frank Murphy, to eject strikers. Skirmishes erupted along the picket lines while Murphy temporized, tried to get the parties to negotiate. General Motors convinced police to attack, but pop bottles, metal pipes and other missiles drove off the lawmen. Murphy refused to commit the National Guard, and eventually General Motors recognized the union.

At Ford, where Henry Ford had obdurately announced he would never recognize a union, the company's labor goons beat up two organizers, Richard Frankesteen and Walter Reuther, on a bridge that led to the River Rouge Plant. But by spring, Ford too capitulated. In Chicago, labor strife was bloodier, with Chicago cops killing 16 strikers at Republic Steel in a springtime melée.

In Florida, a black man who held up a gas station was seized from the jail by five hooded men and shot to death. A Connecticut Negro, accused not only of murdering a sheriff but of yelling "to hell with the law," was taken by a mob, shot and hanged.

Abroad the carnage piled up bodies on a scale appropriate to international affairs. Spain provided a testing ground for weapons and ideologies with volunteers assisting the Spaniards in slaughtering one another. The Japanese continued to gore China, entering what was then called Peiping with an orgy of executions, rape and plunder.

In that Depression year of 1937 even attempts to uplift man by heroic accomplishments seemed doomed to disaster. In May, the mighty dirigible *Hindenburg* arrived at Lakehurst, New Jersey, to complete its first transatlantic crossing. A spark ignited the flammable hydrogen and a monument to progress became a torch of destruction. During this year, aviation heroine Amelia Earhart disappeared while on a round-the-world flight, leaving behind no trace and endless speculation on whether she had been forced down by the Japanese who wished to conceal their military expansion in the islands of the South Pacific.

Although the United States economy had made some gains since Roosevelt took over, the fall of 1937 would see a recession that wiped out much of the gains.

Joe Louis, as the year 1937 began, was battling to prove

his credentials as a contender for the heavyweight championship. Early in January he disposed of Steve Ketchel, in Buffalo, with a two-round KO. Less than three weeks later he was matched against Bob Pastor at Madison Square Garden.

Pastor's manager was Jimmy Johnston, whose achievements as fight promoter for the Garden had been a dismal failure largely because the Boy Bandit failed to appreciate the potential of Joe Louis. (It did not seem to occur to the State Athletic Commission that holding the dual posts of fight manager and promoter for the largest indoor arena in New York posed any conflict of interests.)

Jack Blackburn, flashing his mouth of gold, told an interviewer, "I call it one round. That ol' Pastor man won't hear but one bell and that's the one that starts the first heat. My Chappie's ready and he's burning!"

The reference to Louis's burning state of mind may have been brought on by Johnston's constant denigration of Louis before the fight, though the black boxer himself showed little resentment of the remarks. "Jimmy's all right," insisted Louis. "He's just sayin' these things to make us a little money."

The liveliest part of the fight occurred shortly before the boxers emerged from their dressing rooms. Roxborough reported that shortly before the fight, while he waited with Louis, Blackburn and four bodyguards he had hired, Jimmy Johnston, followed by a quartet of tough-looking men, burst into the dressing room. "Get those bandages off his hands," Johnston yelled, according to Roxborough.

The Louis bodyguards reacted by yanking out their pistols and Blackburn shoved Louis behind a locker and tried to shield him from any stray bullets with his own frail body.

"You guys was just here watching us put them on," Roxborough replied. "Get those bums out of here." At this point, one of Roxborough's hired protectors slipped up behind the manager and whispered in his ears, "Boss, I recognize those guys. They're New York City detectives."

Roxborough, however, refused to give ground. "We aren't scared. Now get the hell out of here."

"Don't push me," said Johnston.

"I didn't push you. If I do, I'll hit you on the Goddamn jaw. Joe, get dressed. We don't need this fight. We're getting out of here."

Johnston now paled. This was a pretty fair pay night for him and Pastor. In addition, a pullout at this juncture could cause a nasty investigation. "Don't get sore," he pleaded.

"Out, you bum," stormed Roxborough, now aware that he had won this confrontation, and the visitors left. Exactly what Johnston's motivation was for this scene went to the grave with him; it may just have been psychological warfare, keyed to worries common to the fight game in this period that a fighter would load his wrapped hands with plaster-of-paris or some other rock-hard substance.

Whatever his failings as an entrepreneur and psychological warrior, Johnston apparently knew the strengths and weaknesses of his fighter, as well as those of Louis. He instructed Pastor to keep moving, to stay away from Louis throughout the fight. As a technique for survival, the bicycle routine employed by Pastor worked effectively. Louis's punching power was neutralized, since he could never close on Pastor. While the method prevented a knockout, however, it also meant that Pastor himself could not score points. Louis won a 10-round decision.

"He just run a race," said the victor. "I couldn't hit him because he wouldn't stay put. Jack got burned up. He said for me to pin Pastor in a corner, but I couldn't do it. Nobody got hurt but the people who paid money."

As a revenue-producing venture, the fight was a modest success—Louis's share came to $36,000—but it offered no evidence to compel boxing authorities to recognize Louis as the leading challenger for the championship.

A more conventional match, and one with a far more satisfying conclusion, was Louis's February meeting with Natie Brown, the clever boxer who had forced Louis to a decision in their first encounter. Brown lasted only four rounds in Kansas City on his second meeting.

Well before these 1937 triumphs, however, a subtle web of intrigue had settled over the boxing world, as Mike Jacobs schemed to arrange a Louis confrontation with champion James J. Braddock.

The obstacle to Louis's crack at Braddock's title was an exclusive contract for Braddock's services held by Madison Square Garden. The arena, with Johnston as matchmaker, had been doing poorly. And if Louis captured the championship, the garden would lose its last asset in the battle against Mike Jacobs. Also standing in the way of a Louis–Braddock match was a signed contract for Braddock to meet Max Schmeling on June 3, 1937. It could hardly be argued that the German did not have a legitimate right to be called the leading contender for the championship.

Jacobs's first move was to try to arrange a return between Louis and Schmeling. But the German saw no particular value to such a replay. Schmeling had nothing to gain beyond his share of the gate. He could lose his chance at Braddock, felt by most experts to be an over-the-hill combatant who had beaten a poorly trained, poorly motivated Max Baer.

With no success in inveigling the German into his plans, Mike Jacobs shifted his attention to the Braddock camp where he found one set of willing ears, those of Joe Gould, the manager. Gould, another up-from-poverty conniver, had been partner with underworld figures such as Pete Stone, alias Pete the Goat. When Owney Madden left Sing Sing in 1933, one of the pair of friends that met him at the gate of the prison was Joe Gould.

While Mike Jacobs dickered with Gould, the Louis management became impatient. Shortly before Christmas of 1936, Roxborough had come to New York to discuss with Mike Jacobs the chances of arranging the fight with Braddock. Negotiations appeared to be stalled and it was Roxborough's recollection that he advised Jacobs, "I think that we should line up a fight for Joe in Miami." Jacobs reportedly agreed that the more Louis fought, the more pressure there would be on the Braddock people to confront this challenge.

On that uncertain note, Roxborough left Jacobs's office. Outside on the street, he immediately observed a pair of men staring at him; one he recognized as an Owney Madden soldier. Since such specimens often hung out around Madison Square Garden, Roxborough thought nothing more of it and moved toward the curb. Suddenly the two intercepted him. "Got a man wants to see you," informed one of the thugs. "Let's go for a ride."

Roxborough accepted the probability that both of his companions were armed. If he had any hopes of escape, they vanished when a large black Buick pulled over to the curb and the second man ordered, "Get in, it's icy on the street and you may fall down and hurt yourself."

The black manager complied and for an hour the car wandered through the canyons of Manhattan without any destination. Finally, they halted in an alley, and now Roxborough feared that perhaps he had been marked for assassination. He was led down the alley, through a back door of

147

a building and then into a corridor that ended at an office. Roxborough realized that he was actually in the backroom of a nightclub. Then he found himself facing his host, Joe Gould.

As perhaps the greatest anticlimax of Roxborough's life, Gould stuck out a welcoming hand, "Hi, Roxy, I was afraid you might not make it."

Roxborough could afford to be indignant, since it seemed obvious that he had not been brought to the office to be assaulted. He irately demanded to know the reason for Gould's caper.

"Don't get sore," assuaged Gould. "I figured if I called you, you might not be able to find the place." He invited his guest to relax and smoke. Then he offered his proposition. As best as Roxborough could remember, it went: "You want Braddock, you got him. You want the title, you got it. It's all set, a 12-round exhibition in Atlantic City. . . ." Roxborough reacted at the word "exhibition." He summarily dismissed the proposition.

Gould, unabashed, continued, "It will be billed as an exhibition, but you know that if a heavyweight champion is knocked out in a fight, no matter what they call it, he still gives up the title. Braddock won't last 10 rounds. He hasn't fought in 18 months. He's sick. He's stale. He's fat. Louis will knock him dead. I'll give you a guarantee."

Roxborough inquired whether Braddock was aware of this proposal and Gould replied that all he would have to know was that he was defending his title. To Roxborough, one thing remained unmentioned: How much did the Braddock camp want in return for their largesse?

"All we want is 50 percent of Louis," was the answer. "We're going to let you keep half."

Roxborough summoned his courage. "No 50 percent, not

148

50 cents. Nothing. We don't need Braddock. If he had 10 fights he couldn't make as much as Joe can in one. He needs us. You need us. No deal and no exhibition." What Roxborough said was mostly true. A nonfighting champion such as Braddock earned nothing for himself or his management. At 31, with a history of injuries, Braddock seemed very unlikely to stand up against any strong challenge. On the other hand, Louis people hadn't been making big money in recent fights. Only the Pastor engagement did more than pay expenses.

Roxborough claims that the two thugs who remained during the conversation warned that failure to accept the terms could have unfortunate consequences. But Roxborough remained adamant, even as Gould dropped his demands to 25 percent, then 20. Roxborough suggested that if the Braddock people wanted to profit from Joe Louis's future, they should dicker with Mike Jacobs and see if he would be amenable to a contribution from his end. The meeting ended on that note.

And eventually it was Jacobs who agreed to a 10 percent slice of his profits on Louis for a decade, to go to Joe Gould and Braddock. Jacobs's tailor also supposedly was enlisted to sweeten the relationship with some suits. Before the 10 years was up, though, Jacobs forced Gould and Braddock to accept a settlement.

Still there remained that troublesome contract between Braddock and Schmeling, for June 3, 1937. Madison Square Garden and the German refused to renounce their claims upon the champion. The resourceful Gould began a propaganda campaign against a fight for Schmeling, now that more Americans had begun to find the Nazi government distasteful. Gould announced that he had taken a poll and discovered that fight fans would boycott any meeting between Braddock and Schmeling. Not so coincidentally, stories appeared in which it was suggested that the Anti-Nazi League to Champion Human Rights, headed by Samuel Untermeyer and Jeremiah T. Mahoney, thought a chance at the championship for Schmeling might lead to that emblem of superiority disappearing forever into the evil darkness of the Third Reich. Later, Mike Jacobs would find the anti-Nazi group an opponent, instead of an ally.

Bamboozling the public was one thing, and an easy one for hustlers like Mike Jacobs and Joe Gould. A legal document posed more serious obstacles. Sol Strauss, the legal counsel to Jacobs, poured over the contract between Madison Square Garden and Braddock. Strauss proposed that the agreement was invalid because, while it bound the fighter, it placed no obligation upon the arena. The matter went into court in New Jersey, not incidentally beyond the reach of politicans friendly to Madison Square Garden and in the backyard of both Jacobs and Braddock. A judge named Guy L. Fake found for the heavyweight champion, and the final roadblock had been cleared. Louis and Braddock signed to contest the championship at Comiskey Park in Chicago, again well out of range of any last-minute legal ploys by the New Yorkers, close to where the protection of the Chicago politicians could be expected. Still, in a zany charade, the New York State Athletic Commission persisted in holding a weigh-in ceremony for Braddock and Schmeling on June 3, but the principals were phantoms.

Louis, training at Kenosha, Wisconsin, plunged into perhaps his most vigorous schedule yet. He ran 10 miles a day and he belabored his sparring partners with an untypical ferocity. He turned 23 in camp and Bill Bottoms baked a birthday cake. But Marva Louis was not in camp. Louis stayed away from golf and stuck to his regimen, which included continued instruction in the avoidance of right hands.

150

At Grand Beach, Michigan, heavyweight champion James J. Braddock strove to recapture his powers. Apart from the fact that he was approaching 32 years of age, and that he had a history of injuries and illness, Braddock had not had a scheduled fight for nearly two years. Long layoffs devastate a fighter's timing. The Cinderella Man, he was called. In the eyes of most experts Braddock was doomed to hear chimes that would send him back to obscurity well before midnight.

A Hell's Kitchen kid, Braddock was born a few blocks from Madison Square Garden. He ran with the tough kids of the area, swam in the then unpolluted Hudson River. At 13 he quit school to deliver messages for Western Union. The family had by then crossed the Hudson and lived in Hoboken, New Jersey. An older brother, Joe, boxed as an amateur, and while Jim Braddock was still in his middle teens he made the error of unauthorized use of Joe's sweater. A family brawl followed, and although he took a beating, Jim was apparently encouraged enough to try the sport seriously. In his first fight under an assumed name, he performed at a Loyal Order of the Moose Benefit and earned three dollars. Coached by his brother and a friend, he entered the amateur lists. In 1925, weighing 161 pounds, he won both the amateur light heavyweight and heavyweight championships of New Jersey.

Early in his pro career, Braddock met Joe Gould, who happened to be at a gym in the company of two beer barons interested in Harry Galfund, a fighter controlled by Gould. The manager was willing to sell his share in Galfund for $2,500. But the bootleggers wanted some demonstration of Galfund's skills. Spotting the skinny Braddock hammering on a bag, Gould offered him $15 to go three rounds with Galfund. It did not occur to Gould that this gawky young-ster would pose any problem, or undoubtedly he would have

151

instructed Braddock to make Galfund look good. Instead, Braddock used his left hand so effectively that when the demonstration was over, Gould was forced to unload the fighter for only $1,200.

But Gould recognized talent and he asked Braddock, "Who's your manager, kid?"

"Don't have one," answered Braddock.

"You do now," said Gould, and for all of the knavery in his life, Gould showed a constant loyalty to Braddock. For several years, the fighter slowly climbed the ladder of contention, adding weight and experience. But in 1928 he broke a knuckle on his right hand in a fight. It was to be reinjured several more times. "It healed badly," said Braddock. "A surgeon wanted $1,500 to fix it and Joe Gould and I didn't have the money." Fortunately Braddock broke it again in a fight and a surgeon this time set the bone correctly.

But, for the next three years, the Cinderella Man never looked more like the chimney sweep. He lost more than he won, and against a staggering array of nonentities. By 1933, he had performed so poorly, that the Illinois Athletic Commission insisted he spar for inspection in a gym before it would declare him eligible to fight in that state. In Philadelphia, against Al Ettore, Braddock worked so ineptly that the referee banished him. A few months later in Mount Vernon, New York, he and his opponent, Abe Feldman, proved so ineffective that the referee ordered both of them out of the ring and it was declared no contest. Only after Braddock produced medical evidence of another injured right hand was his purse for this match released. But the battered right hand meant he could not pass a ring physical.

In the fall of 1933, Braddock returned to Weehawken docks to eke out a living. He made from $5 to $12 a week, barely enough to support his wife and three children. When he was able, he tended bar at the North Bergen Social and Athletic Club. Braddock hit near bottom as he faced a shutdown of gas and electricity and a bill from the milkman who would extend no more credit. With a dime to his name he walked several miles to the Weehawken Ferry, rode the vessel for four cents, and with another six cents still barely jingling in his pocket walked several miles to Joe Gould's office. The manager kept himself alive selling car radios. Gould managed to borrow $35 for Braddock.

But even that could not stretch very far. The ex-fighter found a job swinging a hook as a stevedore lifting railroad ties. The work was too spotty to keep the family going and Braddock, like Louis, applied for home relief. "I did pick-and-shovel work for the WPA and got $18 a week." But the work on the docks produced an important side effect. To give his sore right hand an opportunity to heal, Braddock relied on his left, until it matched the right in size and power. And finally his right hand recovered. He called Gould, "I'm in good shape. Get some fights for me."

Gould had pestered Jimmy Johnston for a bout and finally in the spring of 1934 the promoters became convinced that Braddock would offer a prestigious win for a rising young heavyweight named Corn Griffin.

There were 56,000 present to see the fight, but they had come to see Max Baer bloody Carnera for the championship. Corn Griffin and the 28-year-old Braddock were in a preliminary. In the first round, Griffin banged the older man to the canvas and the script appeared to be as ordered for those pushing a new sensation. But Braddock got off the floor and began to pummel Griffin. In the third round, Braddock sent the young hopeful back to obscurity.

When Braddock and Gould conferred in the dressing room, the fighter declared, "I did that on stew and hamburgers. Get me some steaks and see what I do."

Gould continued to haunt the smoke-filled rooms where matches were made. Finally, through Owney Madden, he got a match with John Henry Lewis, a young black heavyweight.

Altruism had not been entered as a distinguishing characteristic on Madden's record by police. But he and Gould were thick. "I don't know what arrangement Gould had with Madden," said Braddock in his retirement years. "It didn't affect me; if Madden got any money, it was from Gould's share."

Although Lewis had even beaten the light-heavyweight champion, Braddock boxed well enough to win in 10 rounds.

The performance elevated Braddock to the rank of a contender for the heavyweight crown worn by Max Baer. Braddock struggled to a decision in 15 rounds with Art Lasky, another highly rated challenger. The New York State Athletic Commission rewarded Braddock's pluck. It nominated him as the number-one contender for the honors held by Baer.

The champion professed a great lack of interest in the new threat. Baer was perhaps still unhappy over Braddock's remark at the time Braddock visited Baer's leisurely camp before the Carnera fight. "This fellow must be training for the junior prom."

Pressure for the fight grew. Mike Jacobs urged Baer to take the match because it would complete Baer's obligations to the Madison Square Garden, and Jacobs dangled visions of huge promotions before Baer. He promised Baer a big pay night with the winner of the Louis–Carnera fight.

Finally, Baer capitulated. On the day of the weigh-in Baer continued his clowning. "He made the beginnings of a move to hit me," recalled Braddock. "If he had swung, I was going to hit him back. Baer stopped and grinned. I smiled, but not as much as he did. I knew Baer could throw a punch, hit pretty hard. But I also knew I could stand up to him."

The newspapers declared Baer a 10 to 1 favorite and Joe Gould tried to rush his fighter past the newsstands plastered with discouraging headlines. Braddock remembered, "I remarked to Joe that if I had money and was a betting man I could clean up at those odds. I didn't care if the odds were 50 to 1, I thought I could win."

In the dressing room before the fight, Braddock loosened the tension with a tale of a telephone call home in which he vowed to his wife that he would "bring home the title." His children became visibly excited because they thought he promised to return with a "turtle."

As time wore on during the fight Braddock saw that Baer could not maintain his pace. "I said to him," remembered Braddock, "Max, you're way behind. He didn't smile, he tried to belt me."

Braddock's victory over Baer was a popular one; the underdog had triumphed, the has-been had come back. Promoters and officials of the industry also looked with favor on Braddock. Baer's mercurial behavior had threatened to jeopardize whatever dignity the sport could muster. Jimmy Johnston was well aware that if Baer triumphed he would defend his title under the banner of Mike Jacobs's promotions.

But the heavyweight champion didn't defend his title for two years. When he did, he deserted the Garden for the Louis match in Chicago, causing Johnston to lose his post eventually. Now Braddock faced the tough black man from Detroit, who in four rounds did to Baer what Braddock could not accomplish in 15.

There was in Braddock no trace of racial hostility toward his favored opponent. "I never thought about whether a fighter was white or not. What you were interested in was your own ability. Louis was a good one, but I didn't think he took a punch well." George Nicholson, a northern-born black heavyweight, who never advanced beyond prelims, served as a sparring partner for Braddock. "He was a wonderful guy," said Nicholson many years later. "Always treated everybody the same. When we put rocks in the beds of the guys in training camp, we would put them in his too. We ate together, showered together, all equals."

Nicholson actually worked with the champion for a few weeks at Loch Sheldrake, New York, during the period when Braddock thought he might go against Schmeling. But when Braddock signed up to fight Louis in Chicago, the management selected Grand Beach, Michigan, as the site for training. Braddock informed Nicholson that the area was largely closed to Negroes. "Braddock said he didn't want me to feel any discrimination and if we couldn't all be together there, be treated like equals, he thought too much of me for me to go there."

Nicholson's immediate loss turned out to be his long-time gain. "Al Douglas," said Nicholson, "one of the guys in Louis's group, then came over to me at Stillman's Gym where I was working out and asked me if I'd like to be sparring partner for Joe Louis at $25 a day. I told him I'd have to ask Braddock. He said it was fine, and he didn't begrudge me the opportunity, even though he was going to fight Louis." As a result Nicholson traveled to Kenosha to begin an association with Louis that lasted through the Brown Bomber's World War II service.

The former Braddock aide, however, found the going stiff at first. Told to throw those right hands, Nicholson smashed one through to Louis, "so hard, he didn't know what struck him. Joe was a little peeved with me, but Jack Blackburn said that I was okay. After that Joe and I got on fine."

With Nicholson, among others, to keep him alert and Jack Blackburn to wheedle, nag and scold him, Louis readied himself for Braddock, then drove from his Kenosha, Wisconsin, training camp to Chicago, his adopted home town, for his assault on the championship.

In a blue bathrobe, trimmed in red, Joe Louis walked down the aisle of Comiskey Park in Chicago on the night of June 22, 1937. Some 45,000 people were on hand to see him meet Braddock. As the two fighters prepared to square off in the first round, Jack Blackburn supposedly whispered, "Chappie, this is it. You come home a champ, tonight."

Although he was a distinct underdog, Braddock thought he had a chance. "Joe always had trouble with guys who stayed low and I figured I might catch him." But Braddock's chances were not helped by an undisclosed attack of arthritis in his right arm. "I had to get a shot in it so I could hold it up for the fight," recalled Braddock.

During the initial moments of the round, the challenger's vulnerability to that right hand almost made a liar of Jack Blackburn. Braddock drove a punch that some say caught Louis's jaw and he went down. Sportswriter Frank Graham thought the right hand missed the chin and struck the neck. But wherever it landed, the punch failed to dim Louis's senses and he rose instantly. Braddock rushed to pursue what he thought was his advantage but the younger man fended him off easily.

When Louis returned to his corner at the close of the round, Jack Blackburn whispered in his ear, "Chappie, when you is knocked down, you stay there until the count of nine. You can't ever get up so fast they can't see from the bleachers that you was down."

Inexorably, Louis's skill and quicker reflexes sapped Braddock. Round after round the champion absorbed punishment, particularly around the head. Lacerations and bruises turned his pleasant Irish phiz into a distorted mask. But he kept himself vertical, if wobbly.

Braddock was a man whose route to the championship had been a torturous one. Unlike the king of England who six months earlier had given away his inherited throne "for the woman I love," Braddock did not intend to abdicate. He was of the school that knew Lear's mistake, that the king must pay a price before he is permitted to yield. When Joe Gould suggested he signal surrender, Braddock replied through his bloodied lips, "If you do, I'll never speak to you again as long as I live."

In the eighth round Louis ended Braddock's brave stance with a left to the head, a left to the body and then a right hand that sent the champion to the floor face first.

In the dressing room, Joe Gould first offered homage to the courage of his fighter, and then said, "Joe Louis is a good boy. Joe has done more to bring boxing back than anyone in the game today. He deserves to be champion." It was a handsome tribute, though perhaps marred by the fact that Gould was to share in the future profits of Joe Louis.

The new champion told newsmen he expected to defend often and that he wouldn't consider himself fully established until he met Max Schmeling again. There was a small celebration at the apartment of Joe and Marva Louis. Jimmy Cannon dropped in and found the new champion a diffident host, uneasy about association with the revelers. He urged the reporter to pull up a chair in the kitchen and he cooked pork chops for Cannon.

Saluting the new champion, one newspaper wrote, "The next six months tell the story. If Joe Louis forgets his resolve to be an ambassador of good will for his race and to wipe away the stigma which Jack Johnson brought on colored champions, he'll never make the grade." For the nonwhite fighter, prowess was not enough.

11

Little more than two months after the erstwhile shoeless youth from Alabama became heavyweight champion, he re-entered the ring to defend his title for the first time. The challenger was a Welshman, Tommy Farr. Farr held the rank of British Empire Champion, which was a modest credential; the sun set on British pugilism long before it went down on the empire. Though hardly a household name in America, Farr had outpointed Max Baer and Bob Olin. And a week before Louis defeated Braddock, Farr put away a highly esteemed German, Walter Neusel, in three rounds. Still, Farr figured to be a long shot against Louis. Among other deficiencies, he bore the reputation for cutting easily, a condition seemingly as endemic to British fighters as hemophilia among some branches of the Spanish royal family.

Meanwhile, Max Schmeling, considering himself bamboozled out of his rightful crack at Braddock, had returned to Europe with a plan to gain world, if not United States, recognition as the legitimate heavyweight champion. Negotiators for Schmeling managed to convince the German Boxing Commission, the French Boxing Federation and the British Boxing Board of Control to recognize Schmeling as the true world champion—what effect Louis's dark skin played in this dark decision is impossible to know. But the result was to invest Schmeling with the title on the strength of his having beaten Louis before he became champion and before Braddock's wiggle out of his contractual obligation to Schmeling.

Actually, Mike Jacobs had begun to dicker with Schmeling for a Louis rematch after Louis won the title. Schmeling's money demands and insistence that the fight be held in Europe stonewalled any agreement.

But Schmeling made a pitch to the New York Athletic Commission to force Louis to meet him instead of Farr. He was on the defensive immediately, however, because German newspapers had printed a story that accused New York Governor Herbert Lehman of bribing the Commission with $7,-500 to shunt Schmeling aside. The German fighter denied any knowledge of the sources for the newspaper story. Major General John J. Phelan, head of the Commission, pointed out that his agency had spent all of $23.50 on a telegram to Schmeling proposing a match between Schmeling and Louis but had received no reply. General Phelan then scolded the challenger for his 1930 foul success: "You won the title on the floor, you could have gotten up." The indignant Schmeling responded, "How do you know I could have?" To the surprise of none, Schmeling's protest failed to affect the scheduled meeting between Farr and Louis.

Although the challenger was considered to be simply a three-dimensional canvas on which Louis could demonstrate his art, Louis's fight with Farr, his first defense of his title, drew 32,000 to Yankee Stadium. Instead of running away, Farr actually brought the fight to Louis and stayed on his feet while doing it. He cuffed the champion often and Louis failed to score an impressive victory. In the fourth round, however, the black man crunched a blow to Farr's nose, and ringsiders claimed they heard the sound of bone-breaking. Years later,

Louis offered one of his rare alibis: "I might have done better if I hadn't hurt my hand on top of his head."

Although Farr stayed up for the 15 rounds and gave a good account of himself, the verdict went to Louis for superior boxing skill. The Englishman looked much the worse for the match, with a swollen nose and bleeding from cuts under both eyes. There was immediate talk of a rematch. Jack Dempsey, continuing to ballyhoo any dim sign of a white hope, claimed that Farr would win, now that he understood Louis's style and knew his weaknesses.

In fact, Louis suffered so little trauma from the 15 rounds that he rushed off to Newark Airport to catch an airplane for Detroit in order to see featherweight Henry Armstrong beat Orville Drouillard. Jack Blackburn professed no concern about his pupil's progress. "I figga he's three years short of his prime. I ast him what he thinks about bein' the champion and all that, but he says it ain't no difference." To those who already mentioned retirement, Blackburn scorned, "He'll retah when John Roxborough says he can retah. Roxborough's the boss around heah."

Tommy Farr called the champion, "the best and cleanest fighter I ever met," but the verdict elsewhere was less enthusiastic, since Louis had disappointed expectations for a savage knockout.

Harry Grayson of the Newspaper Enterprise Association insinuated that Louis might be gun-shy: "Louis, I fear, was a study in American mob psychology. The Alabama born darky was rushed to the front at a time when the field was unbelievably bad, even for heavyweights." Grayson then said of Schmeling, "The plodding Teuton was more than a little passé but he was never much of a hand for taking a nine on a dirty look."

The experts were so dumfounded by Farr's survival that

162

they ranked his failure to take the count the biggest surprise in sports for 1937. Speculation on the intrinsic weaknesses of Louis captured the imagination of many.

Jim Tully, in a piece for *Liberty* magazine entitled "Why Joe Louis Will Not Be Champion Long," extrapolated from the Farr fight: "Louis was gunshy. Schmeling had written with a hot iron, the fear of a right hand across his brain." According to Tully, Farr, having shaken off the best of the champion's punches, called him "yellow" and "a name reflecting on his ancestry." Seated next to Farr, Jack Dempsey concurred that Louis could not beat the Welshman, and in Tully's prose, "His eyes narrowed as an ex-King's will who sees the abdication of another." (The occasions on which Tully got to observe the reactions of former monarchs contemplating the vicissitudes of other kings is worthy of speculation.)

Tully considered the decision awarded to Louis to be manifestly unfair. He concluded with a rather original observation: "Farr had learned: *by blinking his eyes each time, Louis telegraphed his punches*" [italics by Tully]. This was the only time anyone every discovered that Louis's eyelids semaphored in conjunction with his fists. As a footnote, *Liberty* offered a comment from Dempsey: "His [Tully's] article gives the clearest possible picture of the state of the heavyweight championship today. I heartily agree with its conclusions."

For all the puffery and the fine fight he did put up, whatever chance Farr had to meet Louis again slipped away in 1938. Jim Braddock, in his valedictory performance, clearly outpointed the Briton in New York. Then Max Baer, and a new heavyweight contender, Lou Nova, both won decisions over Farr.

As 1938 opened, the stock market was again in full slide.

Government figures showed as many as 10 million unemployed. The U.S. Supreme Court was finally approving legislative programs and agencies designed by FDR, but the recession only deepened. From the heads of the automobile companies came gloom. General Motors said the year-end decline in sales was the most severe on record. A conference of 1,000 "small businessmen" demanded the demolition of FDR's New Deal, which offered a grandiose $12 billion federal budget.

Summer suits were advertised for $17.50, and Kentucky Bourbon sold for $1.59 a fifth. A 1938 Nash automobile could be purchased for $900 but the situations-wanted outnumbered the help-wanted ads in the classified section of the newspapers. For blacks, conditions continued to be even more desperate. Figures for the period showed nonwhites in the South earned one third that of their white counterparts, and in the urban North, blacks made half that which whites collected.

Another attempt at a federal anti-lynching law failed to pass the U.S. Senate after six weeks of southern filibuster.

The newly created Congress of Industrial Organizations put into its constitution a clause "to bring about the effective organization of the working men and women of America regardless of race, creed, color or nationality."

Abroad, fascism continued to grow. In Spain, the fascist rebels under General Franco, helped with arms from Germany and Italy, gradually won control of the country. A handful of Americans who had enlisted in the Abraham Lincoln and George Washington brigades suffered death, defeat and disillusionment as communist elements often appeared more concerned with the international fortunes of the Party than beating back the Franco troops.

In Germany, Adolf Hitler demanded annexation of

Austria, and that German-speaking land tried to accommodate by bringing pro-Nazis into the government.

Joe Louis, more than likely not aware that such a place as Austria even existed, worked twice in the first three months of 1938, while seeking the opportunity to confront the one professional who had defeated him. In New York, Louis took only three rounds to KO Nathan Mann, a wholly owned subsidiary first of Dutch Schultz and later of Owney Madden. And in Chicago, Louis destroyed Harry Thomas in either five rounds, according to the Illinois Boxing Commission, or four rounds, according to the champion's corner.

During the fourth round, Louis flattened Thomas. His seconds climbed through the ropes, into the ring and dragged the senseless Thomas back to his corner before the bell rang. The handlers started to resuscitate him. Meanwhile the referee declared the fight over, a KO in the fourth. At ringside, Joe Triner, head of the Illinois Boxing Commission, thought otherwise. He saw Thomas now revived in his corner and overruled the referee. To the fury of the Louis people, the champion was forced to smash Thomas to a 10 count in the fifth. As a result, Louis fought no more in Chicago, except for exhibitions.

Although the Farr fight had earned better than $100,000 for Louis, almost as much as he earned against Braddock, Nathan Mann and Harry Thomas together only brought $56,000. Because of the stock-market staggers, only a premium foe could attract top-dollar customers. Obviously the best pay night would be Max Schmeling.

Some observers have suggested that Mike Jacobs pursued a Schmeling match for Louis at a measured pace. The Farr promotion and the two lesser engagements that followed might not have produced the revenues of a grudge fight, but for the promoter, the returns were sizable and safe ones.

Jacobs probably did worry about the possibility that the German would prove an inescapable nemesis for the young black champion. And that could end Jacobs's domination of the fight business, which he had only recently achieved; following Louis's ascension to the championship, Jimmy Johnston had lost his post as matchmaker for the Garden and been replaced with Jacobs.

Eventually, however, Jacobs negotiated the kind of contract that would satisfy his needs. Louis and Schmeling were scheduled to meet June 22, 1938.

Much had changed on the international scene in the two years since Louis and Schmeling had met the first time. *Anschluss,* the absorption of Austria, occurred in March of 1938. Only two days after Adolf Hitler paraded in triumph through the streets of Vienna, alleged spokesmen for the Sudeten Germans, people of Germanic extraction who lived on the periphery of Czechoslovakia, called for union with Nazi Germany. Joseph Goebbels announced, "We won't tolerate any longer the 3.5 million Germans being tormented. Austria has shown what could happen. All we want is peace, but not the peace of the graveyard."

Inside Germany, oppression of Jews grew. More of their possessions were confiscated, the professions were closed to them, and many were consigned to Dachau and other concentration camps. An orgy of synagogue and shop-window smashing by Nazi toughs that became known as "Crystal Night" followed a passionate speech by Goebbels that bore the refrain, "Out with the Jews, out with the Jews."

Even in the United States, the Nazi seed sprouted a rank weed. In 1936, while Max Schmeling was delighting his friends in the United States and in the homeland, the Friends of the New Germany turned into the German American Bund with a naturalized American and World War I German army lieutenant named Fritz Kuhn as führer. That year the Bund rallied in Madison Square Garden, site of many Louis triumphs and Mike Jacobs's home grounds. The theme before the packed house was the virtues of Hitler's Germany. The Bund made common ground with several native American fascist groups. Kuhn spoke for all of them at a Bund rally in 1939 when he denounced FDR, Secretary of Labor Frances Perkins, and Treasury Secretary Henry Morgenthau, Jr. and said, "If you ask what we are actively fighting for under our charter, I will repeat here the declaration I made public some time ago; A socially just, white, Gentile ruled United States." There appeared no room in that structure for a black heavyweight champion.

Some stories about the period insist that brown-shirted Bundists came to the Pompton Lakes camp of Louis to sneer at him. Neither Julian Black nor George Nicholson, both of whom were at the training camp during this period, remembered any such incidents. "I heard they were around," said Black, "but I never saw them." It was Nicholson's understanding that in the event any troublemakers tried to show up, the state troopers who guarded the training camp would turn them away.

For Mike Jacobs it was not the Bund itself that seemed a threat, but the reactions of people to what the organization and its spiritual father represented. In 1936, Adolf Hitler had not gone down to the docks to wish Max Schmeling good luck for his duel against the black man. By 1938, the Nazi hierarchy saw Schmeling in a fonder light. (Unfortunately, only weeks after Schmeling had asserted Aryan superiority over the black race, Jesse Owens and other blacks in the Berlin Olympics had run and jumped their way to an embarrassing number of gold medals, leaving the Aryans to mumble about physiological deformities in the heel bones that

167

permit African descendants to run faster.) Indeed, immediately after his triumph the craggy-browed Schmeling and his handsome Czech-born actress wife, Anny Ondra, spent a weekend as guests at Berchtesgaden, the Bavarian resort where Germany's elite clustered around their leader. In 1938, a newspaper reprinted a photograph of Schmeling, Anny Ondra and the Nazi hosts during that 1936 vacation. Mike Jacobs, on seeing the picture, growled, "That Nazi sonovabitch." But like International Telephone and Telegraph, which sold to both sides even during World War II, Jacobs recognized that business knows no ideological favorites, and he suffered no personal qualms about the possible outcome of the fight.

Once again, however, he faced a massive boycott of the fight. Ten women appeared with picket signs in front of Jacobs's office. The promoter conferred with a delegation of people from the American Jewish Committee who urged him to cancel the fight. They suggested to him that the heavyweight championship, if it passed into the hands of the German, would disappear into the Nazi propaganda machine and become a weapon aimed at United States morale.

Jacobs responded that to deny Schmeling his rightful chance to contest for the heavyweight championship would make him a martyr whose unbloodied shirt could be waved before the world. Furthermore, Jacobs assured the anxious civil leaders, Louis would destroy the German in the ring, thereby turning the battle into a rankling defeat for the Third Reich. As a pacifier, Jacobs also offered to turn over part of the receipts to a nonsectarian refugee group which aided those driven from Germany by Hitler's forces. That was a compromise, some petitioners wanted Schmeling to award a percentage to the Anti-Nazi League. Although newspaper accounts sporadically carried warnings by some Jews that thousands of uniformed Bundists would be on hand to create a riot at the fight, the promoter continued with the project. And no demonstration of United States Nazi strength ever occurred.

The fight's overtones of international politics reached even into the White House. In the spring of 1938, Louis had been invited to attend an Elks Convention in the nation's capital. The Benevolent and Protective Order of Elks actually did not extend its grace to nonwhites, an exclusive condition of chapter charters lasting into the 1970s. But in pursuit of white values, black citizens had created the Improved Benevolent and Protective Order of Elks to cover themselves and the rituals. Social and eleemosynary purposes remained the same as those for the white clubs. Louis rode in an open car as part of the Elks grand parade in Washington. Meanwhile, Julian Black, active in Democratic politics, had spoken to Alicia Patterson, then a publisher of the *Washington Times Herald* and a supporter of FDR. She advised the White House of Louis's availability and the heavyweight champion was invited to 1600 Pennsylvania Avenue. The meeting between the Harvard-educated, polio-afflicted aristocrat from New York and the black 25-year-old sharecropper's son creaked with artificiality. About the only common ground lay in the development of the upper torso and arms. Compensating for the loss of lower-limb strength, the president had built up his pectorals and biceps in order to support his body. Toward the end of their tête-à-tête, FDR supposedly said, "Lean over Joe, so I can feel your muscles." Having satisfied himself of their mass, the president continued, "Joe, we need muscles like yours to beat Germany." Newspapers fleshed out the quote to say, "Joe, beat Schmeling to prove we can beat the Germans." Julian Black was present, insisted that Louis was properly impressed with

169

meeting the Chief Executive and only his natural restraint kept him from enthusing about the occasion. However, Earl Brown wrote that Louis, when asked about his session in the White House, said, "I didn't think nuthin' of it."

While FDR fretted over United States morale, the spirit of Nazidom infested Schmeling's training camp at Speculator, New York. Jack Dempsey said that he actually saw a swastika banner peeping out of a trunk in the Speculator camp, though he could not identify the owner of the baggage. Harry Sperber, a Jewish refugee from Germany and a reporter for a German-language newspaper in the United States, happened to wander through the rooms of a cottage at the Osborne Hotel where the Schmeling group lived. He glanced inside a closet and discovered a full Nazi uniform, complete down to the swastika armband. The room belonged to Max Machon, Schmeling's trainer and confidante. Machon, who carried on the stereotyped manner of the imperious German, required no such discovery to make himself unpopular with the press. What had been largely whispered became more noisily bruited.

Reporters and others carried quotes allegedly made by Schmeling or on his behalf by representatives. Among these bright sayings was "I would not take this fight if I did not believe that I, a white man, can beat a Negro." "The Negro will always be afraid of me." There were references to Louis as "the black amateur" and "dumb animal." Oddly enough, most of these pejoratives turned up in print some years after the fight, which may be attributable to either the timidity of newspapers to go beyond the most narrow interpretation of relevance or to the belated discovery of social significance after the United States and Nazi Germany became confirmed enemies.

Surely, Schmeling sallied forth with far more support from the founding fathers of the Third Reich than on his initial campaign against Louis. The Nazi radio system dispatched Arno Helmers to supply a ringside blow-by-blow shortwave to the home folks. Helmers, who appeared to have been picked by a casting office for Teutonic nastiness, displayed his credentials with a report to Germany that the Jewish governor of New York, Herbert Lehman, was part of a plot to ensure Schmeling's loss.

As further evidence of affection for the German knight errant, two days before the fight, der Führer himself cabled, "To the coming World's Champion, Max Schmeling. Wishing you every success. Adolf Hitler."

Paul Gallico, in Europe for coverage of the Olympic Games, worked with Louis's conqueror on the two-part piece for the *Saturday Evening Post*. In the notes from Gallico that preceded Schmeling's account, the reporter described the fighter's home. He noted a basket of flowers with a red swastika ribbon, sent by Adolf Hitler to Anny Ondra. A photograph of der Führer with a personal inscription by the subject hung over a trophy case.

In his preface, Gallico called Louis "nerveless," "emotionless," "ice cold killer." To Gallico, however, Schmeling confided, "He [Louis] says nothing with his mouth that colored fellow. He says it with his fists. I like that kind of man." But continued the German in his first-person story, "They [writers who snickered at his chances] must know that I have saved my money, that I do not need to come to America to be knocked out by a colored man for the sake of some thousands of dollars."

The Black Uhlan then spelled out his tactics, "After I have taken his left, my right hand which drops from my chin,

171

must land before his can. I must be in shape, taking Louis's iron left fist in the face 10 or 15 times in a round is not a pleasure."

At the end of the fourth round in which Louis first went down, Schmeling says he ruminated, "And so it is over with the idea of a superfighter. A superfighter does not go down, but if he does, he is smart enough to stay down and take a count of 8 before he gets up. I think he is just a hurt, bewildered boy who does not know what he is doing at the moment." According to Schmeling, his friend Max Machon agreed, "So now we have the superman *(übermensch)* in our pocket."

After Louis landed several punches that the Germans thought were low, Machon complained, "They are sending him out to foul." Schmeling also said Louis stuck his thumbs in his eyes. However, until the 12th round, Schmeling said he considered the fouls accidents due to Louis's dazed condition. But in the 12th, Schmeling thought Louis hit him a left hook below the belt that seemed deliberate. "Under New York rules you could not win on a foul claim" (in fact the rule had changed, because this was the way Schmeling had earned his championship).

One interesting point in the piece was that Mike Jacobs had tied up Schmeling in the event that he won. Having cornered the heavyweight market, Jacobs was not going to permit any other operators to get any leverage. Uncle Mike would then have a piece of the future.

That Schmeling ever made any of the more rancid comments about Louis attributed to him is unproven. No reporters in the United States ever coaxed from him any derogatory remarks about Louis in 1938. Evidence of his affection for, or closeness to, the Nazi Party and its leadership also is ambiguous. In 1936, while training for the first fight against

Louis, Schmeling entered into a casual conversation with Harry Markson. The discussion touched upon the recently announced presidential candidacy of Norman Thomas on the Socialist ticket. As Markson recalled it, Schmeling inquired about the influence of Thomas in America. Markson dismissed him as unimportant. "He ran four years ago and he polled under a million votes."

Schmeling, however, was quite impressed, thought Markson. "Under a million votes," he remarked. "We had one like that, under a million votes and now he runs the country." Markson's memories of Schmeling's diminution of Adolf Hitler did not become public until well after World War II when the German had achieved a sort of unofficial denatured Nazi status. Even at that, Hitler polled as high as 13 million votes in the last free German election and he could hardly be said by 1936 to have been without general public support.

Jack Dempsey, speaking to columnist Joe Williams in 1946, before Schmeling became cleared of his Nazi taint, remembered a different kind of attitude. Dempsey had promoted the 1933 battle between Max Baer and Schmeling. In what Dempsey spoke of as partly a publicity stunt, he suggested to the German that he take out United States naturalization papers. Said Dempsey, "He leaped to his feet, gave the Nazi salute, barked [a description that seems more Joe Williams than Jack Dempsey], 'Jack Dempsey, do you know what you are asking, for me to disown my country and my leader. You have insulted my friends. I will still fight for you but I'll remember the insult. Heil Hitler.' "

That incident apparently failed to diminish Schmeling as a fighter in Dempsey's mind. In 1938, the former champion put his byline on a magazine piece that predicted Schmeling as an easy victor over Louis. However, when interviewed by sportswriter Jack Cuddy a few days before the match, Dempsey rated Louis the winner with a first-round knockout. Unfortunately for Dempsey the seer, both the magazine article and the newspaper piece appeared the same day.

During World War II, Schmeling's ties to Nazism clouded even further. He became a sergeant in the *Werhmacht*'s paratroops. Author Curzio Malaparte, a former fascist journalist, wrote an unfavorable story of Schmeling's behavior in Poland as the Germans began to tighten the pressure on the Warsaw ghetto. Given the climate of Germany in the early days of World War II, the ability of a Schmeling to express his distaste for the horrors of the Warsaw ghetto may have been zero. (Very few Americans saw fit to question the behavior of the United States immediately after Pearl Harbor when thousands of Nisei and Issei were packed off to "relocation camps," the United States version of concentration camps, although to be sure the treatment could not be rated in a class with the murderous Nazi programs.)

On the other hand, after being injured in Crete, Schmeling was supposedly interviewed by a United States correspondent on what he had seen there. He almost immediately fell from Nazi grace for a failure to admit to witnessing any British atrocities, which had been part of Goebbels's propaganda. After World War II he protested that he had never had any real sympathy with the Nazi leadership and, like many other good Germans, had been used. Certainly, the post of sergeant in the paratroops for a 33-year-old hero is hardly recognition of meritorious service to a political movement, except maybe in the eyes of those who believe war the finest expression of human endeavor.

In 1946, the German heavyweight's wife, Anny Ondra, a Czech by birth, wrote Dan Parker of the *New York Mirror*, "My husband stubbornly refused to join the Nazi party or even honorary ranks such as *Schreustuemführer* in the stormtroopers or the SS. He refused to deliver propaganda speeches to the Hitler Youth or on the air or to write in that sense for the newspapers. . . . Max . . . exposed himself to some extent by intervening for citizens and foreigners who were being prosecuted by the Gestapo or military courts. He never flinched in his attitude toward Jews, as you know he kept his Jewish manager, Joe Jacobs under contract up to the time of his death in 1940, unregarding all persecutions." (Joe Jacobs seemed to have the same tolerance for Nazi policies that Schmeling had for those they oppressed. The fight manager was quoted as having said, "Most of the trouble with the Jews over there, is caused by Jews in this country. Everybody's happy over there. They are treated like anyone. Synagogues are still open.")

Anny Ondra's defense continued, "He never severed his relations with his other Jewish friends in Holland who had to leave Germany and he posed for photographers with German Jews." She offered the names of some Allied P.O.W.s who had benefited from Schmeling's intervention on behalf of better treatment of prisoners.

More than likely Schmeling was neither a dedicated Nazi nor actively opposed to the government. Like many Germans, he may have accepted the rule of the Nazis at first, and then when the nature of the beast became obvious, been unable to resist openly. After he had been rehabilitated by the press in the late 1940s and "de-Nazified," Schmeling became a successful businessman.

At the time of the fight in 1938, some blacks saw in Schmeling and his homeland the threat to them as well as the Jews. "We could see Schmeling as the mouthpiece for the German idea," said Joe Bostic, a sportswriter and sometime promoter. But adversity occasionally offers its route to reward. "I was writing a column for a black newspaper then," remembered Bostic. "And I had been trying to get black basketball played in Madison Square Garden. Once they signed up Schmeling [even though the fight would not be held there], I started giving them hell, calling the place the Sports Palast. They eventually gave in."

Bostic also led the battle for working-press credentials for black newspapermen. "They would turn us off by saying that working press tickets were only for people from the daily press. Until the *Atlanta World* came along there was no daily black newspaper. We would get what they called tax tickets; you still had to pay a tax but there was no admission price. The seats were far from ringside. After Louis fought Brescia, we got our first boxing press credentials [1937]."

In the black community a certain ambivalence toward the Nazi ideology could have been present. Sufi Abdul Hamid, born Eugene Brown, had organized the Negro Industrial and Clerical Alliance. Sufi Abdul Hamid preached that Jews were responsible for the Depression troubles in Harlem, and the Alliance picketed white-owned shops (many of the proprietors were Jews), demanding tribute. The Alliance fell apart under pressure from merchants but anti-Semitism was a persistent feature of some black thinking.

On the other hand, A. Philip Randolph advised, ". . . no Negro is secure from intolerance and race prejudice so long as one Jew is a victim of anti-Semitism. . . ." (Randolph was far more forthright in his perceptions than many southern newspapers which vigorously attacked Hitler's oppression of the Jews while remaining stone silent about the repression of the blacks in their own towns.)

Many nonwhites considered the fight simply a sporting proposition. A lively commerce in bets moved between Harlem and Yorkville, the section of New York that housed Germanic Americans.

Bostic thought that the champion lacked any real social conscience. According to Bostic, Louis could recognize racism if directed at him personally, even when cloaked in the traditions of the period, but he was not sufficiently interested or learned in the world-power stakes. When it came to Schmeling, Louis of course needed no cause to represent beyond his own. He was defending not only his gold stake but he had personal pride up front. Schmeling had humiliated him in their first encounter.

At a reunion with Schmeling in 1973, Louis denied that there was ever any feud between him and the German. Some of those who spent time in the 1938 Louis camp at Pompton Lakes report differently. After the fight, Louis, referring to the slurs published under the Schmeling imprimatur, said, "Maybe they put words in his mouth, but he didn't deny them." Billy Rowe, like Bostic a newspaperman of the period, said, "People in camp were far more emotional about Schmeling than Joe was. I told Joe that they were no super race but Hitler was making all this talk just to cover the problems of German people." According to Rowe, Louis answered, "I want to prove to the world that there are black men better equipped, better able to do things. I'm going to beat him good." (His friends as well as his enemies almost invariably tripped over their attitudes when they attempted to render Louis's speech.)

Whatever fueled his passion, Louis was determined and confident. To sparring partner Freddie Wilson he murmured, "I feel wonderful, I'm afraid I might kill him."

To Jimmy Cannon, Louis predicted, "It go one." To Damon Runyon, Louis backed off, "Ah'll knock Smellin' out in two rounds."

Actually, as late as 1963, Louis said in an interview, "Max Schmeling said a good German could beat any colored man in the world. And that night I felt like every colored man in the world."

In any event, at Pompton Lakes, Louis maintained the serenity of single-mindedness. He ran his four to five miles per day, sparred under Jack Blackburn's discerning eye. George Nicholson and Willie Reddish, eventually to train Sonny Liston, when he became heavyweight champion some 24 years later, obligingly threw right hands to remind Louis of Schmeling's potential. There were no females in camp, and no golf was played. As many as 5,000 people showed up twice a week to see the champion train, and admission came to a dollar a head.

The international flavor of the match was kept boiling by the doings of Nazi sympathizers. Germany's role as arch enemy was boosted by an indictment of 18 people, two days before the fight, as members of a Nazi espionage ring.

For Mike Jacobs, the affair became a gusher of money. Interest in the fight surged, demand quickened and Jacobs made his accommodation. He had boosted ringside prices from $30 to $40 a seat. In a typical Jacobsean gimmick, he disguised the number of ringside rows, officially running from 1 to 37 but interspersed with such fakes as 6 A, 13 A and so forth. Several thousand choice seats he skimmed for the use of his ticket brokerage agency, dealing them off for as high as $200 a piece. Not the biggest grosser of his productions, the second Louis–Schmeling show may have been Jacobs's most profitable personally.

Following the weigh-in on the day of the fight, Louis retired to the Theresa Hotel in Harlem until time to head for Yankee Stadium. Extra precautions were taken by the police that evening in the event that any of the Bund decided to show the flag. Cops filled the streets as Louis silently rode through Black Harlem to the Bronx arena, just off the Grand Concourse, in that period sort of the Champs Élysée of Bronx Jews. Reminiscing on the era, Harry Markson described the night ride through black New York as one graced by cheery greetings from the residents. In sharp contrast, some 20 years later, driving to a Floyd Patterson fight, Markson remarked, "We kept the windows shut, doors locked. There was such hatred in the faces of people, it was sad." In Harlem itself, the streets were almost deserted that sultry 1938 evening as the clock approached 10 P.M. A whiff of rain hung in the heat. The traditional Friday-night promenade of Harlem suspended as the residents gathered around stores that sold radios, clustered in poolrooms and steamy tenements by the Philco or Atwater Kent, waiting to hear from broadcaster Sam Taub at ringside.

Officially, attendance registered 70,043, with crowd estimators putting the number at near 80,000. How much of this was pure exaggeration and how much part of Jacobs's unofficial receipts is immeasurable. In the streets, political activists, labeled "radicals" in the press, carried posters, "Oust Hitler's Agents and Spies," "Down with Hitler and Mussolini." Once again freebie fans loitered on the downtown section of the subway platform, craning for a glimpse of the action several hundred yards away. The City of New York, pushed by Jacobs who could not abide any leakage of his show or else because of complaints from owners of the building about outsiders crowding on the roofs, posted guards that prevented any high-rise viewers.

In his dressing room, Louis made certain he was ready. Ordinarily, he shadowboxed in the dressing room for four or five minutes before he headed for the ring. This time, said he in a ghosted memoir, "I pranced around and warmed up for

179

40 minutes. The Chappie put on my flannel robe first, and my blue silk robe over that to keep as much of my body heat as I could."

When he reached the ring, Louis kept moving about the ring to keep himself limber and his body warm. "I didn't look at the crowd of 70,000, I just looked at Schmeling." According to reporter Caswell Adams, the introductions brought a greater volume of cheers for the challenger than for the champion. There were, of course, far fewer blacks in the audience than whites.

When referee Arthur Donovan called the two men to the center of the ring, he instructed them on the rules of New York State, warned the handlers about their behavior, specifically ordering them not to come bounding through the ring ropes with any protests, and then he called upon Joe Louis and Max Schmeling to give the crowd "the greatest fight in heavyweight history." The two men separated to return to their corners, ready to battle. It was exactly one year since Joe Louis had thumped Braddock to the floor in Chicago to become the new king.

Immediately after the bell, Louis committed his forces. There would be no probing patrols to feel out the resistance. The champion jabbed with his left hand several times, almost an invitation to Schmeling to come over with the right, which had been so devastating in the first fight. The German looped a right but it missed. Louis jabbed again, harder, with three more lefts. Schmeling struck him with a right but it failed to deter Louis. Louis jabbed again, four times by his memory, and then smashed his right fist to Schmeling's jaw. The blow stunned the challenger, propelling him against the ropes. As Louis swung a heavy right to the body, Schmeling turned slightly so that the blow caught him just below the rib cage toward the back. Those at ringside heard a yelp of pain

180

from the German, who now hung on the ropes for support. Referee Donovan motioned Louis away and commenced counting; he scored it a knockdown, even though the man was still on his feet, because he still clung to the ropes.

After a count of one, Schmeling staggered toward the center of the ring. Louis fell upon him and a right to the jaw put Schmeling down for a three count. When he pulled himself erect, Louis fired a left and right to the head and Donovan began tolling again, the downed man on his knees, his gloves barely touching the floor, like a penitent in supplication before the superior he had wronged. Schmeling came up at two—as experienced as he was, he could not collect his senses enough to follow the count and rise at nine. Louis banged him with a left hook and then a right cross to the jaw. Schmeling was down for the fourth time. As Donovan began counting, Max Machon hurled a white towel into the ring, the traditional sign of surrender but unrecognized in New York State. Donovan continued to count, until he realized that Schmeling could not recover. He threw his arms apart to signal the end of the fight. The numbed Schmeling embraced Louis and then the champion went to his dressing room to meet the press; the long-hungered-for revenge had been delivered. One observer recorded 41 punches by Louis during the 2.04 minutes of the fight.

Among the first to extend his congratulations was the governor of Michigan, Frank Murphy. "Michigan is proud of you, Joe. You'll never know how my heart thumped during that round," said the man soon to become U.S. Attorney General and later one of Roosevelt's liberal Supreme Court appointees. Louis only returned an awkward "thanks."

"I got what the folks call revenge," said Louis to the newspapermen. "I had to throw only three good punches to get him. I shook him up a bit with a right. But the body punch that came right afterwards was the one that started him down the hill."

Indeed, that blow to Schmeling's abdomen aroused considerable furor. Joe Jacobs, in the loser's dressing room, ranted, "He never hit Max a good punch in the head. He never hurt him there. That kidney punch paralyzes him. That's an illegal blow in the kidneys." Joe Jacobs was still in the "foul" business.

"Such a terrible blow," gasped Schmeling, in what was described as broken English, but mercifully the dialect was not reproduced. "He hit me right here in the kidney. Like a cramp it was. I couldn't think, I couldn't move." Someone asked if it were a foul.

"Yah, yah, it was a foul."

Louis denied any illegal strike. "Shucks, that was a body lick and not a low one at that. It was a good punch."

More in character, Louis was quoted, "You makes them easy by getting a guy on a string and I got that Max on a string early. I didn't hit him too hard. I hit that Baer twice as hard."

Schmeling trotted off to a hospital, leaving behind the possibility of a foul claim. But in Harlem and the other black environs of the country it was a big win. According to the accounts, a good many Harlemites headed for Yorkville as soon as the fight ended, to collect on their wagers. There were no incidents; the Yorkville burgers paid with good grace.

On their home turf, the blacks flooded the streets in celebration. Police Commissioner Lewis Valentine announced that he was banning automobiles along 7th Avenue, from 125th Street to 145th Street. "It's their night," said the Commissioner. "Let them have their fun." The statements accurately reflect the era's racial separatism and the security felt by the white power structure.

During "their night," 20 cops received minor injuries, including a brain concussion suffered by a mounted officer knocked off his horse. Exuberant Harlemites leaped aboard running boards of taxicabs and private cars venturesome enough to pass through the territory. Ashcans standing in front of crumbling tenements toppled, bottles and tin cans sailed off rooftops.

New York was not the only city where blacks reveled. In Cleveland, a mob in the streets performed the Big Apple, the day's ballroom craze. One man was struck by a bullet as several shots were fired into the air. Chicago blacks also danced in the steamy streets, and bullets ripped the night air there as well. Some sports tore trolley-car wires away.

In Detroit, the joyful occupied St. Antoine Avenue, Grafiot Avenue, Adams Avenue and Hastings Street. For 30 minutes a local band kept the celebrants amused with a single tune, "Flat Foot Floogie." The unofficial mayor of Paradise Valley, Albert Pakenham, said there had been little betting there due to a shortage of Schmeling backers. A banner read, "Joe Louis Knocked Out Hitler."

The writers of the day drew from a palette with varying shades of purple. Said Bob Considine, "He [Louis] was a big lean copper spring, tightened and retightened through weeks of training until he was one pregnant package of coiled venom."

Cas Adams clung to the Louis-the-less-than-human vision. "Louis was evil last night, a vulture slithering in, abandoning all science and newfangled lessons, fighting as he must have done in the Alabama canebrakes . . ." (which the champion left before his teens and where he did very little fighting according to those who knew him there).

James Dawson in the *New York Times* stuck to good gray prose. "With all due respect to Schmeling's thoughts on the subject, the punches which dazed him were thundering blows to the head, jaw and body in bewildering succession."

When the champion arrived at the office of Mike Jacobs the following day for the ritual receipt of his share of the gate, reporters questioned him about his opponent in the hospital. "I was a little bit sore at Smellin' for some of the things that he said, but no, I ain't going over to see him at the hospital. I just guess he was just the only man I ever been mad at. I'm sorry if he was hurt, thas all; I don't like to hurt nobody." (It was probably one of the most accurate reproductions of Louis's speech.)

Schmeling, who spent two weeks in a hospital with what was diagnosed as a fracture of the third lumbar vertebra, rode in an ambulance before tottering up the gangplank to sail for home. There was no sense of disgrace; condolence messages came from the rulers of Germany and the people at home were told that the black man succeeded through illegal means. Fight films, shown in Germany, were skillfully edited with the portion that showed Schmeling turning his back excised. All that the viewers saw was the champion hammering at Schmeling's kidney region.

The citizens of Germany had stayed up until 3 A.M. to hear Arno Helmers's description. But immediately after Louis landed his first hard punch and Schmeling appeared groggy, by coincidence or by design, the power supply for the broadcast supposedly was cut off. And it was not restored until the fight was over. However, there was no suspense on the outcome. The Berlin Associated Press report (which does not indicate any shortwave failure) said that gloom enveloped the taverns where the Schmeling followers gathered to listen. Comments there echoed Arno Helmers's closing words, which were heard in Germany, "We sympathize with you, Max, although you lost as a fair sportsman. We will show you on your return that reports in foreign newspapers that you would be thrown into jail are untrue."

Within a short period of time, Schmeling withdrew his own assertion of a foul and the canard survived only in the minds of those who could not accept defeat of an Aryan by what they considered a member of an inferior race.

12

After the Schmeling fight, amid a downpour of admiration for Louis's performance, O. B. Keeler, an Atlanta newspaperman, drove off to look for any remnants of the champion's background in the Buckalew Mountains. From a hotelman named Robert Charles Riley in Lafayette came unsubtle reminders of Jack Johnson. "He's more popular with the white folks than with his own people. But they don't get much steamed up over his fights these days. Joe's always behaved himself well and that goes a long way around here."

Keeler discovered a five-year-old cousin named Alfred Lee Barrow whom he described as a "ringer for Louis . . . automatically two little fists like aces of clubs are flying." And an Aunt Cora spoke of the atmosphere at the time of the second Schmeling fight. "Dey wás goin' to town to hear de radio. . . . Not me! I know what dat Smellin' done done to him oncet. An' I tell 'em dey comin' back wid hung down heads an achin' heart. An' dey druv off in de oxcart."

According to Keeler, the journey to Lafayette by oxcart required three hours there and three back. He quoted Aunt Cora on the jubilance of the voyagers after the fight: "Dey was bustin' wide open."

Louis's long-missing father, thought to be dead many years, had suddenly been discovered, on his death in a state

186

mental institution. Although the son had not seen his parent since he was a toddler, he wired funds to cover the internment.

The Atlanta white man, after recording Aunt Cora's comments on the expense involved in the burial of Mun Barrow, remarked, "Cullud folks set great store by funerals."

Still patronized in the South, and basically condescended to in the North, Joe Louis nevertheless now stood as an undisputed heavyweight champion of the world. Those in his immediate circle recognized, if not maturation at least an assertion of independence, and not always with happy results. He returned to the game of golf, avidly pursuing the sport to the dismay of Jack Blackburn and others. The trainer viewed the pastime as harmful to the muscles most appropriate for boxing. Others in the camp saw golf drain away the champion's money. Freddie Wilson remembered, "He used to play with people like Tony Martin, Al Jolson, Bob Hope and Bing Crosby and lose money to them. I saw him drop a lot of money on a golf course to a fellow named Bill Spiller who drove better and had a better putting game.

"I said to him, 'I'm sick and tired seeing Spiller beat you. Why don't you quit it?'

" 'How long you been working for me, Fred?' Joe said.

" 'Bout 10 years,' I answered.

" 'Where were you 11 years ago?'

" 'I only worked for you 10.'

" 'I didn't need you 11 years ago, and I don't need you now.' " Since Wilson drew as much as $1,000 a month while Louis was in training camp, plus "walking around" money when the champion was not actually scheduled for a fight, he dropped the subject. However, Wilson has said that he knows of a former Pullman porter who paid for his house with money taken from Louis in golf.

Writer Billy Rowe contended that Louis never actually dropped much money betting on golf. "All those stories about him being ripped off in golf are nonsense. I remember when Joe owed Charlie Sifford [first black golfer to bend the color line] about $10,000. They went out and at the end of the day the guy owed Joe about $3,000. It was that sort of thing, nobody ever had to pay off."

Louis found more serious ways to throw away his money than in a country-club game. In 1937, in one of his first attempts to invest, Louis created the Chicken Shack in Detroit. Friends and some notables arrived dressed in tuxedos; it was New Year's Eve as well as a restaurant opening. Unfortunately, nobody remembered to order any chicken. With management of that caliber, the business was doomed to failure. Its prolonged life only meant a greater loss of capital.

In these early days of big money, Louis also indulged himself in another of his favorite sports. As a youngster he had worshiped the Detroit Tigers, apparently oblivious to the lily-white character of baseball. After he became champion, he posed for photographs with such local heroes as Hank Greenberg, still unresentful that baseball denied the opportunities to blacks that his own field permitted. As a half-lark, half-investment, Louis, against the advice of his management, put together and played for a black softball team. The 22-man show toured the country in gaudy uniforms and Louis dropped about $30,000, much of it on replacing the aggregation's bus.

While the heavyweight champion suffered a financial shutout, some people who were involved scored heavily. Big crowds turned out to gawk at the touring softball team. In Washington, D.C., the Louis squad defeated a gang of local all-stars, 8–1. The center of attraction for the 5,000 specta-

188

tors, "mostly colored" according to the newspaper account, struck out twice, walked twice. In Philadelphia, a mob of about 12,000 descended on the ballfield. They jumped fences, scaled walls with ladders and then washed onto the field from the stands to touch their hero. Eventually, the exhibition was canceled because the Louis idolators refused to leave the field and permit play. He escaped only by the help of the police. In Fresno, California, Louis performed before 1,200 and played errorless ball as a first baseman. He struck out three times, however. The whole enterprise collapsed on the West Coast as the champion decided to control his indulgences temporarily. What the softball tour showed, however, was that Louis had already become a rallying figure for black Americans, simply through his presence.

For a time Louis focused his potential as a cultural model upon aping segments of the white upper class. He participated in an attempt to create a horsey set for blacks. Shortly after the Braddock fight, he posed for photographs at the first all-black dude ranch, some 70 miles outside of Los Angeles. In July of 1938 he competed in the first United States Negro horse show at the Utica Riding Club, outside of Detroit. Among his companions were John Roxborough, State Senator Charles C. Diggs, and a dentist, Dr. Paul Alexander. Julian Black was a spectator in the grandstand. Riding MacDonald's Choice, a horse on which he had spent $1,500, Louis took a third-place yellow ribbon in the five-gaited saddle class. This kind of activity reflected the influence of Roxborough and Black, both of whom, whatever their business interests, clothed themselves in middle-class dignity that would have been acceptable at Grosse Pointe or the Gold Coast. Marva Louis, too, followed these standards.

The champion also took time to make a film, *Spirit of Youth,* a thinly veiled misrepresentation of his life. Max

189

Baer's thespian work in the *Prize Fighter and the Lady* was far more successful, and so was the white fighter's film. There was no market in the 1930s for movies that featured non-whites; only a pitiful few blacks could afford even the 10-cent admission fees of the day.

None of these activities, however, satisfied a basic restlessness on the part of Louis. He much preferred to spend his money and time on a headlong pursuit of his own pleasures. One of these pleasures was buying things. By 1940, he had not only bought his mother a home in Detroit but he and Marva shared an expensive eight-room apartment in Chicago. He owned 25 pairs of shoes, 30 suits at $100 apiece. According to Earl Brown, Louis preferred "swagger models with huge square shoulders, ripples in the coat backs and cut in waists. His taste in materials runs to checks, stripes and plaids with green predominating. In socks, he also liked bright colors." Other possessions included two apartment buildings, a large black Buick, two show horses, 80 Hereford cows, 100 Poland China hogs, a Chow dog and a 477-acre farm at Spring Hill, Michigan.

But while some of these items might fall under the heading of investments, the champion engaged in a series of hedonistic sprees that brought no return beyond the immediate pleasure. Considering Louis's background as the son of a sharecropper, the joy of glittering materialism and ostentatious spending was as natural as his table gluttony. It was not just a matter of race culture; many highly paid white athletes and show-business people were just as careless with their money.

The chief recipient of Louis's largesse was Harlem or, more properly, residents of the area. His taste for this community, rather than Chicago or Broadway, was not simply a black man's seeking a safe area in which he could satisfy his appetites. Harlem was something more.

In the first 20 years of the century, Harlem changed from a middle-class white semisuburb to a black urban center. Then, in the 1920s, other blacks were drawn to the area by what became known as the Harlem Renaissance. Black musicians, poets and intellectuals came together and created a thriving, vibrant culture in Harlem.

Then came the Depression, and by the late 1930s, only the afterglow remained. As in a once flourishing garden, only the rankest kind of life survived.

But it was precisely this crepuscular glory that favored the tastes of Joe Louis. Whites came uptown to join blacks in sampling the lusty night life, the music and dance of the clubs and theaters, the vices not permitted elsewhere in the city.

Some watering holes, such as the Lenox Club, had a mild amount of desegregated action. But the larger, more famous ones, like the Cotton Club where Duke Ellington poured out his music, refused to admit mixed parties. Whites and blacks sat at separate tables. Places like the Cotton Club belonged to whites, men like Owney Madden, and until Repeal had been uptown speakeasies.

Harlem was still basically more of a plantation than a ghetto. The white massas came and went at their pleasure and felt reasonably secure in the black enclave. Business belonged to whites, even the better jobs in Harlem were filled by whites.

Louis, by virtue of his privileged standing, was completely free in Harlem, however. He hung out at Smalls, the Mimo Club, Johnny Cobb's the Nest and a place called Jimmy Daniels where whites and blacks elbowed one another for room at the bar. After a fight, Louis would have an entire floor reserved at the Hotel Theresa. He would bounce from room to room, escaping from Marva's eyes by using the room of one of his friends.

191

Louis never drank, nor did he smoke in this period. He was content to trade talk with sporting bloods and circulate among the women. With tens of thousands of dollars available to him Louis proved an easy mark for anyone with a hard-luck story. "It wasn't unusual," said Earl Brown, "for him to start out the day with $2,000 in his pocket and by evening he'd be calling, perhaps to Marva, and say, 'Honey, have you got any money?'"

Billy Rowe has said, "When Joe would walk into a place, the price of everything went up right away. People would figure he could make the money, that he had the money, why shouldn't he pay it out. And he would invite it. He had been a guy who had nothing and now suddenly he had millions, or at least thousands. So he would never look at a check, just put his hand in his pocket and pay."

Mannie Seamon, an assistant trainer to Blackburn, commented, "They should have called him 'can't say no Joe.' He was his own worst enemy. He liked fun and laughter and guys clowning around and he paid for all of it. Anyone could give him a hard-luck story and as soon as it was over he'd reach in his pocket and pay." Age failed to make Louis wiser when it came to his handling of money. As he grew older he tossed away ever larger amounts on good times.

It was not a case of Louis being victimized by high rollers and confidence men. Marva Louis has said, "Nobody cheated him of his money. He just spent it." And Joe Bostic supported that view. "The newspapers and the business people uptown wanted Louis around because he was good for business. They weren't after him to invest. The racket people, the numbers guys, they just wanted to be with him and bask in his glory. In Harlem, the top echelon of the black sporting crowd was not what you would call underworld (the black community has always recognized gambling as a legitimate

192

business). There were some people up there who did dislike Joe, because he only made his money downtown. For most of them, Louis wasn't a person, he was a commodity."

The spirit of fun and games so avidly sought in Harlem also pervaded the training camp. Once Louis had whipped Schmeling, he became far less single-minded. The resident comedians, who often traveled with Louis, were Freddie Wilson and Freddie Guinyard, Louis's boyhood chum. "Most of the time, when we weren't working out," says a man who was in the camp, "we'd sit around telling jokes and stories, mostly lies and mostly about our experiences with women. Freddie Wilson told most of the stories. Joe loved to hear these lies and he would laugh and laugh."

Matters sexual seem to have preoccupied Louis. "Before the Schmeling fight," said a black reporter who hung around Louis, "Joe had this girl at the training camp and he was laying her every night." That may well be an exaggeration; Louis himself denies that he spent the months before his disastrous first encounter with the German cavorting with women, and his managers made a strenuous effort to keep predatory females away from the training camp. Still, according to one source, shortly after Louis had established himself as a figure of note through the Carnera fight, he began a lifelong career of consorting with women.

"He would come into town, go up to a club in Harlem," said an acquaintance from the period. "The manager would bring out all the girls in the show. Joe would pick out one and spend a day or so in the Hotel Theresa with her. Meanwhile, Roxborough would find out he was in New York and call Mike Jacobs and tell him to find Louis. They were terribly worried that something might happen to him, some pimp get his hooks into Joe. Mike always tried to get Joe to stay in a hotel downtown but he preferred the Theresa."

It is the memory of a sparring partner that, even when Louis was in camp, there was a heavy demand for his attention from women. "There were girls from Washington, D.C. and from Pennsylvania who would come up to see Joe when he was training at Pompton Lakes. There was an actress and a singer who also came out to the camp, but most of the time Joe led a very clean life while he was in camp."

Apart from the fear that Louis might become entangled with an unsavory crowd and the possible dilution of his physical resources, his counselors worried most about a replay of the Jack Johnson script. "There were white women involved," said one follower, "but it was all very discreet. They would come up to Harlem to meet Joe. He never flaunted it, never made a public thing of this aspect."

It is part of the traditional white mythology that blacks possess an excess of sexual energy (a stereotype accepted without complaint by blacks). Lust appears more often than not, however, to be part of the professional athlete's syndrome. Perhaps the almost exclusively physical achievement demanded in sports infects the life away from the playing field. Athletes may feel the need to keep competing against other men by conquests of women; it is as if they somehow feel the exploits in the boxing ring or on the golf course lose currency so quickly that they must prove their masculinity at every opportunity. Some women see in the physical power demonstrated in sports a possible equivalency in sex, and they chase athletes. Easy availability heightens the sexual promiscuity of performers who often spend a great deal of time away from home.

The jokes in training camp, too, largely centered on sex but there was an awareness of race, said George Nicholson. "One joke that brought big laughs was about the monkey coming up the highway when a car driven by a white man came along. The driver stopped to let the monkey cross over. Then a car driven by a black man came along and it damn near run over the monkey. The monkey picked himself up out of the dust and said, 'These people, they always putting us down.' "

"Another favorite that often was repeated was to imitate first a white girl combing her hair and singing a hymn. She would go 'Nearer my God to thee,' and the comb would go all the way to the back of the head. Then the black girl would do the same thing and she'd only sing 'Ne' and the comb would already be through her whole head of hair."

The black humor was carefully hidden away from outside eyes. "Poor Mannie Seamon," said one ex-sparring partner. "We'd be talking about niggers in front of him and he wouldn't know what to think, whether we were serious or what."

Sam Langford also entertained Louis during his occasional visits to camp. "He would come to Pompton Lakes," remembered Louis, "and tell a lot of fantastical stories while we were all lying under a tree. He talked about Betsy which was his left hand and Sue his right. He told us about being in Mexico in a fight to the finish and he showed up carrying his lunch," laughed Louis, "cause he says he didn't know when the fight would end. When he fought Harry Wills he said he was knocked down. And while on the floor, he looks up at Wills and says, 'I'll be up to see you soon.' "

Black jack and other card games offered some diversion in the many nonworking hours at Pompton Lakes. "Sometimes we shot dice," remembered Nicholson "but for small money, just to make it interesting. Mike Jacobs and Roxborough joined in occasionally, long enough to drop a couple of dollars or so. Ping-Pong, which had been discovered by Americans during the 1930s, also passed time.

"Sometimes we'd walk into town to see a movie or to the ice cream parlor" said Nicholson, "or maybe Mike Jacobs would invite us all down to his house for a meal."

Confined to the limited recreation of the camp, the group concocted wagers to test one another. George Nicholson said, "One time, Louis bet me $75 I couldn't go three days just on liquids and not eat. He'd plant sandwiches in my room and then he'd find them and say to me, 'I caught you when you fixin' to eat.' But he never caught me eating and he paid off."

Practical jokes pierced the monotony of the routine. There was an electrically wired chair, and there were fake telephone messages, usually attributed to women eager for a night with the butt of the joke. Once, Carl Nelson, a black Chicago policeman who also worked as a bodyguard for the champion, provoked a loud quarrel with Freddie Wilson. To the terror of the latter, Nelson pulled his pistol and started shooting. While Wilson dived for cover, Louis hooted for joy; he and Nelson had contrived the argument and loaded the bodyguard's weapon with blanks.

One camp follower, seeking a smile from the camp's principal figure, put a chicken in the hot seat. When the fowl plaintively squawked over its electrical jolt, Louis glowered. He scolded the fun-seeker for tormenting an animal.

Much of the evening, Louis would be on the telephone. The calls generally were to female friends all over the country. "One month, our bill was $1,500," remembered Nicholson. "He never wrote a letter or sent a telegram." In fact, one of the few if not the only letter in any archives is in the file of former Governor Frank Murphy at the Michigan State Historical Library in Ann Arbor. Signed by the champion, it read, "This will introduce Miss Eulalia Gaines, my sister who is applying for the position of inspector of beauticians."

The working part of the day would begin at 5 A.M.; Louis would do five or six miles on the road, accompanied by somebody like Nicholson, or on occasion Jack Blackburn would follow the fighter in a slow-moving car. Wild oats grew alongside the track. Occasionally, Blackburn would improvise an exercise. For a while he made Louis stoop, pick up a rock, bowl it 20 or 30 feet ahead and then sprint to catch it before it stopped. "Roll dem stones," commanded Blackburn. On return, the champion dried off with an alcohol rub and returned eagerly to his bed. At 10 in the morning he had his breakfast. The champion was as aggressive at the table as in the ring. He would down a chunk of American cheese, cereal, ham, four eggs, celery, half a dozen slices of toast and a quart of milk. With a companion, the fighter would again take a stroll and then perhaps spend an idle half-hour tossing a baseball about. Jack Blackburn did not care for this form of entertainment either, fretting over the possibility of a finger injury. Eventually, he convinced Louis to put away his baseball and use a softball. By noon, Louis would be back in his bed for another nap.

The intensive part of training began around two P.M. After some calisthenics and loosening up on punching bags, the champion and sparring partners would enter a ring and do from three to six rounds. George Nicholson often drew the assignment of imitating the next scheduled opponent.

"When we were getting ready for the second fight with Bob Pastor, I tried to imitate his tricks," Nicholson recalled. "Joe caught me on the chin, knocked me down on my panties. We figured that Pastor wouldn't do so well the second time around."

At five P.M. the camp sat down for dinner and again Louis

197

attacked with determination the vegetables, slices of bread, perhaps two pounds of steak, fruit and ice cream, a favorite that he could consume by the quart.

Although he now indulged himself considerably while away from his profession, Louis defended his title with impressive frequency in the three years before World War II. Between the Braddock and Pearl Harbor, Louis had 19 title fights.

It was, however, eight months after the Schmeling fight before Louis returned to practice his trade. The opponent was John Henry Lewis. He was the light heavyweight champion at the time, and quite obviously overmatched against Louis. The two men had something more than a nodding acquaintance and supposedly John Henry was signed to help him escape financial ruin. Some whispered rumors suggested that rather than embarrass John Henry, Joe would carry his foe for a number of rounds. It was John Roxborough's belief that Blackburn advised Louis that he would do John Henry a favor if instead of carrying him and inflicting punishment over a number of rounds, that Louis would be merciful if he simply ended the fight swiftly.

On January 25, 1939, John Henry Lewis succumbed in a one-round knockout and immediately retired from boxing, undefeated at least as light heavyweight champion. For his abbreviated work, Louis received $34,000. The sum represented the champion's share of a near full Garden.

Only a few years earlier, the arena would never have staged a match between two black men. Still it was not a great success. Jacobs had kept his ticket prices scaled low to weaken customer resistance, and the bargain opportunity to see a heavyweight champion brought the spectators if not the money.

Three months later, in Los Angeles, a lanky challenger

198

named Jack Roper stepped into the ring to challenge Louis before a small crowd. Officially, Roper rated as a 10–1 shot. Whenever a longshot fights a heavyweight champion, some member of the alleged cognoscenti could be counted on— sometimes purely from perverted opinion but often to promote the fight—to predict an upset. Jack Dempsey had touted Roper. He was counted out in two minutes and 20 seconds of the first round, leaving behind him only a boxiana fragment: "I guess I zigged when I shoulda zagged."

From an Orange, New Jersey, saloon brawler, meanwhile, came the insistent cry of "I'll moider da bum." The boast belonged to paunchy 29-year-old Dominick Anthony Galento. Joe Jacobs, now that Schmeling had returned to Germany as a reputable citizen of the Nazi-governed land, guided "Two-Ton Tony."

An authorized biography of Galento reported that when he turned professional in 1929, Galento avoided black fighters because, during an amateur match against one, he had suffered a badly cut lip. When he was enticed to meet a black in the professional ranks, Galento again found himself bloodied. He avoided nonwhites when possible after this experience.

His career faltered, partly because Galento insisted upon catering to his own whims about diet and training. In 1932, just before going up against Arthur DeKuh in Newark, Galento on a $10 bet consumed 50 hot dogs. When it was time for him to dress for the match, his handlers were forced to slit open the waistband of his trunks and fasten it with a safety pin in order to accommodate the frankfurter bloat. Thus repaired, Galento KO'd DeKuh.

Becalmed as a fighter for several years, Galento served as a bouncer in a saloon. The chief advantage, according to him, was the three meals per day. For a period, Jack Dempsey tried to manage Galento into a proper white hope but surrendered when he discovered he could control neither the eating nor training habits of his charge. Galento refused, for example, to do road work. "What do I need that, I don't dance around in the ring."

Finally Joe Jacobs became Galento's seventh manager of record. Galento punched out some of the standard stalking horses of the mid-1930s and seemed well on his way to a fight with Louis in 1938. But an attack of pneumonia cost him weight and time. He returned to the wars against Nathan Mann, the mob-controlled heavyweight, who took a satisfactory count in two. Then Harry Thomas went down in three. Pennsylvania boxing officials declared Thomas ineligible to compete in the state in the future. Years later, Harry Thomas claimed that he had been paid to take a dive for Galento.

A barrage of challenges to Louis emanated from Joe Jacobs, while Galento, opening beer bottles with his mouth for the amusement of reporters and tavern customers, insisted, "I'll moider da bum."

Popular opinion made Galento a candidate for another one-round knockout. But Blackburn warned his charge, "He fights in a crouch and throws that left hook from the floor. If you let yourself open, he'll tag you." Galento made Blackburn's advice stand up. In the opening round, Galento sprung up from his squat and stunned Louis with a left. The champion shook it off and in the second round appeared in total control as he floored Galento. But in the third round, Galento charged in and struck Louis with another left. Louis fell to the canvas. "I was dazed and wobbly," remembered Louis to one of his ghosts, "but I struggled to my feet at two." Galento's undisciplined attack permitted Louis to ward him off. In the fourth round, Galento collapsed under a series of combinations and the referee halted the fight.

Unlike the previous ventures, the meeting with Galento was worth considerable money; the Louis organization collected $114,000.

Before 1939 ended, Louis worked one more evening. Jimmy Johnston's fighter Bob Pastor, on the strength of having stayed for 10 rounds against the champion, petitioned for another meeting. At Briggs Stadium in Detroit, 33,000 people turned out to see Pastor, a light heavyweight stuffed to 183 pounds, try again to make Louis look foolish.

Pastor, however, chose to follow a different script. He came out swinging instead of boxing. As a result, Louis knocked him down three times in the first round, once in the second. That convinced Pastor that he was operating on the wrong plan. He reverted to his keep-away tactics and hung on until the 11th round before he dropped with a left to the jaw.

On the following day, while Jim Braddock, a spectator at the match, sat with sportswriter Frank Graham during breakfast, the defeated Pastor appeared. He stopped and explained that he would have won except that blood from a cut over one eye blinded him. Braddock smiled, "Yeah, he sure hits hard, don't he?"

The Pastor fight occurred on September 20, 1939, 20 days after Germany had invaded Poland, igniting World War II. On the day that Joe Louis put away Pastor, German military officials had already arrived in Moscow to discuss with the Soviet Union the method for carving up the supine territory of Poland, now ravaged by both Nazi and communist troops. Closer to the apparent interests of Joe Louis, Marian Anderson, the black contralto, had been denied the use of Continental Hall in Washington, D.C., by the proprietors, the Daughters of the American Revolution. Eleanor Roosevelt quit the organization and Marian Anderson sang at a large

201

Lincoln Memorial Easter Sunday service. She also appeared at the White House to entertain King George VI and Queen Elizabeth. The singer had visited Louis at Pompton Lakes at the time the D.A.R. suddenly discovered the Hall was not available for her. He invited her to render the national anthem before one of the fights.

The economy of the United States began to recover in 1940, as the Allies' needs for war materials and Franklin D. Roosevelt's increased spending for military defense pumped dollars into the system. For most black Americans, however, the advances were slim. Some substantial improvement came from U.S. Supreme Court which ruled against government salary differentials based on race, and the first erosion of restrictive-housing covenants came as a result of a court decision. In an effort to boost defense production and enlistment, Congress restricted bias against Negroes in some defense-appropriation bills and encouraged training in some military specialities. But it was more shadow than substance, the provisions being easily evaded. The Negro tenant farmer faced particular hardship as agriculture continued to be extremely soft in the economy.

To open his 1940 campaign, Louis met an import from Chile, Arturo Godoy. Less than 16,000 people for a meager gate of $88,000 came to watch the champion batter the South American. But Godoy approached Louis in a crouch throughout the fight and the style baffled Louis. Unlike Uzcudun, Godoy never lapsed into careless curiosity. He remained hunched over and after 15 rounds he was hardly marked by Louis. When the fight ended he rushed across the ring to bestow a public kiss on Louis's mouth. Frustrated enough to declare the encounter with Godoy "my worstest fight," Louis considered the gesture acutely humiliating. "I ain't never had no man kiss me," he complained in disgust.

The Godoy fiasco was followed by another aesthetic failure. An Iowa fighter aptly named Johnny Paychek, anointed by both Jack Dempsey and Benny Leonard, exuded such emanations of fear as he came down the aisle that Caswell Adams wrote, "Did you ever see a dream walking? Well I did, in Madison Square Garden tonight." If Paychek threw a single punch at Louis it went unobserved and he fell in the second round.

Contenders were becoming increasingly difficult to locate. From the Paychek match the Louis share amounted to less than $20,000, which hardly paid for expenses. Al Weill, who handled Godoy, agreed to a rematch. Bolstered by savants who saw in him some mysterious ability to fell Louis, Godoy openly bragged how he would destroy Louis. Clem McCarthy pulled from the champion another quote that became part of the Louis legend, "Any dog can wag his tail."

During the fight, which drew only 26,000 people, not much of an improvement over the first match, Godoy decided that he must demonstrate more aggressive tactics if he were to win. He came out of his crouch to throw punches, but that permitted Louis to retaliate with short blows to the face, opening up a lacework of lacerations. In the eighth round, Louis dropped the South American twice and the referee stopped the bloodshed. The enraged Godoy tried to continue, only the desperate clutch of manager Weill and trainer Whitey Bimstein saved referee Billy Cavanaugh from assault.

Louis was beginning to become a victim of his own successes. To Mike Jacobs's dismay, challengers worthy of higher-priced tickets could not be located. As the country geared up for war-materials production, starting in December of 1940, Louis also embarked on a program of plenty, the so-called bum-of-the-month campaign.

At Boston Garden in December 1940, Louis stabbed away at the New England Heavyweight Champion, Al McCoy, until McCoy's bloodied eye prevented him from heeding the bell for the sixth round. On the last day of January 1941, it was Red Burman's turn at Madison Square Garden. He lapsed unconscious in the fifth. In February, Gus Dorazio lasted only to the second round.

Louis celebrated the vernal equinox at Detroit meeting with an amiable giant named Abe Simon, whose 254 pounds gave him 52 more than the champion. Simon only weighed 10 to 15 pounds less than Primo Carnera, but giantism as a ticket seller had lost its power and it was another lean crowd. In the first round, the big man was downed by a punch. He was, however, hardly dazed, for even as he lay on his back, legs pointed toward the ceiling, and gloves similarly outstretched, a grin swept over his face. Asked about his reaction, Simon answered, "It was the first time in my life I'd ever been knocked down cleanly. And when I lit on the seat of my panties [curiously, a word commonly used by fighters to describe their trunks] the thought struck me, 'Abe, what a funny looking sight a big hulk like you must be to those people sitting out there.' "

Simon put in another 12 rounds for the benefit of the people sitting out there, going down twice and ending up draped over the ring ropes, obviously unable to continue.

Less than three weeks later, in St. Louis, Tony Musto, the "Baby Tank" whose main justification for appearing as a challenger appeared to be that he was available, went nine rounds for the pleasure of St. Louis fans.

The earnings from the bum-of-the-month-club operation hardly fit championship traditions. As challenger against Jess Willard, Dempsey settled for a picayune $27,500 on a gate of better than $450,000. As champion, however, his poorest night was against Billy Miske in the obscure setting of Benton Harbor, Michigan, where the receipts amounted to $135,000 and he received $55,000. In contrast, Louis got less than $20,000 on five occasions—Paychek, McCoy, Dorazio, Simon and Musto. The Jacobs plan to keep the champion fighting often failed to generate huge profits, possibly because Louis was black and less of a draw. The frequency of the Brown Bomber's appearances and the ineffectiveness of his foes probably depressed interest and attendance, too.

The earnings of the Louis operation took a marked upturn starting in May of 1941, however. Buddy Baer, the younger brother of Max and at 6 feet 6½ inches the tallest specimen Louis ever fought, drew a good crowd to Griffith Stadium in Washington, D.C. Buddy Baer had fought a prelim on the night that Louis demolished his brother. The younger Baer had also lost that evening and his credentials for meeting Louis had more to do with blood lines than with achievements. He had knocked out Abe Simon, Nathan Mann and Tony Galento, but on the other hand had lost to such as Gunnar Barlund and Eddie Blunt.

In the first round, after several exchanges, Baer put together a three-punch combination and sent Louis reeling through the ropes for a knockdown. He scrambled back for action, without any helping propulsion from ringsiders as in the Dempsey–Firpo match. Louis began piling up points, although in the fifth round Baer centered his attack on a puffed eye. Any hope for capitalizing on the injury ended in the next round. The champion sent Baer down with a right to the face. Shortly after he rose, Baer was driven back to the floor. He stood up at nine only to be smashed to the canvas again, just as the bell that ended the round sounded. Ray Arcel, Baer's trainer, and Ancil Hoffman, who managed the younger Baer as well as the senior one, vigorously protested the final knockdown, claiming it came after the bell and Louis should be disqualified. In the midst of the argument, Freddie Guinyard suddenly materialized in the ring. Assuming the fight officially over, he danced over to Louis to congratulate him. That brought further laments from Arcel and Hoffman. When they refused to let Baer answer the bell for the seventh round, the referee declared Louis the winner, the challenger disqualified. Louis's share for the night's effort amounted to just under $37,000. Even better returns lay just over the horizon.

Billy Conn, a Pittsburgh stripling who had held the light heavyweight championship, and his manager Johnny Ray agitated for an opportunity against Louis. Officially, Conn had fought and won as a heavyweight seven times. None of his victims could have terrorized the division, but Conn had some things that were always resistible in boxing. He was a skillful boxer, and he had the Irish gift of gab.

Enough people were impressed by Conn's abilities to bet the odds down to 18–5, a price shorter than any of Louis's title defenses except for the second Schmeling encounter. A near capacity mob of 54,000 struggled inside the horseshoe-shaped Polo Grounds in New York to see if the Pittsburgh sapling could somehow prove mightier than the oaklike Detroiter.

If betting confidence still rested heavily on Louis, his trainer was smart enough to know a challenge ahead. "This fellow is mighty fast, Chappie," said Blackburn. "You've got to stalk him until you get him in a spot to nail him." Louis took the advice perhaps too much to heart. He decided on his own to come into the ring light, thinking that the fewer pounds he carried, the better able he would be to keep up with the nimble Conn. He weighed in at less than 200 for the first time in six fights, and later analyses suggested that the champion had "dried out" in the attempt to control his weight.

For the first two rounds, Conn backed away from Louis, but the champion appeared to be making points with his aggressiveness. Starting in the third round, Conn began to stick Louis with his quicker left jab and his right fist. By the fifth round, Jack Blackburn saw command slipping from Louis and he urged him to more vigorous pursuit. Obediently, Louis hammered his challenger for the next two rounds, but the pace, combined with his physical condition, sapped his strength. Conn recovered from the damage of the fifth and sixth and for the next six rounds proceeded to peck away at Louis, harder and harder. At the end of the 12th round, the youth from Pittsburgh appeared to be in control of the fight and ahead on the cards of the officials. Awaiting the start of the 13th round, Louis received a pessimistic appraisal of the situation from Blackburn and assistant trainer Mannie Seamon. Later, it was reported that the aging Blackburn said, "I'm tired of going up and down these steps. Go knock that son of a bitch out."

In the 13th round, Conn, who in the minds of some experts would be a winner if he simply avoided trouble for the remainder of the fight, came out with a full-fledged attack. In the first exchanges he delivered five solid blows to two from Louis. Louis jabbed a left that brought blood from Conn's nose and the two then stood toe to toe hammering at one another. It was a fatal mistake for Conn. Louis, the far heavier puncher, saw an opening and fired two right hands that struck flush on the jaw. When the referee completed counting, there were only two seconds left in the round.

In his dressing room, Louis grunted, "They told me if I was going to win, I had to knock him out. I knew they were right and I was waiting for him to lose his head. He's a real smart fighter and you got to admit he's faster than I am."

Caswell Adams in the *Herald Tribune* wrote: "If he hadn't been Irish, he'd been boss this morning. But being Irish he wasn't content to coast and dance in the last three rounds." Conn's manager had put it a different way: "If he hadda Jewish head instead of an Irish one, he'd be champ."

For Jacobs the evening had been most gratifying. He had taken the precaution of tying up Conn's future in the event that the challenger won. In fact, some believed he would have welcomed an upset as injecting fresh interest into the sport. But the results fully justified a return engagement for Louis and Conn that would do substantially better at the box office. And this match had grossed $450,000.

But while good times appeared ahead for boxing, the world was falling apart. On the morning of the fight, the newspaper headlines had reported, "Nazi War of Nerves on Russia." Four days later, Nazi Panzer units rolled into the Soviet Union.

When it was time for Louis to fight again, at the end of September, Nazi troops had pushed to within 220 miles of Moscow. United States-owned freighters with cargoes of war materials destined for Britain were being torpedoed by Nazi U-boats. Charles A. Lindbergh addressed a rally of America First (an organization ostensibly created to keep the United States out of the European war) and said, "The three most important groups which have been pressing the U.S. toward war are the British, Jewish and Roosevelt Administration." The United States had its first peacetime military draft, and among those to be classified 1–A in September was Joseph Louis Barrow. Sole supports of their families ordinarily received a deferment and Louis was the source of sustenance for his mother and several relatives. He was paying his sister

208

Vunies's way through college, but he did not object to his classification.

The ring fodder for September was a largely ballyhooed product named Lou Nova. Among other things, Nova advertised that he wielded a "cosmic punch," which was not to be confused with a simple left hook or right uppercut. Nova, claiming strength through Eastern philosophies, insisted that his cosmic punch carried some sort of spiritual sock with it. As a fighter, Nova exhibited unsubstantial evidence on behalf of his theory. He had knocked out the shell of Max Baer twice, but Tony Galento had in turn done him in. Nevertheless, thanks to the pre-fight publicity and the surprise showing of Conn, Louis was only a 13–5 favorite. This time the Polo Grounds held 56,000 people. The fight went into the sixth round before Louis reduced the possessor of the cosmic punch to human rubbish.

The time for the golden rematch with Conn appeared to be shortly after the new year. But less than three months after Louis's win over Nova, Japanese warplanes interrupted the breakfast quiet of Pearl Harbor and scrambled not only the assembled naval vessels but the plans of Mike Jacobs as well.

13

Immediately after Pearl Harbor, long lines of men patiently waited to enlist at recruiting stations. Jack Dempsey was rejected, but the U.S. Navy embraced Gene Tunney, for physical-conditioning supervision. Celebrities from the entertainment and sports worlds put on uniforms. Some eventually found convenient arrangements that suited the publicity needs of both the services and the individual. Others drew less comfortable assignments; some went to combat and became casualties, a few died.

Little better than one month after Pearl Harbor, the sports community launched its own modest war productions. The National Football League, for example, put on a game between its All-Stars and the Chicago Bears. Some 17,000 spectators showed up on a raw January afternoon and raised $26,000 for Navy Relief.

Of much more sporting interest was a meeting between Joe Louis and Buddy Baer at Madison Square Garden on January 9, 1942. It was advertised that Louis's entire purse would go to Navy Relief and that Mike Jacobs would contribute his profits. The heavyweight champion was rewarded with great doses of patriotic affection. Jimmy Powers of the *New York Daily News* informed his readers that the heavyweight championship was worth $1 million to its owner. Powers remarked that to risk such an asset at no return was truly a magnificent gesture. Powers recalled the sins of athletes in World War I. Jack Dempsey had evaded the draft by pretending to be a defense worker, posing at a shipyard in a famous photograph, his pretense of being an honest laborer belied by his patent-leather shoes.

Powers awarded the devil his due, noting with approval Max Schmeling's participation in the German paratroops and the invasion of Crete. In that vein, Powers applauded Louis a second time. There had been some talk of Louis enlisting in the army air corps. Said Powers, "We'll have a much better army if we have Joe Louises in the Air Corps. Colored men can see much better at night than whites."

The *Daily News* writer remarked, "You don't see a shipyard owner risking his entire business [as Louis was doing]. If the government wants a battleship, the government doesn't ask him to donate it. The government pays him a fat profit." Powers concluded, "The more I think of it, the greater a guy I see in this Joe Louis."

Louis trained at Greenwood Lake for the second Buddy Baer fight and he was more nearly on his own than at any previous period in his career. In 1940, John Roxborough, along with others including former Detroit Mayor Richard Reading and 88 policemen, were indicted by Judge Homer Ferguson who sat as a one-man grand jury investigating corruption in Detroit. Roxborough was convicted in December 1941 as a policy operator and received a two-and-one-half- to five-year sentence to Jackson State Penitentiary.

Almost among the missing from training camp was Jack Blackburn. Suffering from a variety of cardiovascular troubles, Blackburn barely participated in the program at Greenwood Lake. Manny Seamon handled most of the duties. So weak did Blackburn feel that he advised Louis before the

211

fight, "I don't think I can make those stairs [up to the ring] tonight."

Louis assured him, "You won't have to climb those steps but once, Chappie."

Whether it was of concern for Blackburn, distraction over a divorce suit filed by Marva, the probability of being called for military service soon or just that Louis invariably performed more efficiently against a man the second time around, the champion made good on his promise to his trainer. In the first round, he ripped into the 250-pound challenger in a devastating attack and floored him three times. Buddy Baer tried to pull himself up by one of the ring ropes the last time around, but he was erect only after the toll of 10 had been signaled.

The newspapers reported that Louis contributed $47,100 to Navy Relief, Baer gave $4,078 and Mike Jacobs $37,229 from a gate that grossed $189,000. Other sources put Louis's share at $65,200. In addition, no figures were released concerning the income from fight films or the radio broadcast, nor was there any mention of whether the Louis management relinquished its claims to these. Still, as Powers indicated, Louis had risked a $1 million asset for at best a tiny dividend.

John Kiernan in the *New York Times* cautioned readers not to expect such largesse from other boxers because "they are not as well off as J. Shufflin' Louis." Newspapermen were apparently ignorant of Louis's growing financial troubles, and might have accorded him even more praise had they known how poorly off he actually was.

One day after the fight, the heavyweight champion of the world received a notice for induction into the army. Louis accepted the summons gracefully and asked only that he be

212

allowed to take his physical examination and begin service from New York.

With the working press in attendance, Louis endured a physical examination at Governors Island and was subsequently ordered to report to Camp Upton, Long Island, for active duty. Louis arrived at the post in a chauffeured limousine with Julian Black, meeting his fellow inductees who came out from the city on a bus. The citizen soldiers all went through the initial processing and then, in the words of a reporter, "Louis was assigned to Company C, a colored outfit." But he was still enough of a special case to be granted a pass his first day in camp in order that he might appear on the Eddie Cantor radio program.

The armed forces of the United States during World War II were almost totally segregated. There were few black combat units. Most black servicemen worked in supply or construction units, and were often commanded by white officers. There was an all-black air cadet school at Tuskeegee which furnished good copy on the contribution of blacks to the war effort, but the opportunities for nonwhites to participate in combat were sharply restricted.

For several months, Louis soldiered at Camp Upton. While he enjoyed some special favors, passes that allowed him to attend a testimonial dinner and rallies in New York City, he spent most of his time absorbing the basic requirements of an army private. In the early days of United States participation in World War II the uses of all manpower, including celebrities from the sports and entertainment fields, remained confused. The chiefs of staff were still trying to determine where to deploy their ill-trained, poorly equipped men in early 1942. They were even less certain of the uses to be made of a Joe Louis.

213

One obvious employment was seen in fund raising for the proper charities. Navy Relief had profited from the Baer fight and now it was proposed to do the same for the army with a fight against Abe Simon. Louis transferred to Fort Dix, New Jersey, where a special gym had been constructed. While doing minimal military duty he spent most of his time training under Mannie Seamon. Jack Blackburn was now too ill to come East at all and spent most of his time in hospitals or convalescent homes.

The fight with Simon occurred on March 27, 1942. Louis knocked his opponent out in the sixth round. This time, Louis gave up $36,146 to Army Relief. He also bought $3,000 worth of tickets for soldiers to witness the fight. With the contributions from Mike Jacobs and Simon, the total for eleemosynary ends amounted to $55,000. The entire affair drew public approval. Actually, Louis's wartime fights were more for morale purposes than money. The amounts of money raised were comparatively insignificant. The federal budget for military purposes had leaped to $55 billion, would go higher.

In keeping with the practices of the period, the *New York Herald Tribune* subhead read: "Negro Stops Opponent in . . . Sixth Round." The race of a white boxer rarely ever became the descriptive adjective.

While Louis was on the rifle range at Camp Upton, Jack Blackburn died in Chicago. The bereaved fighter was granted leave to attend the funeral. "This is the worst shock of my life. Jack started me in the boxing game and followed me all the way through," Louis announced to interviewers. "He made a fighter of me and did more for me than anyone else."

The funeral minister, J. O. Blackburn repeated a version of Blackburn's snapper to Louis. "You were born with two strikes on you. Swing with the third and don't foul out." The dead man left a modest estate valued at $6,500.

While Roxborough served his time at Jackson State, Louis remained loyal; Freddie Wilson remembered accompanying the champion on a visit to Roxborough. "Roxy had a radio in his cell along with a big sign, 'Don't give up hope.' " Julian Black also suffered some reverses. He was indicted on a charge of income-tax evasion but the case was dismissed. Joe Gould, Jim Braddock's manager and associate of Owney Madden, was not so fortunate. He had wrangled a commission in the army that put him in a pivotal position to negotiate contracts with military suppliers. Gould was accused and convicted of accepting bribes to pass on contracts for liferafts. In a memorable apologia, Sam Taub, the veteran ringside radio announcer praised Gould as a friend for many years but added, "He shouldn'a done it in wartime."

There was one more move for Louis to defend his title while in uniform. In September of 1942, he became embroiled in a situation that exemplified the uneasy partnership between commerce and patriotism. It was announced that the heavyweight champion would defend against Billy Conn, also in the service. The proceeds above expenses were all destined for the Army Relief Fund. To ensure that the project would be above reproach, a committee of sportswriters became co-promoters with Mike Jacobs under the listing of War Boxing Inc. That the sportswriters' presence eliminated the possibility of venality is another mark of the innocence of the age. The project had received the blessing of the War Department and the fight was tentatively scheduled for Yankee Stadium on Columbus Day.

Within a few days after the initial announcement, Billy Conn appeared at Mike Jacobs's Rumson, New Jersey, estate and started to train in quarters constructed on the property. The National Broadcasting Company, with P. Lorillard,

215

makers of Old Gold cigarettes as the sponsors, bid a record $71,200 for the radio rights. A committee of sportswriters accepted the offer.

The next newspaper story in the *Times* recounted that War Boxing Inc.'s operators had decided to permit the two fighters to draw from the receipts enough to pay off some outstanding debts. Otherwise, said War Boxing Inc., it would be difficult to stage the fight because of possible claims from sources owed money. Louis was reported beholden to manager John Roxborough for $41,146 and obligated for $59,805 to the Twentieth Century Sporting Club, Mike Jacobs's promotional corporation. Conn owed Twentieth Century $34,500. War Boxing Inc. was saying that Roxborough and Jacobs, who in effect were already a part of the proposed fight arrangements through Louis and the promotion of the fight, might block their own enterprise if their IOU's were not dissolved. No mention was made of the amounts due the United States Internal Revenue Service, which by 1942 had dunned Louis for $117,000 in back taxes. If he were to receive the roughly $100,000 proposed as his slice of the Columbus Day fight, Louis's obligations to IRS would better than double the original sum.

Solemnly, *New York Times* correspondent Joseph Nichols detailed these allocations. He mildly hinted at the justice of the modifications of the original concept that had donated all to charity. He did not mention that after the sportswriters arrived at their decision, the elected head of the organization, Grantland Rice, resigned in protest. His place was, in fact, taken by the *Times*'s own John Kieran. The Nichols story did say that the War Department had approved the latest fiduciary arrangements. Louis was already training at Greenwood Lake, New Jersey.

On September 25, with advance sales of nearly $300,000

and a million-dollar gate in prospect, Secretary of War Henry L. Stimson abruptly canceled the fight. The *Times* said that with the fees apportioned to the fighters, the total cut from the gate would have been $250,000, leaving a not inconsiderable three-quarters of a million for the charity. Stimson, however, declared the affair unfair to other men in service who would not be given an opportunity to work off their civilian-incurred indebtedness while in uniform. (Few of them could have earned and donated $750,000 to Army Relief and none would have jeopardized anything similar to the heavyweight championship.)

Stimson publicly stated that his decision ought not to be construed as faulting any of the principals. He held them innocent of any knavery or low scheming. Along with his ban on the fight (which remained in effect even after all parties announced they would participate with the entire proceeds to charity) Stimson also outlawed further fund raisings by the military relief funds, saying that their resources were adequate for their purposes. The first whiffs of patriotism at a profit had begun to reach Washington and one avenue of such fraud, the charity affair, was now proscribed.

Louis emerged with his integrity intact. Even if he had been granted the $100,000, he would have received less than 10 percent of the gate, a fraction of what he ordinarily ought to command. The whole affair had, though, brought to public notice his financial troubles.

He was beset by other problems in the war years. Although a reconciliation with Marva had occurred and one newspaper columnist announced that Louis "has made a thumping success of his marriage which less than two years ago was in divorce court," the relationship was deeply troubled. Another myopic observer said, "The Joe Louises are a happy and devoted couple—a credit to their race, their nation and this city." For a brief period Marva Louis tried the nightclub circuit as a singer. She met only indifferent success, touring 38 cities, netting $15,000. Their first child, Jacqueline, born in 1943, failed to bind the pair. In 1944, Marva told columnist Earl Wilson that the marriage was solid: "He's a lover again." But she obtained a divorce March 28, 1945, asserting her husband deserted her in the fall of 1943. She lamented, "Joe thinks I ought to be happy because I've got all the material things any woman could want. But it's no fun being alone all the time." The manner in which she received support proved to be another blunder that dropped the fighter into a deeper pit of debt.

Though Louis's fights failed to pay anything substantial toward the alleviation of wartime suffering, he had begun to be noticed as a rallying figure for the nation. At a January 1942, dinner the New York Boxing writers awarded Louis the Edward J. O'Neil trophy. The plaque was in honor of a former New York sportswriter who had been killed while covering the Spanish Civil War. (Less than 10 years later, those who had fought for the Loyalist cause would be marked as subversives.) Former New York mayor, James J. Walker, the man who had negotiated the legislation that permitted boxing to thrive after World War I, declaimed an eloquent speech about the honor guest. "Joe, all the Negroes in the world are proud of you because you have given them reason to be proud. You never forgot your own people. You are an American gentleman. When you fought Buddy Baer and gave your purse to the Navy Relief Society, you took your title and your future and bet it all on patriotism and love of country. Joe Louis, that night you laid a rose on the grave of Abraham Lincoln." Revisionist historians had not yet pointed out that the Great Emancipator had been willing to go along with slavery if that were the price of preserving the Union.

A few months later, Louis was asked to appear at a benefit show for the Navy Relief Society. Harry Markson remembered Louis visiting him in his office at Madison Square Garden. "I said to him, Joe, they're liable to call on you to say a few words. Would you like me to write something out for you?' He said, 'Naw, they won't call on me.' He was that modest."

But during the affair, celebrity Louis was indeed singled out and asked to say a few words. He mumbled a few phrases and then concluded, "We can't lose because we're on God's side."

The audience adored it. Billy Rowe pointed out to Louis that he had actually flubbed the line, that the right thing to say was "God is on our side." But when newspapers the following day praised the sentiment expressed by Louis, he teasingly asked Rowe whether he still thought he'd made a mistake. The idea was not original with Louis; Lincoln, for one, had said the same thing. But newspapers, magazines and commentators all seized upon any encouraging words. Public-relations expert Carl Byoir took the Louis quote and made it the centerpiece of a poem. Patriotic fervor was one commodity that suffered no rationing.

The war caused some public gestures to be made toward blacks. The D.A.R., three years after it had barred Marian Anderson, now invited her to give a series of concerts at Constitution Hall. To the merchant marine was added the liberty ship *Booker T. Washington.* With manpower resources critical, black Americans were now essential to the wartime effort. By 1944, two million blacks worked in war industry, many in jobs formerly restricted to whites. In spite of the patriotic fervor of the time, friction grew as blacks left the South to work in the northern factories. In the summer of 1943, race riots left 34 dead in Detroit, five dead and 500 arrested in Harlem. Of all blacks, Louis stood out as the one who could pacify both members of his race and whites concerned about blacks forgetting to know their place. To one interviewer he had remarked, "There's a lot wrong with this country, but Hitler ain't going to fix it." When Louis was questioned about putting his title on the line with no return to him, he answered, "Ain't fightin' for nothin', I'm fightin' for my country."

Even his critic Paul Gallico pointed to Louis as the exemplar for all Americans: "Citizen Barrow has set us a lesson. Can we learn it, we are saved. Should we ignore it, we shall reap what we deserve."

Louis was again what Joe Bostic called "a commodity." This time he was packaged in patriotism. The beauty of the Louis product was that it served advocates along all points of the spectrum. In July 1942, the left-wing *New Masses* printed an interview with Louis by Blaine Owen in which the subject allegedly unburdened himself on a number of issues, all duly supporting the orientation of *New Masses.*

Owen, tracing Louis's origins wrote, "Down in Chambers County, Alabama, the 'kinfolk' of a great fighter joined the Sharecroppers' Union, now part of the CO Agricultural Workers' organization. I spoke of this union, of their struggles, to the serious faced boy [the boy was 28 years old and by the 1950s no sensitized left writer would employ "boy"] whose proportions made the rest of us look small."

"Sure a union's good for folks," Louis supposedly told Owen. "They can get together and help themselves." Owen then told of white sharecroppers who named their babies for Louis, how on fight night "it was the hungry, the dispossessed and the unpossessed grouped about the radios from coast to coast who were in there cheering for Joe, the group of boys in a Dusseldorf sports club who wrote asking that Louis beat Schmeling—those boys may have been put into military uniforms now, but I don't think they want to fight against Corporal Barrow."

Owen recalled a night in 1936 at the training table in Louis's camp before the first Schmeling fight. Owen said a discussion arose over the coming Olympic Games in Berlin and fund-raising problems for the United States Olympic Committee. There was talk that the lack of money would keep some of the black athletes from making the trip. Owen quoted Louis, "They asked me for somethin' to help them out, but I sure don' feel like doin' it. . . . Any other year they wouldn't have no trouble but who'd want to help them go there? . . . Any American that believes in fair play and the rights of people ought to feel that way, I sure don't want to help that sorta thing. 'Course I'm a Negro, but it's not only that. . . ."

When asked if he had contributed to the Olympic fund-raising campaign, Louis replied No. "There was no mistake about it; Joe Louis was opposed to American participation in the Nazi Olympic Games," revealed Owen six years after the fact.

At another point Owen brought up the subject of the rules at the Illinois Athletic Club in Chicago where Louis fought many of his amateur bouts.

"The colored fighters had to go up the back way, Joe told me. 'They wouldn't let us go in the front with the others. I'd tear the damn buildin' down before that'd happen again.' "

Many years later when asked about the backdoor policy for blacks at the Illinois Athletic Club, Louis answered, "That entrance was the one nearest where I got off the elevated train. It was more convenient. To go in through the front I woulda had to walk all the way round the block. I didn't know then that I wasn't supposed to use the front. It was Ray Robinson who broke the color line there, he refused to go up the back stairs."

That incident, the naïveté of Louis, tells more about his race consciousness than all the World War II propaganda pieces. Meyer Berger, in his 1936 column for the *New York Times,* flatly stated that the young Detroit hopeful showed no interest in the fortunes of his fellow blacks. Given his background, the meager education tended him and the attitudes of the principal media of the day, it would have been far more surprising if Louis had exhibited to Berger or any other reporter a profound sense of race consciousness.

The men around Louis—Roxborough, Black and Blackburn—could not have been called Uncle Toms. They moved more easily, more independently in the white mainstream than most blacks. But they had all learned how to evade situations that brought indignity. It was asserted by one black reporter that both managers of Louis consorted with white women. Jack Blackburn, raised in a southern-oriented border state and less educated than the two businessmen, was always conscious of the power invested in whites but he retained his integrity.

Through Roxborough, Louis had become a contributor to the NAACP, "I made my first appearance for the NAACP in Cincinnati in 1935," said Louis. "There were thousands of people there, including Walter White. I gave it a big boost." Louis was also an early backer of the Detroit Urban League.

The former heavyweight champion believed that he first began to appreciate what being black meant after his family moved to Detroit. "I started to know about the South then

222

but 'course I couldn't have learned much when I was in Alabama. I was only a kid." Undoubtedly, Roxborough, Black and Blackburn, aware of the potential threats to a successful young black fighter, counseled Louis on his behavior. He, however, dismissed these efforts, saying, "I got all my coachin' on being black from my mother."

Lillie Barrow Brooks, bred in southern traditions of black behavior and religion, may have helped give her son his early image of forebearance and leadership through example rather than rhetoric. Explaining the effect of his mother's coaching, Louis said, "After I got beat by Schmeling, she told me, 'You did your best, don't feel bad. You didn't embarrass your people. You do your best, that's good enough.' "

Billy Rowe cited a typical Louis reaction: "Louis possessed a sort of silent knowledge of what was going on and what he represented. He had an ongoing knowledge of the street that was fantastic. People tried to use Joe. But he did things his own way. The *Pittsburgh Courier* was hot for a statement from him about World War II discrimination in the Navy and Air Force. Joe said I won't do it. Then he decided to do a benefit for the Navy. His attitude was now let's see them do things right. By putting them on the spot he did more to call attention to unfairness than all the words that could have been printed." The record of the U.S. Navy in World War II when it came to treatment of blacks was abysmal, and there is little evidence that the heavyweight champion's appearance at a benefit caused any ameliorating efforts.

In the opinion of Joe Bostic, the young Joe Louis was aware enough of racial attitudes to detect any personal snubs. But prior to his World War II experience he was unlikely to have felt any deep commitment beyond himself.

Bostic thought Blaine Owen's account of Louis and the Olympic fund raisers less than credible. On the other hand, Bostic accompanied Louis on a tour of the South in 1937. "We were some place in Alabama and this white man kept talking to Joe, 'Boy this, Boy that.' Joe say, 'If you don't stop talking like that, this "boy" is going to kick you in the ass.' "

For the most part, Louis was isolated from the oppression visited upon his fellow blacks. From the moment he came under the guidance of Roxborough and his black team, he became a protected member of the species.

From the observations of participants in the training camps, the subject of race was not ignored, but neither was it a burning issue. Mike Jacobs had stuck to his promise to give Louis the shortest possible route to the top and there was no sting of discrimination to poison the swift success. As a result the status quo had come to be at least tolerable. Freddie Wilson described an incident that explains the acquiescence. "We were driving along; I was doing maybe 70 miles an hour in Ohio. A state trooper stopped us. I figure we're in for real trouble. He comes over to the car and starts to bawl us out. Then he sees Joe. 'Oh, it's you, champ. Well, cut it down a little, huh fellas?' " That was hardly the typical experience of a black man halted by a state trooper in the 1930s.

George Nicholson who also traveled with Louis remembered their adventures together as basically free of unpleasant incidents. The secret lay in knowing where to go and under what circumstances. "Everybody around Pompton Lakes knew us," said Nicholson. "We could go to the shows or the ice cream parlors. We never tried any of the other places, avoided spots where there might be feelings against blacks. When we went to a big city, the fellows all had a tendency to go into the black section of town."

The Louis experience of the period was not entirely free of humiliations, however. Nicholson recalled, "When Louis and I were in Wisconsin for a boxing exhibition, we were told we'd have to eat in the store room of a restaurant. The owner said he didn't want to upset the public. Joe bought us some sandwiches and we ate in the car. The same thing happened to us in San Antonio. We had our choice of eating in the back of the restaurant or on the street. We ate in our car."

Even before World War II, it had become apparent that Louis was more than just another heavyweight champion. E. Franklin Frazier, a black sociologist, discovered in 1940: "Joe Louis enables many lower class youths (in fact many Negro youths and adults in all classes) to inflict vicariously the aggression which they would like to carry out against whites for the discriminations and insults which they have suffered."

Frazier cited a 19-year-old Washington, D.C., high school graduate who said, "I've tried to follow in Louis's footsteps but I'm not big enough. I've heard all of his fights and seen him several times here in Washington. I've thrilled at every damned 'peck [Peckerwood, derogatory for whites] he knocked over and helped raise hell in the street celebrations after each one. When he lost, I felt pretty bad, though I'll never feel something was wrong—crooked."

The sociologist drew from several other examples: "Likewise a 10-year-old son of a laborer would rather be Joe Louis than any other Negro in the country because he 'would get a lot of fun going in the ring and beating up somebody.' "

From a 17-year-old collegian, Frazier obtained this memory of the first Schmeling fight: "I was hitting every blow with him and taking with him those he got. And when he lost, I really felt sick. Somehow I didn't even want to go on the street the next day. One thing he's done, he's certainly

225

made the so-called white fighters have a wholesome respect for his fists. I suppose symbolically that's the only way white people can be made to respect Negroes in other walks of life."

Historian Charles S. Johnson noted the reverse side of the coin. "In a few areas of the South, the disposition of Negro youth to celebrate too jubilantly the fistic triumphs of Joe Louis has been brusquely and sometimes violently discouraged, indicating that the symbolism was as significant for the white as for Negro youth." When Swedish sociologist Gunnar Myrdal interviewed black students in a one-room Georgia school he discovered that none knew the name of the president of the United States; only one thought he knew of Booker T. Washington; all were ignorant of Walter White, William DuBois and the NAACP. But several could identify Joe Louis, Ella Fitzgerald and Henry Armstrong.

Before World War II, Louis made one attempt to use his popular stature for a cause. On occasion, Louis traveled with Charles Roxborough, brother of the fighter's co-manager, later a Michigan state senator. He suggested to Louis as early as 1936 that the fighter might find some friends in the Republican party. Jesse Owens had been recruited by Ohio Republicans. The activity did not interest Louis at the time, but in 1940, he agreed to campaign for the GOP presidential nominee, Wendell L. Willkie.

"I liked the way he talked," said Louis. "Color didn't mean nothing to him. He believed everybody was created equal. And he lost with more votes than any President ever got up to that time." The decision to go with Willkie brought a mild dissent from Julian Black. "I thought it unwise for a fighter to get involved in politics. He has fans in both political parties," said Black, who happened to be a member of Chicago's Kelly–Nash Democratic machine.

To aid Willkie, the heavyweight champion visited several

cities and delivered short speeches. Announcing his support for the challenger to FDR's third term, Louis told Detroit newspapers, "I'm in Willkie's corner because I think he will help my people."

At St. Louis he told listeners he backed Willkie because he could give the country something Roosevelt failed to—an antilynching law. "I am just Joe Louis. I am a fighter, not a politician. This country has been good to me, has given me everything I have and I want it to be good to you and give you everything you need. I am for Willkie because I think he will help my people. I figure my people ought to be for him too." None took offense at Louis's possessiveness over blacks. But when he came to New York to campaign in the beginning of November 1940, he ran into some vigorous counterpunches. Support for FDR grew as the World War II closed in on the United States.

Walking the Manhattan streets to drum up votes for Willkie, Louis confessed that he found political campaigning "almost as bad as fighting five men in one night." He chewed a candy bar as he paid a public-relations call on a black city policeman, James Sloan, who in a minor incident had been kicked in the groin by FDR's press secretary, Stephen Early. To the chagrin of Louis and his Republican guides, Sloan remarked that he remained a Democrat and would vote for Roosevelt.

Louis admitted to reporters that he had failed to vote in 1936, and reiterated his reasons for backing Willkie: "Because he promises my people more jobs, more jobs and better jobs. He promises them better jobs in the government." The fighter insisted, "I was born Republican [in the Alabama of his youth such an affiliation was a joke]. My mother was a Republican, a Republican and a Baptist."

Then Louis, probably schooled by an adviser, said of

227

Roosevelt, "He's the cause of my people being on WPA, because when the NRA made the Unions, they raised the pay $3, or from $19 a week to $22 a week, and white people got the jobs. It was a bad thing that wages were raised that way.

"Take a janitor. The union made them pay a janitor $22 a week. A white man says for that much money I'll take the job. The result was that colored people were put on $15 a week on relief. I think Mr. Roosevelt is making a lot of lazy people out of our people. They sit around waiting for the $15 a week. You all know that jobs are better than relief."

As a lesson in economics it was simplistic at best. Still, 30 years later, better-educated people continued to argue that raising the minimum wage automatically throws the young and unskilled, the poor and nonwhite out of work. What was most offensive to Louis's critics was the notion that those on relief were lazy, particularly as it was applied to "our people."

The correspondent from the *New York Times* who accompanied Louis while he loosed these sentiments called the delivery "halting and embarrassed." The audiences were reported "enthusiastic," but it was agreed that the personality and not the words were the source of the affection. Throughout, the news account said, Louis was "unsmiling."

Spokesman for the National Black Cross of America, a black-organized civic-improvement group, said, "The colored people of America appreciate Joe Louis as a heavyweight champion but not as a spokesman on political matters."

In Philadelphia when he stood up for Willkie, Louis cringed under a shower of boos. "Listen you fellas," protested Louis, "I don't really care whether Mr. Roosevelt or Mr. Willkie gets elected. It don't concern my business. Neither one'll get in the ring with me."

An unkinder cut at Louis came during a Madison Square Garden rally for FDR. New York City Mayor Fiorella La-Guardia, nominally a Republican but a backer of the president, coupled the support for Willkie from the head of the United Mine Workers, John L. Lewis, and the heavyweight champion. Sneered LaGuardia, "Willkie has the arrogance of John L. and the intelligence of Joe."

Louis's final salvo for Willkie was a telegram to the candidate that read, "Win by a knockout. It will mean freedom from the WPA and for American Negro rights."

When the election returns counted Willkie out, Louis commented, "The fight is over. I never alibi after a fight."

His brief encounter with politics left him unmarked, but in the opinion of many individuals closely associated with Louis, it was his military experiences the next four and one-half years that matured him. Louis agreed. "Talking about things, being in the service really started that," said the fighter. "I would never want another war, but it taught me a lot. In service you had to do things for yourself. Fix your shoes, see that you got your food, keep track of your clothes and where you had to be. I enjoyed that about the army." Few of his contemporaries found that the army gave them more responsibility and independence than civilian life. But Joe Louis was that unique specimen, a professional athlete. Pro sports tend to remove a sense of self-responsibility from the athlete for anything more than performance. Training camps sequester men from outside influences. Promoters, publicity men and road secretaries arrange transportation, housing, meals, personal amenities. Athletes in the name of discipline and concentration upon athletic achievement live childlike lives under the control of others. They become schooled to behave like Scott Fitzgerald's Tom and Daisy Buchanan, people who go around smashing things and use their money, or in the case of athletes, the promoters and clubs to paper over the damage. The system even becomes self-defeating, as when a pair of sprinters arrive late for their Olympic heats because instead of learning for themselves their starting times, they are trained to depend on some other person for the information. High rates of failure in the management of money and in marriage are among the social consequences when the athlete is forced to leave the zoolike atmosphere. One corrective measure of recent years has been the resort to skilled financial representatives who attempt to preserve the performer's sudden wealth. While the new keepers may indeed prevent the athletes from turning into rotting fiscal hulks, they only build more walls around the human being, replacing the one erected by the professionalized sports system. Financial security does not necessarily create a human being capable of functioning in a free society.

For Louis, the period in the army put him beyond the reach of keepers like Black, Blackburn, Roxborough and Jacobs. It enabled him to begin an independent life. Beyond anything else, life in the army forced Louis to confront his racial identity, for Jim Crow served in the United States forces throughout World War II.

Several months after his arrival at Camp Upton, Louis had received orders to Fort Riley, Kansas. The Defense Department had still not determined how to handle personalities like Louis. At this point in his military career he was only accommodated in his wish to serve in the cavalry. Louis may have thought there was still room in the army for horses, but the cavalry at Fort Riley retained only vestigial remnants of an equestrian unit. Louis was, however, photographed astride a horse for p.r. purposes. While Louis was at Fort Riley, the decision was made to use Louis as a morale builder for troops through a series of boxing exhibitions and personal appearances.

Meanwhile, Louis had discovered a friend in a very important place. Judge William Henry Hastie, the first black federal judge, had been named an assistant secretary in the War Department to deal with the problems of black servicemen. Serving as an aide to Hastie was Truman Gibson. Gibson had done legal work for Julian Black, and Louis had known him for several years. It was, in fact, Gibson who had arranged for Louis to be assigned to Fort Riley, and Gibson was also deeply involved in the abortive Conn fight. When Judge Hastie, in 1943, resigned his post in outrage at the policies toward blacks, Truman Gibson stayed on at the War Department.

By coincidence, Fort Riley had another black recruit, Jackie Robinson, a graduate of UCLA and a highly regarded football player. Less advertised, Robinson had also shown a talent for baseball. Robinson had applied for Officers Candidate School and it seemed he would be accepted for the token program of black commissions. Then, according to Truman Gibson, Robinson bumped into a peculiar problem. "They wouldn't permit him to play on the Fort Riley baseball team but it was okay for him to play football," Gibson explained. "Robinson refused to accept this kind of restriction." (The authorities at Fort Riley were apparently in harmony with the civilian sports patterns; football practiced a limited amount of integration but baseball remained totally segregated.) "As a result, his entrance to OCS was delayed."

When word of Robinson's predicament reached Louis, he called Gibson. Through the intervention of Judge Hastie, approval quickly came through for Robinson to attend OCS. Gibson said that Robinson's problems did not end there. "Jack was involved in some incident with a white officer who finally said, 'Nigger, don't talk to me like that.' Robinson punched him out, damn near left him dead and there was hell to pay. Again Joe reached me and an investigation cleared Robinson."

After Robinson broke the color line in baseball he said that Louis had not only been of enormous help during his difficult days in the service but that Louis's conduct had been a powerful force in his breakthrough. Robinson told Harry Markson, "As rough as my first year was, I might never have been able to make it if it hadn't been for Louis. He paved the way."

The War Department had created a troup out of Louis, who eventually became a sergeant, George Nicholson, who also held sergeant's stripes, and Corporal Walker Smith— Sugar Ray Robinson. Almost everywhere the group went, they ran into the kind of troubles that required the intervention of Truman Gibson and company or some other policymaker.

"We went to an army camp in Virginia," said Louis. "Right over the entrance they had that sign, 'Give me liberty or give me death.' But they had all the black troops in the worst seats, and there weren't enough places. I told the general, 'I'm not going to box. You can order me to fight but I won't get in the ring.'" Accommodations to satisfy the black soldiers were made.

In another instance, a telephone call went to Gibson. "'Goddam, this is the limit,' Louis said to me," laughed Gibson. "'They not only got separate buses but separate bus stations at this camp.' I went to Assistant Secretary Kenneth Royall, who denied that such conditions could exist. I told him to call the commanding general. He did and things were changed."

In Alabama, Ray Robinson and Louis failed to observe the "whites only on the front benches" sign where they waited for a bus. In the ensuing altercation with military policemen, the more volatile Robinson grabbed one of the soldiers. Robinson wound up in the stockade and was released only after Louis had once again protested to Washington.

Overseas, the group encountered the same discrimination that plagued them at home. While they were walking in an English town with some white girls, a group of United States sailors attempted to force the women to go with them. "I don't give a damn if it is Joe Louis. You're white girls, and they are just a bunch of niggers. We don't want to see any white girls making fools of themselves over any niggers." Shore police got rid of the sailors.

Were it not for their painfulness, some of the confrontations might strike an observer as dark comedy. On one occasion, Louis needed a driver to take him to a nearby airfield. A captain had been assigned as his escort, and along with a major, Louis waited patiently for the tardy automobile to arrive from the base motor pool. When it finally came, with a black sergeant at the wheel, the captain remarked, "No wonder the car is late. I didn't know they were sending a nigger driver. They're always late." Louis's reaction was to demand another escort officer, even though the captain tried to deny the invective that had only moments before spouted from his mouth.

During one visit to a military camp in the South, Louis was actually arrested by an MP for using the telephone booth designated for whites. The fact that no separate but equal facility existed for blacks failed to impress the MP.

At a small private party for Louis in England, a white colonel accompanied by a female friend attempted to barge in on the festivities. Thrown out, the officer yelled at Louis's friend Eddie Green, "I can hardly wait till I get back to my hometown in Mississippi. There we know what to do with niggers like you and Joe. We'd tar and feather you for not obeying a white man."

Time and again, Louis was forced to complain to commanding officers about the unequal opportunities for black servicemen to see him demonstrate his ring skills. Louis also observed that United States whites abroad created a good deal of apprehension about black soldiers by bad-mouthing them to the local residents.

Among the pleasant experiences for Louis was a reunion with Billy Conn in the British Isles. They flew together from London to Liverpool and, according to Louis, both men smacked their chops as they speculated on the lucrative prospects for a second fight, once the war ended. "Billy said to me," remembered Louis, " 'The least you could have done was to let me have the championship for a while. We'd have done even better in the second fight.' I told him, 'Billy, you had it for 12 rounds and couldn't hold on to it,' " chuckled Louis.

Shortly after this repartee, the pilot advised his passengers that there seemed to be some equipment problems and they might have to crash-land. "Billy says to me, 'Oh my God, we done lost the money,' " said Louis. Some time later, when Louis was back in New York, a reporter after hearing the anecdote asked whether the aircraft had indeed crash-landed. "I'm here ain't I," growled Louis.

America and Joe Louis came out of World War II in somewhat different shape. Both had indeed demonstrated a new independence and strength. But while the nation might fret about the size of its national debt, it was easily able to generate enough product to manage its obligations. Louis, on the other hand, came out of World War II a financial disaster —and short on time and opportunities to recoup.

14

After Germany surrendered on May 8, 1945, the war in the Pacific appeared headed for a conclusion, and the itch to cash in on deferred potential of a Louis–Conn rematch gnawed at Mike Jacobs. Truman Gibson visited Jacobs in New York and the promoter, in search of leakproof privacy, drew the War Department official into the fastness of the toilet. After making certain that there were no eavesdroppers, Jacobs offered a proposition. "He told me," said Gibson, "that it would be worth $10,000 to me if I could get Louis out of the service. He asked me how I would like to become Louis's manager, and he told me how much I would make." Gibson could not or would not oblige, and it was his recollection that Louis did not appreciate his failure to do so. "Joe stopped talking to me for three years," Gibson recalled.

Louis, however, didn't have long to wait for a legitimate discharge. With the Legion of Merit "for exceptionally meritorious service," he was honorably discharged in October 1945. Louis was not like other men coming out of the service, forced to start from scratch. But he was, although the holder of a block of gold in the title, a bankrupt.

When Marva sued for divorce, she had agreed to take a $25,000 cash settlement plus the ownership of the Chicago apartment house. But Louis did not have the $25,000 and, he says, he went to Julian Black for an advance. Black turned him down, according to Louis (though Black has denied it). Since the Chicago man's contract as co-manager had already expired, Louis cunningly decided to make Marva his co-manager, guaranteeing her Black's normal share, 25 percent. As Marva's co-manager, Louis accepted a good friend of John Roxborough's, real estate investor Marshall Miles of Buffalo, New York. Louis has explained that Roxborough's difficulties with the law prevented him from continuing as manager.

Louis's debts, made public at the time of War Boxing Inc.'s ill-fated promotion with Billy Conn, had continued to rise. He was deep in debt to Jacobs and Roxborough, among others. The Internal Revenue Service steadily tacked interest upon its assessment of Louis and charged him with income from the Baer and Simon fights, despite his contributions to relief funds. Expenses that Louis felt obligated to incur in his role as champion, the IRS refused to accept. It would not, for instance, permit him to deduct $3,000 worth of tickets to the Simon fight which he bought for soldiers.

Louis and his group hoped that one super extravaganza would get him out of the clutches of the IRS and other creditors. Boxing fans, deprived of their sport for four years, were seen as ravenous to witness the dream rematch between Louis and Billy Conn. Although the economy still suffered from a wartime bellyache, Mike Jacobs calculated the hunger of customers for Louis and Conn as financially insatiable. He set an unheard-of $100 price of ringside, which covered considerably more territory than the immediate tier around the ring at Yankee Stadium.

Among the annoying problems that faced the promoter was construction of the infield seats. He secured some 40,000 feet of spanking new yellow board lumber at a time when such items were in short enough supply to be under control of a federal agency. When word circulated that the new lumber might be declared illegally obtained—a midwest realtor raised a hue and cry of foul—the sly Jacobs arranged to have his order spend many hours soaking in water. The suspect pile of wood took on the dull appearance of second-hand stuff, exempt from controls. Jacobs escaped that peril. As ringside seats got off to a good start, Jacobs decided to add 5,000 to the 10,000 planned. "He took the cost of those 5,000 seats out of our share," said Marshall Miles.

The gate panned out as the richest of any Louis fight. Still Jacobs, for the first time in his history, grossly overestimated his projections. On June 9th, 10 days before the fight, the promoter clacked that he already had $1.9 million in the till. But that was the figure for the gate when the fight was actually held. Jacobs made a mistake with the $100 price. When on June 19, 1946, Louis at 207 pounds and Conn at 182 stepped into the ring at Yankee Stadium, only 45,000 fans, 9,000 fewer than had witnessed their first battle, were present.

Equally disappointing was Louis's performance. He stood revealed as a slow-moving 32-year-old, who, if the target were obliging enough to stand still, could yet develop enough leverage to knock a man senseless. Conn, although nearly four years the champion's junior, seemed even more deteriorated by time. Louis told friends later than Conn was a shadow of the man he had met five years earlier. It was Conn's plan to tire his elder by gliding around the ring out of reach. But unlike the first fight, Conn landed few blows, and by the eighth round he had even lost his ability to dance away. A series of seven punches put the challenger away in a satisfactory ending to what was otherwise "an exercise in slow motion," as one critic called it.

The returns from the fans amounted to $1,925,564, disappointingly short of what had been hoped would be a $3 million gate. Louis's share amounted to $591,116, plus a few thousand from the sale of the fight movie. What happened to the radio money, Louis failed to say. The IRS was not yet in the practice of tying up fight purses until its end was paid, so Louis got his money immediately and used much of it to wipe out some of his obligations. He paid Jacobs the full $143,000 he owed him, and Roxborough his $31,000.

Less than three months later, Louis went up against Tami Mauriello, 198 pounds of trivial opposition, so hampered by a deformed foot he could not back up easily. The fight went one round, but Mauriello stunned Louis with a punch, before the champion KO'd him. Only 38,000 customers, with prices scaled far below the Conn game, paid $335,000. The champion's share totaled $103,000. Louis escaped with only a 25 percent cut for Marshall Miles and company; a month after the Conn fight, he and Marva had remarried. Out of this marriage came their son Joe, Jr., known as Punchy.

In an effort to reduce the tax bite for 1946, it was arranged that the entire $103,000 should remain in the custody of Mike Jacobs until after the first of the year. In January 1947, Marshall Miles came to New York and headed for Jacobs's office. Uncle Mike, who had suffered a stroke that would eventually drive him into retirement, revealed that only $500 remained of Louis's money. The champion had withdrawn the rest. "I was really sore," said Miles. "Jacobs should never have given Joe the money without checking with me."

When the shocked Miles questioned the champion—"it took me three days to find him"—he readily admitted that he had drawn out the more than $100,000, investing $43,000 in the Rhum Boogie Café in Chicago, with his friend and camp joker Leonard Reed as manager. Other sums had gone

239

for the restless satisfaction of pleasures—golf, women and traveling around.

It was both Louis's good fortune and bad luck that in 1947 there was a dearth of suitable heavyweight challengers; there seemed to be no heavyweight around who was capable of either coaxing people to pay premium prices for seats or threatening to defeat the superannuated champion. So Louis toured South America, putting on exhibitions. The choice of Latin America proved a poor one. The people in Bogotá, Panama City and other sites were either unfamiliar with the champion or else disinclined to pay the steep prices necessary for a glimpse of Louis. The show returned to the United States barely in the black.

Louis then concentrated on his investments. In Harlem, he opened the Joe Louis Restaurant and Bar on 125th Street. Like most of his commercial promotions, it got off to a fast start and then died even before it got to the stretch, under-trained, undermanned and undercapitalized. His other ventures included a vocational training school in Chicago, a soft drink called Joe Louis Punch and an insurance company that John Roxborough was supposed to control. None of them survived with any return to Louis. Louis also tried to secure an agency for Ford automobiles. In a memorable incident, he went with Truman Gibson to Detroit to discuss the proposition with Henry Ford, taking along a postwar Ford that he had bought and that was defective.

Said former employee Louis to Ford, "You don't make a car worth a shit." Perhaps it was the failure to show the proper reverence for the family product, but Henry Ford failed to help Louis get a dealership. It was many years, in fact, before any black obtained a car franchise from any of the major manufacturers.

The announcement of each Joe Louis business enterprise carried with it bravado about his future economic security. In the fall of 1948, through the mouth of a pair of ghosts, Louis declared, "I got annuities. I've got Joe Louis Enterprises Inc. going good. [It was to be a catchall holding company.] I've got an interest in the Joe Louis Punch. That's a soft drink that's selling good in 31 cities and in South America. I've got $25,000 stock in it and I get 5 percent in royalties. I may build myself a bottling and distributing plant and sell Joe Louis Punch myself [it was akin to the race-track tout pushing a horse and then becoming so overwhelmed by his own propaganda that he too backed the entry]. I've got my houses in Detroit and in Chicago. I am in the Superior Life Insurance Society with Mr. Roxborough in Detroit." (The former co-manager some years later said of this association "Joe has a lifetime job with my company, the Superior Life Insurance Society of Michigan, of which he is vice president and director of youth activities.")

"In New York I'm setting up to go in business with Ray Robinson to distribute Canadian Ace Beer. In a garage out here in Chicago, I am starting with Chicago School of Automotive Trades."

Part of the purpose behind the invasion of Latin America had been to introduce Joe Louis Punch to what was described as "soda thirsty South America." The heavyweight champion of soft drinks, Coca Cola did not find the cherry-like flavor of Joe Louis Punch much of a contender.

Joe Louis Enterprises served as the payee for monies from tours of South America, Europe and the United States, and royalties on fight films. Louis also claimed during this period to be an investor in a California housing construction firm, to have financial interests in television, and to be backing a black newspaper, *New York Age.* Marshall Miles regarded the California real estate and television propositions as properties of Louis's imagination.

Miles reviewed some of the investments. "He didn't lose much in the place on 125th Street. They just used the name; he didn't put up any money. The Joe Louis Punch was a good drink but they didn't promote it properly. He never really got anything out of Roxborough's insurance, although the company continued to be one of Roxborough's businesses. Louis lost a lot of money in the Rhum Boogie nightclub though. I'd say that the truth is every investment he made was bad. I don't know why he didn't get the Ford agency. Sometimes, in these deals it would be the people pushing Louis who would scare somebody off." One such shadowy deal was Louis's try, with Ray Robinson, to set up a Canadian Ace Beer franchise. It was discovered that a long-time racketeer named Harry Greenberg with ties extending back to Al Capone was a silent partner of Louis and Robinson. As a result the state licensing bureau turned down the application from Louis and Robinson. The vocational school closed when the G.I. Bill, tuition for former veterans, ran dry. *New York Age* failed to capture enough readers.

"And what he didn't throw away on bad investments," said Miles, "Louis spent on good times."

The visit to South America supposedly grossed $132,000 but the entourage gobbled most of it up in living expenses. The heavyweight champion was still hard pressed for cash. Mike Jacobs offered another opponent for the champion, Jersey Joe Walcott. Louis had little reason to fear Walcott, born Arnold Cream. He had been a sparring partner in 1936, before the first Schmeling fight, and was actually a few months older than Louis. Walcott's credentials amounted to a modest three-fight winning streak with no knockouts.

The original proposition was simply a 10-round exhibition against Walcott in a place like Atlantic City (the challenger was from New Jersey). Boxing authorities frowned on this sort of enterprise as deprecating the sport. Equally important, nobody would pay premium prices for such a show. Virtue and self-interest united to agree on a 15-round title match at Madison Square Garden in December.

Walcott bore so little reputation that he came to Madison Square Garden a 10–1 underdog. His threat to Louis seemed to rest on the fact that he had outfathered the champion; there were six little Walcotts at home and he was also referred to as Pappy. The challenger stoically endured the jibes of the writers; it was assumed that he was fair game for both verbal and physical abuse in return for the best pay night of his lengthy career.

From the first round the dancing style of the older man bothered Louis. Walcott pumped up and down, hiding his chin behind his left shoulder. In the opening round he bounced a right hand off Louis's jaw and the champion sat down. In the fourth round it was a right uppercut that put Louis on the canvas for seven. Walcott sprawled on the floor after he threw a right hand in the 13th but it was considered a slip, not a knockdown. Louis was unable to knock Walcott off his feet. When the 15th round ended, the challenger was still dancing. In the view of the majority of the working press, he was the victor. But in an astonishing split decision, two ringside officials voted for Louis while referee Ruby Goldstein, a former fighter himself, awarded the battle to Walcott.

Immediately after ring announcer Harry Balogh held up Louis's right hand, the bruised champion grunted to Walcott, "I'm sorry Joe." It was interpreted by many as an apology for having unjustly been named the winner. Louis later contended, however, that he meant only to excuse an abominable performance. In his dressing room Louis had almost nothing to say.

The next morning, columnists engaged in a competition to determine who could create the best image of Louis's decay. John McNulty may have won with ". . . Louis, slower than a peg legged man crossing a swamp."

From the gate receipts Louis received $76,000 plus $10,-000 from movie films. There was also radio money plus a small sum from the first television broadcast of a heavy-weight championship. Although no one had yet proposed the medium be restricted to closed-circuit broadcasts, there was at the time of the Walcott fight a harbinger of the future with bars in Pasadena, California, proposing to charge $20 for a front-row seat to watch the coming sell-out Rose Bowl Game on January 1, 1948.

There was no question that there would be a rematch with Walcott. Louis said later that if he had decisively beaten Walcott the first time, he might very well have retired at that. Given his penury, it is dubious. But quite apart from the obvious financial rewards of a ballpark production in the spring of 1948, the champion still had his pride. He scoffed at Walcott's pretensions to his role. He insisted that in spite of the opinions of the writers, Walcott had not beaten him. "Man knocks me down twice, he should knock me out if he is to be champion," Louis said, evoking the venerable theory that to become heavyweight champion one must knock out the title holder. But ascending to the throne by parliamentary decision rather than a coup was not unprecedented. Tunney took away Dempsey's title on points. Sharkey did the same to Schmeling, and Braddock decisioned Baer.

In the hiatus before the second fight with Walcott, Louis struck off on the foreign exhibition trail once more, this time to Europe. Again the harvest proved insufficient to the labor in the fields. The gross amounted to only $86,000 and there was some talk that the Swedish promoters, unable to pay off in money, had offered several thousand dollars' worth of skates.

For the rematch on June 25, 1948, Louis trained grimly, though by now he admitted disliking the training routine he had enjoyed in younger days. Following the weigh-in and the usual performance for the benefit of photographers and reporters on the day of the fight, Jimmy Cannon caught Louis alone. The champion, however chagrined he had been after the first battle and almost petulant in his regard for Walcott, had reverted to his basic honesty. "Don't put this in the paper," he told the man from the *New York Post.* "But I stink him out tonight . . . he stink me out the last time."

Early on in the third round, Walcott again slipped through Louis's defenses and sat him down for a short count. But after that the challenger contented himself with staying out of range. Louis meanwhile tried to pin him in a corner. But Louis lacked the necessary swiftness and he was hampered by his own sense of caution. He was not fighting like a young man, who would gamble on a mistake, relying on his resilience and ability to move out of the way if he got in trouble. In the 11th round, to the relief of the audience which had begun to jeer, Louis smashed through with a series of right hands and the evasive Walcott danced no more. He lay on the floor for a full 10 count.

Louis spoke a few words into the microphone afterward, saying that this was his last fight.

A day or so after the destruction of Walcott, Louis entertained Jimmy Cannon in his suite at the Theresa Hotel in Harlem. Although the heavyweight champion now would most certainly have been accepted downtown, he still preferred to make his headquarters in Harlem. A camp follower of the times remembered, "Joe had a whole floor at the Theresa. He had three girls in different rooms, and at that he was always asking for the key to somebody's room so he could use it for a while, to get away from Marva."

To Cannon the champion reiterated his assertion that he would never fight again. When the *New York Post* columnist questioned whether he could afford to quit, Louis became "peevish. . . . He refused to acknowledge that he was short of cash. He explained that he wasn't a millionaire but he was comfortably fixed for life."

Marva Louis was not that convinced her husband's ring career was over. "I hope Joe's right," she said. "But you know how prima donnas are . . . they want another chance."

Instead of formally notifying the various boxing associations of his abdication, Louis set off on six months of boxing exhibitions, displaying his wares before folks around the country and in the Caribbean. A few days before a Jamaica engagement in February, Louis announced he had signed papers permitting Marva to obtain a second divorce in Mexico.

On March 1, 1949, he finally delivered the news that everyone had expected, that he was indeed through as a professional fighter. He filed letters to Eddie Egan, chairman of the New York State Athletic Commission, and Abe Green, president of the World Boxing Association, to certify his retirement. (Editorialized the *New York Times,* "A 34-year-old colored man who was born in a log cabin in Alabama . . . an honor to the ring and his race.") The reason for the delay in Louis's official retirement quickly became apparent, as he announced his sponsorship of a "Tournament of Champions." Louis, it seems, had signed to exclusive contracts the four leading contenders for his title, Joe Walcott, Ezzard Charles, Lee Savold and Gus Lesnevich. Louis later explained that shortly after writing his letters to Egan and Green he had listened to the Ezzard Charles–Joey Maxim fight in Cincinnati and was struck with an ambitious plan: to capture the leading contenders and then sell the contracts to the successor to Mike Jacobs's Twentieth Century Sporting Club, the International Boxing Club owned by Jim Norris and Arthur Wirtz.

Norris, the son of a wheat millionaire, owned the Detroit Red Wings hockey team and a chunk of Madison Square Garden. He was the epitome of the millionaire sportsman, except for an unfortunate predilection for the company of racketeers. During the years Norris was controlling boxing, Frankie Carbo and Blinky Palermo, two of the sports-minded underworld figures, looted and plundered the sport with little restraint. Wirtz, like Norris from Chicago, was a real-estate dealer who had sponsored traveling ice-skating shows.

The Louis account of the Tournament of Champions arrangement, published some seven years after the fact, conveniently overlooked some details. Charles and Maxim fought on February 28 of 1949 and Louis's retirement was announced the following day. Simultaneously with the notice that he abdicated, Louis declared his Tournament of Champions. It is hardly credible that he became inspired on the night of February 28 and by the next day had convinced the four contenders to sign with him.

Government hearings on potential antitrust violations later revealed that negotiations between Louis, the IBC and the fighters had dragged out over an extended period. The first obstacle to the creation of the IBC had been Mike Jacobs. Although enfeebled by his stroke, Jacobs still held a contract with Madison Square Garden. In the Byzantine schemery of the time, the Garden paid Jacobs $150,000 to give up a job he was physically unable to perform. That Jim Norris owned part of Madison Square Garden is the only conceivable explanation.

From the Louis end, the key operators were Harry Mendel, a promoter who had organized events like six-day bicycle races and who was doing publicity for the Louis road show, and Truman Gibson. It was Gibson and Mendel who supposedly bargained for the rights to Walcott, Charles, Savold and Lesnevich.

The government's inquiry into the workings of the IBC brought out some other interesting facts and assertions. A memorandum from General John Reed Kilpatrick, the Madison Square Garden board chairman, to Ned Irish, Garden executive vice president, told of a session at the home of Mike Jacobs in Florida in December 1948. The document stated that Louis had already begun to think in terms of returning to the ring, perhaps in the summer of 1949. But the soon-to-be-retired and then unretired heavyweight champion asked not only for his customary 40 percent of the gate; he wanted $100,000 in a secret payment that would be hidden from the grasping fingers of the IRS. Sol Strauss, Jacobs's lawyer and nephew, was the source for Kilpatrick. Kilpatrick related to Irish, "Sol said that Joe had a terrific fear of being beaten and he asked Sol what he could expect if he were beaten. Sol said that in that event he would put Joe on the 20th Century payroll for $25,000 per year."

General Kilpatrick added, "Joe asked what he would be expected to do and Sol said assist in making matches, to assist in publicity at training camps and talking to newspapermen and so forth. Joe then said, 'You mean I will have to work?' Sol said, 'Yes.' Joe said, 'Then I will work one day a year. . . . I want to play golf, I don't want to work.' "

In any event, the resolution had been for the retired champion to receive $150,000 in return for the four contenders' contracts plus a 20 percent chunk of IBC stock (which Louis later claimed brought him nothing) and an annual salary of $15,000.

Whenever it came to a discussion of his finances, Louis seemed to be a graduate of the school of public relations that finds virtue in everyone, including himself.

The IRS grabbed every Louis asset, including a pair of trust funds set up for the children, unfortunately after the taxmen lodged their claims. Louis declared, "I don't want it to look as if I'm fighting the government here. If the government says I owe the money, I owe the money and they're entitled to it." Many years later someone commiserated that he came 20 years too early, that in the 1960s he would have earned $10 million. Louis shrugged, "Wouldn't make no difference. I'd still end up broke."

Perhaps the strongest expression of Louis's public faith in individuals was that lavished upon those who had been in charge of his money from the start of his professional career. One of the mysteries of the Louis bankruptcy was how the onetime champion managed to dispose of his $4.6 million in earnings from the ring exhibitions and radio and several hundred thousand out of films. In one of his tax suits, Louis reported that his original agreement with Julian Black and John Roxborough gave Julian Black 50 percent off the top of his earnings. Out of the remaining 50 percent, the fighter was expected to pay for his training expenses. Roxborough presumably had a private agreement with Black that took care of his share. Contracts that skimmed this much were common but outlawed by most state regulatory bodies. With the tax bite of more than $1 million, that meant Louis actually could pocket $1 million at best. Still, Louis never publicly criticized his managers nor did he ever complain about Mike Jacobs.

Marshall Miles, who was doomed to fail in his efforts to salvage Louis's treasures because of the strength of other claimants and the nature of his client, spoke bitterly about Jacobs and to a lesser extent Black. "Jacobs never should have lent him that money during the War," said Miles. "And he shouldn't have given Joe the $100,000 after the Mauriello fight." The implication was that Jacobs relied on Louis's extravagance to retain his control, something that Louis continually denied. Friends say Marshall Miles realized nothing financially from his association with Louis. Indeed, he wound up one more creditor.

And while Louis made his obeisances to the IRS, that was the one debt that he made a minimum effort to clear. He had paid off the entire sums due Jacobs and Roxborough. "Joe wound up owing Julian Black $25,000," said Miles. "But he refused to pay him and Julian didn't press it. I think he was afraid to have the whole business become public."

In 1949 and 1950, Louis drew his IBC salary and then toured Central, South and North America, the Far East and the United States. It was worth better than $400,000. But the bill from the IRS had come due and, furthermore, the International Boxing Club needed some heavyweight power at the box office.

The Internal Revenue Service was as implacable as the classical Furies. In 1948, Louis agreed to referee an Albuquerque fight between Chalky Wright and Benny Cisneros. When Louis learned that the match was a charity-sponsored affair for the Barelas Youth Center, he deducted his $1,000 fee. But a year later tax men sought from promoters proof that they paid Louis $1,000. Then they dunned the

250

champion for their share. In vain, Albuquerque people protested this abuse of a good-will gesture. They even considered raising funds to pay the tax owed on the $1,000 but abandoned the drive when told Louis would be taxed for this income as well.

Louis now played a kind of King Lear. He had turned over his title to others while indulging in his pleasures, but he found that a monarch without a kingdom commanded no riches. And whispering in his ear of opportunities to restore his fortunes were Norris, Wirtz and company.

What made up Louis's mind for him was the inevitable decision from the Internal Revenue Service. In 1950, the agency presented its bill for the years 1945–1949. Conceivably, Louis would have been broke without any help from the income-tax officials but he was now accused of owing $1 million. The businesses that had been supposed to pump out income had all wheezed along soaking up money for repairs rather than generating any revenue and were now shutting down.

In 1950, Louis declared himself an active boxer again. The Tournament of Champions concept had collapsed almost immediately after Louis sold his piece of paper for $150,000. Gus Lesnevich and Lee Savold had actually only been promised an opportunity to meet the winner between Ezzard Charles and Walcott. Charles worked a 15-round decision over Walcott in June of 1949 and became champion of the United States except for New York, which refused to recognize the new champion. Great Britain had anointed Lee Savold of New Jersey for knocking out the domestically manufactured product Bruce Woodcock, and the International Boxing Union accepted no one as champion.

To explain his return to the ring, Louis, speaking through another of his many ghosts, said, "The way I figure, championships are won in the ring and ought to be lost in the ring. That was the way I won my title and before I retired that was the way I expected to lose it. Instead I lost it by signing a piece of paper. As a result the heavyweight boxing picture is pretty much of a mess today because Ezzard Charles, who won the title, isn't recognized by a lot of folks. Personally, I think he's the best of the lot. And because he's the best I'm going to fight him in September and prove once and for all whether he's got a legitimate claim to the title." Notably, the Louis p.r. patina shines through. After casting doubt on Charles's right to be champion, Louis had hastened to add that Charles was a worthy opponent—to do less would have been to suggest that the fight lacked epic qualities.

The former champion, however, admitted his money troubles had forced him to return to the only trade that could produce heavy revenue.

Ezzard Charles was a 29-year-old when he and Louis confronted one another on September 27, 1950. He weighed only 184 pounds, the least of any heavyweight champion since Tommy Burns. Charles was not considered a strong puncher, winning less than half of his fights by knockouts in his overall career. But he was swift, a skilled boxer and seven years younger than Louis who weighed in at a portly 218. Sentiment was on the side of the old man; columnists like Grantland Rice and Arthur Daley picked Louis to win and the betting odds established him as a 2–1 favorite. Sentiment was much less obvious among fight fans. The Ring Record Book puts the number of paying customers at only 13,562. The Yankee Stadium seats had been modestly scaled at from $5 to $30 with 15,000 seats at only three dollars apiece made available the night of the fight. The gross gate totalled $205,-000, but the sign of the future lay in the most extensive televised coverage yet of a fight, for which CBS paid $146,-

000 (including radio rights). Estimates of the home-front audience amounted to 25 million. For promoters of boxing, the most significant aspect of the extensive television coverage was a comparison with the featherweight championship match between Sandy Saddler and Willie Pep. The featherweight class hardly fascinated spectator interest in the fashion of the top weight class. Nevertheless, the Pep–Saddler fight drew a $262,000 gate, $59,000 more than the heavyweight match which had the additional drawing card of another opportunity to see one of the superstars of the sport.

The fight itself provided dismal proof of Louis's decline. Louis won perhaps three rounds out of the 15 and Charles received the unanimous decision. The one occasion on which Louis pounded his adversary into trouble, he was unable to pursue his advantage with sufficient quickness.

"After the third or fourth round I knew I was washed up," Louis told reporters. Other journalists reported that the flash of his frailty came later to Louis. "I knew from the seventh round that I couldn't do it. It wasn't a case of reflexes or anything. I just didn't have it." Charles amassed an overwhelming lead on points and received a unanimous decision.

Ray Robinson was there and remembered, "In his dressing room later, blood seeped from cuts above each of his eyes. One of his eyes was swollen shut. I was in there with him but it was like trying to console an old blind man. Squinting in pain and embarrassment, he was unable to put on his pants or locate his shoes. I bent down and worked his feet into his big shoes and tied the laces. I helped lead him out of the ball park."

In his typical style, Arthur Daley wrote, "There was another rush of hope in the tenth round. The Jolter's dread left jab repeatedly rocked Charles. . . . Maybe sentiment has no place in sports. Perhaps there is something to the ancient but

253

stern admonition: 'No cheering in the press box, please.' But a guy wouldn't be human if he remained neutral in this fight. This onetime cotton picker from Alabama saved boxing and gave it some of his own nobility, innate decency, integrity and class. No sir, I rooted for Louis, unashamedly."

". . . a great fighter crushed ignominiously into a defeat," said James Dawson of the *Times.* In his dressing room, Louis said little except to declare himself in retirement. Dawson reported that Louis meant it "positively when he said this au revoir and it can be believed this time Louis means it. He is like the old Louis only in appearance."

Two weeks later, "positively" succumbed. The Brown Bomber said he would continue to make his comeback. Dawson and others had asserted that Louis only went against Charles to square his income-tax bill. But the $103,529 Louis earned from the Charles fight, from which federal taxes would be deducted, could hardly sate the long-deferred hunger of the IRS.

On the basis of his performance against Charles, Louis would have to rehabilitate himself before being granted another opportunity to regain his championship. In Chicago, on November 29, he worked on a South American chopping block, César Brion, and came away a decision-winner in 10 rounds. Few spectators were impressed.

Then Louis brought his show to Detroit where he knocked out Freddie Beshore. In Miami, Amelio Agramonte, a Cuban with a low threshold of resistance, lasted the full 10 rounds. Even though Louis weighed 208 and had trimmed the suet of his belly, he still moved ponderously. At San Francisco's Cow Palace, the ex-champion returned Andy Walker to anonymity with a 10-round knockout. Amelio Agramonte agreeably surfaced again in Detroit and Louis failed to knock him out on the second try, although he

254

preserved his modest winning streak with another 10-round decision.

Louis's next opponent was at least a respectable heavyweight contender. In the incredible tangle of provincial boxing fiefs, former bartender Lee Savold still held the British heavyweight championship. At 35, however, he was only two years younger than Louis, and the experts rated his average talents even more dimmed by time than Louis's. The form held true. Louis's left ended the fight in the sixth round before 18,000 people at the Garden.

For a brief moment, Louis again enjoyed the fealty of a king if not the perquisites of income and title. Into his dressing room to offer congratulations came New York's Mayor Vincent Impellitieri and, more important, the new champion of television, Milton Berle. Then Walter Winchell, still a powerful gossip columnist, seized Louis and called for the *New York Daily Mirror* photographer to get some shots of them together. Winchell magnanimously invited Jimmy Cannon to join the act.

The knockout of Savold might have been enough to get Louis another chance against Ezzard Charles. But unfortunately, a month after the Louis–Savold fight, Charles gave Joe Walcott another title shot (their first meeting ended in a 15-round decision for Charles) and Walcott knocked him out in the seventh round.

Now that he possessed the most valuable piece of property in boxing, Walcott showed no ready desire to risk it against Louis. There was little for Louis to do but slog away and hope that an opening to the truly big money would show itself. On August 1 in San Francisco, Louis used César Brion for a second time as a steppingstone. The *San Francisco Chronicle* headlined its account, "Old Geezer Louis Rips Young Brion." While he did slash his opponent badly, Louis

255

failed to improve substantially upon his Chicago performance, again winning a 10-round decision.

In Baltimore two weeks later, he battered Jimmy Bivins lightly, for another decision. Louis was down to 203 pounds, the lightest since before World War II. But Bivins was little better than a light heavyweight at 180.

The eight-bout comeback since the Ezzard Charles defeat netted Louis less than $200,000, out of which had come his expenses. The tax bill now stood at $1 million and it was estimated that every day that Louis woke up, he owed the government an additional $270 in interest, or $100,000 a year. He was attempting to float a financial sieve.

While Louis still retained the affection of fans and the press, the long-sought messiah of boxing promoters had appeared, a genuine white hope. The Brockton Blockbuster, born Rocco Marchegiano but bearing the ring name of Rocky Marciano, had knocked out all but five opponents in 37 fights. A free-swinging brawler, he offered the International Boxing Club a gate attraction that could endure for years. In the curious boxing-business practices of the day, which led to the antitrust action, the matchmaker for the IBC was an Alsatian immigrant to the United States named Al Weill. The manager for Rocky Marciano was also Al Weill. It was more than a one-hand-washes-the-other type of arrangement; it was one hand passes the money to the other. To confuse people further, Dan Daniel of the *World Telegram* mysteriously claimed that the matchmaker and fight manager were actually father and son when they were one and the same.

Given his choice, Louis would probably have preferred not to fight Marciano. The shortest route to the throne lay in wiping out the occupant, not in skirmishes with other ambitious nobles. But Walcott was distant; Charles couldn't even get the return bout he deserved with Walcott because promoters believed public interest in these two to be minimal. Louis was persuaded to accept Marciano as his opponent with 45 percent of the receipts for him; the Brockton Blockbuster was willing to appear for only 15 percent of the take. Killing even an old king builds one's reputation.

The Madison Square Garden crowd on October 26, 1951, saw probably Louis's best showing since he had left retirement. He won three of the first five rounds, outboxing the younger but less skilled man. But Marciano's crowding, punch-swapping style eroded the older man's strength. Louis had lost his power to generate enough impact to knock down Marciano. In the eighth round, Louis went down twice, the final time on the ring apron, his bald spot visible to spectators as he lay there with only one leg hanging over a rope into the ring.

The fight was worth $132,736 to Louis but only $45,000 to Marciano. Louis also collected something extra from the ancillary income while Marciano drew none of it. But he could afford to bide his time; he was now in line to fight for the championship. For Louis it was the absolute end as a competitive fighter. He was retired; and if he had not done so voluntarily a number of states would have followed the lead of his old adversary, Joe Triner in Illinois, who asked that Louis's license to fight in that state be suspended for his own protection.

Ray Robinson, in Louis's corner immediately after the fight ended, tried to console the loser, while fighting off his own tears. The memory of this occasion haunted Robinson as he faced his own retirement several times.

John Roxborough remembered: "I heard Marciano's

manager, Al Weill, crowing about his fighter's victory. 'My boy knocked out the great Joe Louis,' he chortled. [Roxborough, too, suffered literary ghost troubles.] That made me angry. I went up to him and said, 'Al, your boy didn't knock out the great Joe Louis, He beat Joe Louis's shadow.' "

15

Louis credited his brief stint on behalf of Wendell Willkie and his wartime experiences with developing both his social consciousness and his capacity to exert the leverage of his position. "I learned a lot while campaigning, how to talk a little, meeting people. It felt good, all those people cheering for you. Made a man feel he has a responsibility to his people and to his country."

In the postwar years, he tried to continue that effort. His initial move was to back the Republican candidate for the Harlem Congressional House Seat, Grant Reynolds, against the Rev. Adam Clayton Powell in 1946. A brief statement by Louis called for the election of Reynolds because, Louis said, only a Republican Congress would end the poll tax. Hewing to the Grand Old Party, Louis also plugged Thomas E. Dewey of New York in his bid for re-election as governor. Dewey was returned to Albany by a huge margin. But Powell was an easy winner over the Louis-backed Reynolds. And the 80th Congress, though a Republican one, did nothing about the poll tax, contrary to what Louis had argued it would do.

When Dewey ran for the presidency in 1948, Louis again supported him. As in his investments and his opinions on other fighters, Louis made a habit of backing losers in politics. Backing Dewey was, however, Louis's last act of faith in the GOP.

Truman's surprise win in 1948 and the continued if tepid Democratic commitment to civil rights apparently converted Louis. For in 1952 he supported Adlai Stevenson, the Democratic nominee against Eisenhower. It was, of course, another loser for Louis. In 1960, he supported John Kennedy, and finally chalked up one winner. In 1968, Louis almost went for Nixon but was persuaded to go for Humphrey.

Only rarely was Louis now asked by those in power to speak for black Americans or to black Americans. When the House Committee on Un-American Activities wanted a rebuttal to Paul Robeson's leftist ideas, it chose a more current hero, Jackie Robinson. It was not that Louis had lost the generalized affection of Americans. The sentiment in his favor during his two comebacks testified to his good standing with the public. But there were other black commodities considered to be better current and future values for exploitation.

Of more immediate concern to Louis as he approached 40 was the problem of earning a living. The $20,000 a year from the IBC, plus a few thousand from a milk company that used his name, did not even scratch the great gnawing itch of his needs. Marva had married a Chicago physician, Dr. Albert Spalding, which removed the danger that the children might have become destitute. But that was the only relief granted him.

He tried another series of boxing exhibitions, many of them under the auspices of the armed forces as the war in Korea now put hundreds of thousands of men in uniform. He pocketed only about $20,000 and the search for sources of revenue continued. He toyed with the idea of becoming a professional golfer. Two things stood in his path. While he was a skilled amateur, ordinarily shooting in the 70s, his game was well beneath the quality necessary to make money on the professional tour. Second, the Professional Golfers Association had a whites-only clause.

An opportunity to test the latter barrier arose in California in 1952, during the San Diego Open, which was co-sponsored by the PGA and local Chevrolet dealers. The Chevrolet people invited Louis to enter, as an amateur with a two handicap. However, two black pros, Bill Spiller and Eural Clark, could not enter because as professionals they fell under the PGA jurisdiction (any professionals, including blacks, were automatically covered by the PGA, which then kept blacks out of the professional tournaments).

Even though his fellow blacks had been barred, Louis competed. "I am just beginning to fight. I'm battling prejudice and I'll keep on fighting it. We expect to lick this prejudice, too, just like we've done in athletic contests involving direct physical contact—such as in basketball and football. This is the biggest fight of my life." In another statement he referred to the PGA as "Hitler."

The walls of the PGA did not tumble with Louis's rounds in San Diego. It was some years before the restriction was removed, and the best that could be said for Louis's experience was that he had helped focus public attention on the inequity.

During the next four years he was constantly beset by the demands of the IRS. When his mother died in 1953 she left a modest estate of $5,500. Son Joe's share amounted to $667, and the government, in the spirit of irrigating the Sahara Desert with a drop of spit, seized that as part payment on a debt of what was now estimated at $1,250,000.

In 1955, he was married again, to a woman named Rose Morgan who was in the beauty-shop-supply business. It has

261

been asserted by one acquaintance that both parties were misled in their expectations of this union: Rose Morgan thought that she was not only getting an attractive husband but also someone who could, through the strength of his name, help raise capital for her business. The former fighter, on the other hand, believed that his new wife's income would be enough to provide the pleasures he sought. For both parties, the marriage turned out to be a disappointment. Rose Morgan discovered that her new husband had his own interpretation of the ways of a spouse. To a reporter, Gay Talese, Rose Morgan said, after the divorce, "I tried to make him settle down. I told him he couldn't sleep all day and stay out all night any more. Once he asked me why not, and I told him I'd worry and wouldn't be able to sleep. So he said he'd wait up till I fell asleep before going out. Well I stayed up till four A.M.—and then he fell asleep."

Someone asked Louis why he didn't spend more time at home and he replied, "Home is a place you go when you want to rest."

In 1956, a promoter came to Louis and guaranteed him $100,000 to become a wrestler. To Rose Morgan, her husband's new enterprise bordered on the sleazy. "Joe Louis was like the President of the United States," she explained. "How would you like to see the ex-President of the United States washing dishes? That's how I feel about Joe wrestling." Others, including writers such as Jimmy Cannon and Arthur Daley, took the say-it-ain't-so tack, but it was an economic necessity. One noisy attempt to get the sporting public to pay Louis's tax tab managed to raise only $4,000. To those who begged him not to degrade himself in a series of one-night stands, Louis answered, "It beat stealin' don' it?"

The aroma of disaster hung over the wrestling show like the stink of stockyards in the Chicago beef center. In St.

262

Petersburg, Florida, newspapers openly advertised that no blacks would be permitted to buy seats for the Louis engagement. The late Milton Gross of the *New York Post* broke the news to Louis in his dressing room at St. Petersburg. "He was surprised," wrote Gross. "After so short a time, he is not so adept at wrestling deception that he could feign such astonishment or distress." Louis's first reaction was to refuse to take part. The promoters cajoled him into doing his act, which he performed at a minimal level, even for wrestling. Afterward he donated his share of the gate, $248, to the Miami chapter of the NAACP.

Louis continued with the wrestling exhibitions. In several southern cities, he always threw a black man, not a white. But in Fort Lauderdale, one Whitey Whittler, whose skin matched his name, served as the Louis flopover for the night.

During the long period that he put into wrestling, the former heavyweight champion managed to eke out his guarantee. But as in every endeavor outside the ring, he had arrived on the scene at the wrong time. Better entertainment had begun to find its way onto television, and the wrestling public had already started to shrink. It all came to a thudding halt in Columbus, Ohio. Co-actor Rocky Lee departed from the established choreography and heaved his 320 pounds at Louis while he was still on the floor. A medical examination, after Louis complained of abdominal pain, showed two broken ribs and worse, a bruise to some muscles of his heart. Illinois quickly took away his right to wrestle in that state. Other state boards also recognized that further grappling by Louis might do serious damage to his heart.

While he recovered from his ailment, further troubles fell on his head. Federal Judge Sylvester Ryan, after listening to the testimony on the behavior of the IBC, ordered the corporation dissolved, stripping away Louis's $20,000 salary. He never drew a penny from his 20 percent stock holdings in the boxing promotion company. Then Rose Morgan asked for an annulment on the grounds that her husband declined to have any children.

Louis had one other involvement to which he now turned for financial succor. Shortly after leaving the army he agreed to lend his name if not his energy to a public-relations partnership with his old friend Billy Rowe. When Louis and he first met in 1935, Rowe was a newspaper reporter but had already merged his interests in reporting and commerce. A hat manufacturer promised Rowe some reward if he could get Louis to pose for a photograph wearing one of the hats. When Rowe approached the Louis camp, the backers of the fighter tried to fend him off. "They didn't want anybody to get near him," recalled Rowe. "But I told Joe that I would give him one of the hats and he agreed to appear in the picture. Joe said of me, 'He's the only guy who offered to give me something in New York.' "

Apparently the hat was all the payment Louis received for the implied endorsement.

Louis paid relatively little attention to the firm run by Billy Rowe except to enjoy the hospitality of a potential client for a lunch, evening on the town or small junket. But in the spring of 1960, Louis–Rowe landed a substantial contract, the promotion of tourism for Cuba, now under Fidel Castro. By 1960, relations with the island 93 miles off the coast of Florida could be described as mutually hostile. While Fulgencio Battista ruled as dictator of Cuba until Castro's successful revolt, the United States seemed politely appalled by his excesses but not enough so to aid in his ouster. United States investments in Cuba brought good returns; Battista knew better than to interfere with these, and Havana offered the kinds of vice that were increasingly hard to come by on the mainland. Commerce and sin together easily outpointed distaste for oppression. Once Fidel Castro began to turn off the dividends from United States investment, show a puritanical air toward commercialization of sin and try to export his views to other Latin American nations, he became intolerable to Democrats and Republicans alike.

When the first surprise over Louis's connection with Castro became public, through a spokesman Louis was reported to have said, "There's no place in the world except Cuba where a Negro can go in the wintertime with absolutely no discrimination." That he was nearly 100 percent correct failed to convert his adversaries. To them bigger issues than discrimination at beaches and hotels were at stake. Louis–Rowe had properly registered under the law as a representative of a foreign government. Rowe stressed that Louis would not personally be connected with the account. But this was not enough. Criticism and pressure squeezed down upon the enterprise. Finally, Louis felt impelled to announce his loyalty to the United States and declare that unless Louis–Rowe gave up the account, which was worth better than $50,000 a year to it, he would dissociate himself from the company. Louis–Rowe threw in the towel.

In the early 1960s Louis–Rowe assiduously tried to capitalize upon white business's discovery of the black market. Louis and Billy Rowe would sit with the representatives of race tracks and film producers, for example, and try to convince them, one through his arguments, the other by his massive presence, that for a fee, Louis–Rowe would lift the sluice gates and torrents of black money would flow. But it was an idea whose time had not quite come.

Louis was betrayed time and again by his lack of sophistication as a bargainer. He had consented to the making of a film based on his life in the mid 1950s and wound up receiving nothing for the rights. Talese found himself agreeably surprised by Louis's ability to coax "living expenses" from a television producer while in New York for a program based on his life. But this was just a little more spicy pottage; the birthright still went too cheap to make any improvement in his financial resources.

For a short time Louis held a boxing-promotion franchise in California. Among the attractions he put on was one that featured a bright new prospect named Cassius Clay. But the Joe Louis boxing promotions foundered because the head of the organization granted such generous terms to its performers. He told his wife that he could not do less, knowing how hard the life of a fighter was.

Louis also did what seemed to be some free-lance p.r. work. He made a surprising appearance at one of the trials of Teamster Union head James Hoffa. As on the occasion when Jack Blackburn faced a jury of his peers, Louis simply took a seat in the courtroom behind Hoffa. The fighter had no part in the trial, made no statement. Several blacks sat on the jury, which eventually found Hoffa innocent of the particular charge of the day. Rumors floated that Louis received $2,500 for his appearance. He posed for pictures with Hulan Jack, the black borough president of Manhattan who had been convicted of accepting bribes and within a few years was again indicted for unlawful activities.

Louis and Leonard Reed slapped together a nightclub act. But Louis was not well-enough spoken to play even a straight man. Said one reviewer, "The consensus was that as a song and dance man, he was a tremendous boxer."

He continued to provide copy for newspapers whenever a boxing match of any significance came along. Promoters would hire Louis to show up at training camps, paying him little more than walking-around money. They collected on the amount of newspaper space devoted to the Louis analysis of the coming fight. Sometimes Louis would be announced as a special trainer. On one occasion he was advertised as the author of newspaper pieces on a coming battle. At a press conference with one of the principals, Louis listened to the remarks of the fighter and then said, "I wanna know, did my ghost get that?" As a prognosticator of fights, Louis had an almost perfect record for picking the wrong man. He consistently downgraded Muhammad Ali, not through any dislike of him personally but because he found his "float like a butterfly, sting like a bee" boxing style offensive. "Can't throw a punch when he's movin' like that. Shouldn't pull his head back to get outa the way of a punch." At the time Clay became Ali and announced his conversion to the Black Muslims, Louis did remark, "The things they preach are just the opposite of what we believe. The heavyweight champion of the world should be champion of all the people. He has responsibilities to all the people."

The one fighter of note with whom Louis established some rapport was Charles Sonny Liston. A St. Louis street tough, Liston had served time and it was while he was behind bars that he first learned to fight. Throughout his ring life, including his reign as heavyweight champion (1962–63), Liston was presumed to be a mob-controlled investment. Cold indifference if not hostility usually masked his face. But like Louis, Sonny Liston enjoyed partying and women. Liston's tangled business affairs received the attention of a Los Angeles lawyer, Martha Jefferson. From this relationship developed something more than a friendship between Louis and the woman lawyer. In 1959 they were married.

Martha Louis described her previous husband—who continued to be her law partner even after their divorce—as "a man exposed to books, not life." With Joe Louis she anticipated a man "exposed to life, not books." Her wish was fulfilled with Louis. After somewhat more than 10 years of living with the former heavyweight champion, there must have been days when the former Martha Jefferson yearned for a little less life experience and a bit more of a bookish man.

In the early stages of her marriage, Martha Louis said, "I treat a man right. I treat a man like a king—if he treats me right." When it became apparent that the peripatetics of Louis were not about to yield to marriage, Martha Louis remarked, "If these sort of women like living on the side streets of a man's life, I wish them well. But I am his wife and when I come on the scene they got to get the hell out." Unfortunately, before they got the hell out, Louis fathered a child by one, blew whatever money he had and was introduced to cocaine.

Before he hit bottom, however, Louis exposed himself to other aspects of life. He was hired by the Pigalle Sporting Club in London to serve as a host in the gambling casino. Actor George Raft occupied the same post at another London gaming palace. But Louis lasted only a few months before returning to the United States. He signed on with a new Las Vegas establishment, the Moulin Rouge. The task of shaking hands, scribbling autographs, kibbitzing and dabbling at the gambling tables, playing rounds of golf suited his temperament perfectly.

When the Moulin Rouge underwent a reorganization, Caesar's Palace, a Teamster financed resort, grabbed Louis. The gambling part of Caesar's was directed by Ash Resnick, who had made Louis's acquaintance around places such as Sonny Liston's training camp. Credit for Caesar's recruitment of Louis belonged to Resnick.

A publicity release from Solters/Sabinson/Roskin, Inc.,

which did the p.r. for the hotel in 1973, described Louis's work. "He has one major assignment—to be himself, which the hotel regards as more than sufficient. . . . Breaking Joe's responsibilities down is simple. He greets people at the hotel and all over the country. He plays golf and attends parties. He talks to the press."

Louis himself said, "Call me a greeter. I go round talk to people about the hotel, go to golf tournaments and that sort of thing." Louis paused and grinned, "Other day, the president of the hotel was talking to Ash about me and he say, 'When you find out what Joe does, you tell me.' "

Louis, however, wasn't given the job for charity reasons. Many potential customers would like to rub against the massive shoulders of one of the titans of 20th-century sport. And the black people's market is an idea whose time had finally come. When Muhammad Ali fought Jerry Quarry in Las Vegas in 1972, headquarters for the fight was located at Caesar's Palace. Rooms at $26 to $50 a night filled up with black people and the gambling tables at Caesar's were surrounded by the flash of black high rollers.

That a sports hero such as Louis should wind up as a shill for the home of gambling and a place that is a synonym for United States sin may puzzle some people.

But Louis's work ethic was never based upon the eight-hour day, the desk or a machine. If the ambience of Las Vegas bore the penumbra of organized crime, it would not disturb Louis. Although Roxborough and Black had taken great pains to keep their policy-bank backgrounds divorced from the management of the heavyweight champion, the fighter was well aware of their other activities. During his career in the ring, petty thieves, gamblers and satraps of crime had always been close to the sport. The IBC under Jim Norris had demonstrated an even easier tolerance for the mob than Mike Jacobs when he promoted fights. With "respectable" business closed to his kind of work ethic, Louis had quite naturally come in contact with a great number of workers on the fringe of illegality, if not actually within the underworld.

Martha Louis engineered one major benefit for her husband. She convinced the tax collectors that further pursuit of her husband would only make it futile for him to be gainfully employed. The government, on the strength of her arguments, accepted that Louis would never pay off his $1,300,000 debt. It agreed simply to tax him on his current earnings at the standard rates.

For all of his downward drift, Louis was still called upon in the 1960s to be a spokesman during the racial confrontations of that decade. In 1963, the campaigns by the Southern Christian Leadership Conference and the chapters of CORE brought their sit-in tactics into wider and wider play, occupying not only tables in southern restaurants but construction sites and even roadways in the North. Jimmy Breslin, then with the *New York Herald Tribune,* drew from Louis some comment on the strategy. "Beatniks, that's all a lot of them are," Louis supposedly told Breslin. "They talk like they're the only ones who know anything about racial problems. You know they just discovered the whole thing. Then they go out and do stupid things. . . . What do they think I was doing all the years, sleeping? This problem is going to be fixed and it's going to be fixed the right way. Beatniks, they just get in the way." (There is a rhythm to the quote that smacks more highly of Breslin's style than Louis's.)

A year later, Louis took a more militant stance on what he called "the colored side." He appeared at 117th Street and 5th Avenue in the heart of Harlem, joining with entertainer Dick Gregory and local politician Jesse Gray to celebrate

"New York's Worst Fair" in opposition to the international exposition at Flushing Meadows. Along with the others, Louis posed holding small rubber rats labeled "Souvenir of the ghetto."

"I'm always happy to come back to Harlem," said the fighter, "I'm with this organization 100 percent."

A few months later, in July of 1964, a New York police lieutenant shot and killed a 15-year-old black youth just beyond the fringes of Harlem. Within a few hours, an orgy of violence gripped not only Harlem but another black enclave, Bedford-Stuyvesant in Brooklyn. Police clubbed dozens while stores went up in flames and blacks carried off great amounts of booty. For all the shooting by the cops—officially some 2,000 rounds were expended and the total may well have been much more—just one man was killed, 30 wounded.

While the fires and tempers still smoldered, Joe Louis along with any other individual thought to have a following in the community, was besieged by city officials and reporters who wanted to soothe the residents or to find "what those people want." From Louis came a statement: "I join with the rest of the athletes in hoping a solution is found for this terrible thing which is going on in Harlem. This is too great a city for this to happen in. The basic thing everybody has got to remember is that hoodlums cannot take over because one boy was the victim of a terrible tragedy."

He made his obeisances to officialdom on all sides: "I don't go along with people who say get rid of Police Commissioner [Michael] Murphy. He doesn't walk the beat. He doesn't hit anyone in the head with a stick. I'm sure he doesn't condone it either.

"The various Civil Rights groups, CORE, the NAACP, all of them have a good purpose. It's a shame but sometimes

271

hoodlums take advantage when they can of what good people are doing."

Then Louis struck out on behalf of his own community identity. "Everybody wants the colored side to be quiet. They've been quiet for 100 years. A kid gets shot down in the street. How long can you stay quiet? I believe newspapers should look at both sides. One policeman gets hurt . . . 10,000 colored get hurt. You have to write the colored side, too. It's been going on for years."

By the late 1960s, Louis had begun to show alarming signs of emotional problems. His paranoid concern with Mafia assassins frightened Martha Louis, and he alternated between a frenetic state, in which he disappeared into the company of Harlem whores, and an indolent state, in which he'd lie about the house, too disinterested to attempt even a round of golf. In the midst of these troubles, he suffered a gall bladder attack that forced him to be hospitalized. Once again he became a journalistic oracle on sports-related issues of the day. Angry black athletes talked of passing up the 1968 Olympics in Mexico City, as a protest against racial inequities in the United States. Questioned while in his hospital bed, Louis offered pablum to white America. He termed any boycott by black athletes "a serious mistake." He continued, "Maybe they don't have equal opportunity in America but they're gaining it every day. . . . Things are improving. If they were going backwards, it would be different." Louis made no mention of his alleged position on the 1936 Olympics.

His answer to the other topics on which his opinion was sought at Kirkland Hospital proved less satisfying to the establishment. Muhammad Ali had been stripped of his heavyweight championship following his refusal to accept being drafted. When asked about Ali, Louis remarked that while he thought the young fighter had been mistaken in not

272

entering the army he would continue to regard him as champion "until he goes to jail or retires."

Louis's varying attitudes toward civil-rights issues can be understood in the context of his background. Less easy to understand are the psychoses that gripped him in later life. Looking back over his 60 years, or at least his adult 40, there appears a pattern of symptoms that might indicate a growing disintegration. Almost immediately after he achieved some success, Louis became a wanderer. It was not simply that he would leave whatever he happened to regard as home to see the sights or sample the pleasures, but that he would disappear from view on these excursions. Well before Martha Louis had begun to try to track him down, he had been vanishing for days at a time. Whether it was John Roxborough, Mike Jacobs or Marshall Miles, they could all tell tales of a Louis swallowed up in some warren of the city.

Conceivably, years of punches may have done some subtle damage. His personal physician and Marshall Miles both noticed after World War II a marked loss of reflexes on his left side. One account mentioned a tendency to drool as an indication of damage from blows to the head.

In 1937, his long-gone father, Mun Barrow, was discovered to have died in an Alabama mental institution. That may have preyed on Louis's mind—and science still ponders the possibilities of genetic transmission of the potential for mental illness.

Diagnosed and treated for emotional problems, Louis had spent months in the hospital. He missed a testimonial dinner in his honor in Detroit. Still, he pulled himself together enough to leave the hospital and return to Caesar's Palace. He was not a well man; a chum said, "Even his best friends have to admit he's sick." Whatever his condition, he continued to hustle for Caesar's Palace. And desperate promot-

273

ers still saw him as a marketable commodity. The Garden in 1974 bought some interest in the Joe Frazier–Jerry Quarry fight by hiring Louis to referee, a role he was obviously unfit to fill.

Perhaps one way to try to understand Louis and his career is through the mirror of another time. English authority on the Roman Empire, Samuel Dill, described the progenitors of Louis in *Roman Society from Nero to Marcus Aurelius:*

> The profession of gladiator was long regarded as a tainted one, on which social sentiment and law alike place their ban. It was a calling which included the vilest or the most unfortunate of mankind. Slaves, captives in war, or criminals condemned for serious offense recruit its ranks. . . . But even from the later days of the Republic, men of free birth were sometimes attracted by the false glory or the solid rewards of the profession. Free men sometimes fought at the call of their patrons. . . . The Gladiator oath bound him to endure unflinchingly scouring, burning or death. His barracks were a closely guarded prison, and although his fare was necessarily good, his training was entirely directed to the production of a fine fighting animal, who would give good sport in the arena.
>
> The splendor of the arms, the ostentatious pomp of the scene of combat, the applause of thousands of spectators on the crowded benches, the fascination of danger, all this invest the cruel craft with a false glory. The mob of all ages are ready to make a hero of the man who can perform more feats of physical strength or agility. And the skillful gladiator evidently became a hero under the early Empire. . . . His professional record was of public interest; the number of his combats and victories was inscribed upon his tomb. His name and his features were

scratched by boys on the street walls. He attracted the unconcealed, and not always discreet admiration of women. . . . Sometimes the veteran gladiator might be tempted to return to the old scenes for a high fee or he might become a trainer in one of the schools . . . but the career of ambition was closed to himself by the taint of a profession which the people found indispensable to their pleasures, and which they loaded with contempt.

But as he moved through his 61st year, whatever his fears and ends, Joe Louis had carved out an identity for himself. In spite of all his associations with unsavory people, he had preserved his integrity. Against all the odds, he had taken the abilities given him by nature and turned them to the making of a champion. While he might fear and hate the "assholes" who would blow poison gas upon his vulnerable head, he retained an affection for his fellow human beings that transcended any notion of subservience.

It is one measure of Louis that he maintained his relationship with all three of the women he married, and they entertained one another. That same easy spirit allowed him to speak well of everyone with whom he had associated, including those who exploited or bilked him.

Measured through the earth's age, humans float like wood chips on a river, some bobbing and reappearing, some disappearing to the bottom without surviving the ordinary length of the river. Louis was more than a chip, something like a large thick log that occasionally, when it came to some critical narrowing of the stream, at least temporarily managed to influence the flow. Inevitably that log too would be pushed back into the great flow, heading for the sea where all becomes insignificance.